W9-CNX-909

Writing for the Mass Media

Third Edition

James Glen Stovall
University of Alabama

PRENTICE HALL, Englewood Cliffs, New Jersey 07632

Library of Congress Cataloging-in-Publication Data

Stovall, James Glen.
  Writing for the mass media/James Glen Stovall.—3rd ed.
    p. cm.
  Includes index.
  ISBN 0-13-097965-1
  1. Mass media—Authorship. I. Title
  P96.A8S8 1993
808'.06602—dc20   93-5369
                                    CIP

Acquisitions editor: Steve Dalphin
Editorial/production supervision: Rob DeGeorge
Cover design: Violet Lake Studio
Production Coordinator: Kelly Behr
Editorial assistant: Caffie Risher

**This book is dedicated to
MARTHA ELIZABETH STOVALL
1914-1982
who loved books and taught others to do the same.**

 © 1994, 1990, 1985 by Prentice-Hall, Inc.
A Paramount Communications Company
Englewood Cliffs, New Jersey 07632

All rights reserved. No part of this book may be
reproduced, in any form or by any means,
without permission in writing from the publisher.

Printed in the United States of America
10 9 8 7 6 5 4 3 2

ISBN 0-13-097965-1

Prentice-Hall International (UK) Limited, *London*
Prentice-Hall of Australia Pty. Limited, *Sydney*
Prentice-Hall Canada Inc., *Toronto*
Prentice-Hall Hispanoamericana, S.A., *Mexico*
Prentice-Hall of India Private Limited, *New Delhi*
Prentice-Hall of Japan, Inc., *Tokyo*
Simon & Schuster Asia Pte. Ltd., *Singapore*
Editora Prentice-Hall do Brasil, Ltda., *Rio de Janeiro*

Contents

Preface

Writing is one thing; writing about writing is another.

Like most people, I cannot remember the first word or the first sentence that I wrote. (I am reasonably sure they were not momentous.) I can remember always being encouraged to write, however, by parents and teachers who knew the importance of writing.

I have always enjoyed and admired good writing, and I continue to be in awe of it. How Mark Twain could have created such a wonderful and timeless story as *The Advertures of Tom Sawyer*, how Henry David Thoreau could distill his thoughts into the crisp and biting prose of *Walden*, or how Red Smith could have turned out high-quality material for his sports column day after day—all of this is continually amazing to me. I frankly admit, I don't know how they did it.

And yet, here I am writing about writing. Why should I be doing this? At least three reasons occur to me immediately.

I am fascinated by the process of writing. I write about it so I can understand it better. For me, it is a process of self-education. I hope that some of the insights I have discovered will rub off on those who read this book.

I am convinced that while great writing might be a gift to a chosen few, good writing is well within the reach of the rest of us. There are things we can do to improve our writing.

I care about the language and the way it is used. Those of us fortunate enough to have English as a native language have been given a mighty tool with which to work. It is powerful and dynamic. An underlying purpose of this book is to encourage the intelligent and respectful use of this tool.

This book is the product of many people, some of whom were listed in the first two editions of this book. For this edition, I particularly want to thank **Pam Doyle,** who offered some extremely helpful suggestions on the Writing for Broadcast chapter; **Dwight Teeter,** who contributed part of the appendix on mass media law and had many substantive suggestions about the book as a whole; **Perri Colley,** who wrote another part of the appendix on mass media law; **Mark Arnold,** who uses the book and has a unique perspective on what belongs in it; **Sandra Borden Pigg,** Middle Tennessee State University, and **Janie Bryan Loveless,** Southern Methodist University, who made many excellent suggestions for the third edition; and **Lynnmarie Cook,** who did a wonderful job of copy-editing and helped me out of many tight spots. The folks at Prentice Hall, **Steve Dalphin** and **Rob DeGeorge** particularly, have been marvelously supportive, as usual.

My wife, **Sally,** remains my chief critic and proofreader and always a source of encouragement. My son, **Jefferson,** as I write this, is in the sixth grade and discovering the joys and frustrations of writing.

This book, like the previous editions, is dedicated to my mother, **Martha Elizabeth Stovall,** who was my first editor.

James Glen Stovall

James Glen Stovall teaches journalism at the University of Alabama where he has been a faculty member since 1978. He received his Ph.D. from the University of Tennessee and is a former reporter and editor for several newspapers. He also has more than five years of public relations experience.

1
Sit Down and Write

I have sworn upon the alter of God, eternal hostility against every form of tyranny over the mind of man. (1800)

Equal and exact justice to all men, of whatever state or persuasion, religious or political; peace, commerce, and honest friendship with all nations, entangling alliance with none. . . .
Freedom of religion; freedom of the press, and freedom of person under the protection of the habeas corpus, and trial by juries impartially selected. These principles form the bright constellation which has gone before us and guided our steps through an age of revolution and reformation. (1801)

Enlighten the people generally and tyranny and opressions of the body and mind will vanish like evil spirits at the dawn of day. (1816)
Thomas Jefferson

Ideas carry a society forward. The ideas of freedom, independence, individualism, religion and social order first existed in the minds of men and women but are crystalized for us by great writers and thinkers such as Thomas Jefferson.

The written word is one of the most powerful forces available to humans. It has the ability to carry ideas and information, to entertain and distract, and to change the lives of individuals and nations. The person who wants to write rarely realizes the power contained in writing. Yet it is there—and available to those who have the information and ideas and who are clever and hardworking enough to learn to write well.

How do you write well?

That question defies an easy, quick, simple answer. Yet all of us—at one time or another—have had to consider it. We had begun that consideration at least by the time we were in the second grade when our teachers made us begin writing paragraphs. By the fourth grade, we were learning the rules of grammar and punctuation, wondering what in the world these had to do with good writing. (A lot, as it turns out, although we may be reluctant to admit it.) Outside the classroom, we were writing in our diaries or writing thank you letters to relatives and notes to friends.

At some point, we learned that whatever else writing is—fun, exciting, rewarding—it is not easy. Writing is hard work. As Red Smith, a sports writer for the *New York Times,* once put it, "There's nothing to writing. All you do is sit down at a typewriter and open a vein."

Smith's point is not just that writing is hard but that it requires that we give of ourselves. Writing demands total commitment, even if it is just for a few minutes. We can think of nothing else, and do nothing else, when we are writing. The first step to good writing is recognizing this essential point.

But the question still remains. How do you gather together the words that will convey the information, ideas, or feelings you want to give to the reader? How do you write well?

What is good writing?

Good writing, especially good writing for the mass media, is clear, concise, simple, and to-the-point. It transmits information, ideas, and feelings to the reader clearly but without overstatement. Good writing is writing that outlines pictures of ideas that readers can fill in with their imagination.

Good writing is efficient. It uses only the minimum number of words to make its point. It doesn't waste the reader's time.

Good writing is precise. Good writers use words for their exact meaning; they do not throw words around carelessly.

Good writing is clear. It leaves no doubt or confusion in the reader's mind about its meaning.

Finally, good writing is modest. It doesn't draw attention to itself. Good writing does not try to show off the intelligence of the writer. It lets the content speak for itself, and it allows readers to receive messages directly. Writing should not get in the way of what people need and want to read.

So, how do you do it? How do you write well?

The answer to these questions begins with four of the basic prerequisites for good writing:

Know the tools of the trade. Good writers must know and understand the tools with which they work, just as a good carpenter knows his tools. For writers, a knowledge of the rules of grammar and spelling is mandatory. (Not all writers have to be great spellers, but they should know the rules, and they should always work with a dictionary close at hand.) Writers must know the precise meanings of words and how to use words precisely; although they do not have to use every word they know, having a variety available gives the writer extra tools to use if needed. (Most of us have a vocabulary of about 5,000 to 6,000 words; one scholar estimated that Shakespeare knew about 30,000 words.)

Writers must not only know the language, but they must understand it and be genuinely interested in it. The written word is a powerful instrument with which the lives of many people can be affected. Writers who do not understand this fact do not know what they are dealing with and will not be able to use the language effectively. Writers should also be caretakers of the language, unwilling to see English misused and abused.

Today's writers must also be computer-literate. They should understand the ins and outs of a word processing program, the ways to change and move text, and the proper use of spelling checkers and other utility programs. Writing for the mass media today demands that writers use their time and equipment efficiently.

Know your subject. Writers must have a clear idea to guide them in their writing. If you do not understand thoroughly what you are writing about, your readers will not understand what you have written. Beginning writers frequently have trouble with this most basic requirement of good writing. They sometimes believe that they can "write" their way through a subject, that just getting the words down is enough. Even experienced media professionals sometimes fail to understand their topics. For example, some journalists try to write about events without properly researching the background or checking with enough sources. Some advertising copywriters try to compose ads without understanding the product or the audience to whom the ad is directed. In both cases, the writing misses the mark. It is often confusing and inefficient.

If you are writing about something you do not understand, stop writing and find out what you need to know. Ask questions of people who do know. Look things up. Or just think the subject through more thoroughly. Writing without understanding or without having your subject firmly in your own mind is like writing with a broken pencil.

Write it down. This may be the most basic point of all: You cannot be a writer unless you put words on paper or on a computer screen. People can think, talk, and agonize all night about what they would like to write. They can read and discuss; they can do research and even make notes. But no one is a writer until ideas become words, and sentences become paragraphs. At some point, the writer must sit down and write.

Writing is very hard work for most people, and few have the tenacity to stick with it. Anthony Trollope, a nineteenth-century English novelist, would begin writing at 5:30 a.m. He would write for two and a half hours, producing at least 250 words every fifteen minutes. Trollope responded to the demands of writing with a strict routine. So did Isaac Asimov, a man who wrote books on subjects ranging from Shakespeare to the Bible to science fiction. Asimov would wake up every morning at 6:00 and be at his typewriter writing by 7:30 a.m. He would then work until 10 p.m. He wrote more than 500 books in his lifetime.

Writing is physically difficult because it demands maintaining a stationary position and concentrating for a long time. Writing is mentally difficult because of the effort it takes to know a subject well enough and to think clearly enough to put it down on paper.

In addition, writing involves some risk. We can never be certain that we will be successful in our writing. Something happens to our beautiful thoughts when we try to confine them to complete sentences, and what happens is not always good. Writers must take the chance of failure.

Writers for the mass media have an advantage in overcoming this tendency. Their job is to write, and their circumstances force them to write. They must meet deadlines, often on a daily basis. Working effectively in the mass media environment often requires more discipline than that required of the casual or occasional writer.

Rewrite what you have written. Writing is such hard work that most of us want to do it and forget it. That's natural, but good writers don't give in to this tendency. Good writers have the discipline to reread, edit, and rewrite.

Rewriting requires that a writer reread critically. Writers cannot go through this process patting themselves on the back for all the fine phrases they have produced. Writers must constantly ask if the writing can be clearer, more precise, and more readable. And writers should have the courage to say, "This isn't what I wanted to say," or even, "This isn't very good."

Writers for the mass media often work in circumstances that dictate that someone else read what they have written and make judgments about it. Having another person read what you have written and then give you an honest evaluation of it usually makes for better writing. But writers for the mass media are also at a disadvantage because their deadline pressures often prevent thorough rereading and rewriting.

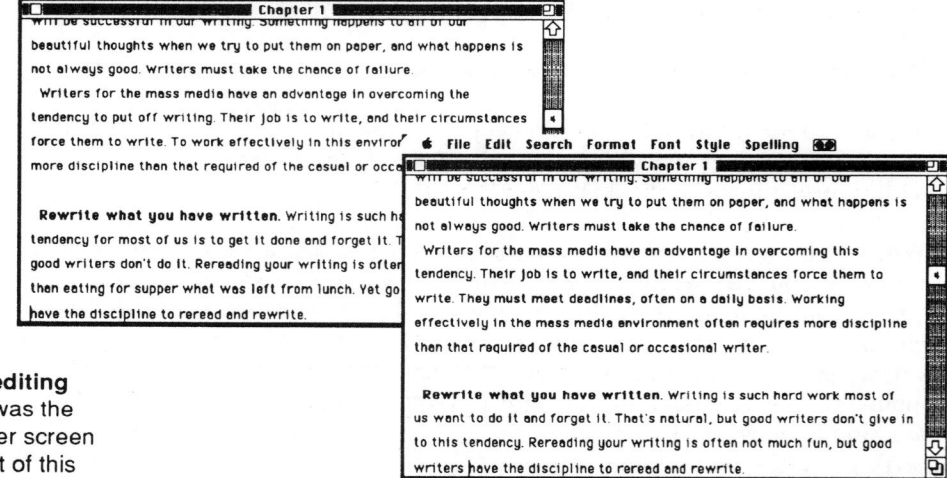

Figure 1-1
Rewriting and editing
The top picture was the author's computer screen for an early draft of this chapter. This section appears on the next page. After some editing, the draft was changed to what is on the second screen. When the draft was converted to hard copy, it underwent additional editing. Compare the top picture to the bottom one, which shows the manscript after one final editing.

Techniques for good writing

The following are some suggestions for improving your writing. Many of them are useful at the rewriting stage of your work, but you should try to keep them in mind as your words are going down on paper for the first time. Not all of these suggestions fit every piece of writing you will do, so they need not be considered a strict set of rules. They do constitute a good set of habits for a writer to develop, however.

Write simply. This is a thought you'll see repeatedly in this book. The key to clarity is simplicity. A clear, simple writing style is not the exclusive possession of a few gifted writers. It can be achieved by students who are just beginning a writing career if some of the following suggestions are kept in mind. The following phrases are famous because they convey powerful messages in clear and simple language:

These are the times that try men's souls. (Thomas Paine, 1776)

A rose is a rose is a rose is a rose. (Gertrude Stein, 1913)

I have a dream. (Martin Luther King Jr., 1963)

Use simple words. "It is a general truth," Henry Fowler wrote in *Modern English Usage*, "that short words are not only handier to use but more powerful in effect; extra syllables reduce, not increase, vigour." Fowler was talking about the modern tendency to use *facilitate* instead of *ease, numerous* instead of *many, utilize* instead of *use*, etc. Many people try to use big or complicated words, thinking it will impress the reader. It doesn't; it has the opposite effect. Benjamin Franklin once wrote, "To write clearly, not only the most expressive, but the plainest words should be chosen."

Mark Twain on using simple words

I never write "metropolis" for seven cents because I can get the same price for "city." I never write "policeman" because I can get the same money for "cop."

© 1993 Jim Stovall

Use simple sentences. Not every sentence you write should be in the simple sentence format (subject-predicate or subject-verb-object), but the simple sentence is a good tool for cleaning up muddy writing. For example, take the following sentence (which appeared in a large daily newspaper): "She was shot through the right lung after confronting a woman married to her ex-husband inside the Food World store on Bankhead Highway shortly before 1 p.m." The confusion could be lessened by breaking this one sentence into three simple sentences: "She was in the Food World store on Bankhead Highway shortly before 1 p.m. She confronted a woman married to her ex-husband. She was shot through the right lung."

Don't use one word more than is necessary. Almost every writer uses too many words on occasion. Even the best writers need to be edited. Go back a couple of paragraphs and look at the Fowler quote; it has at least two unnecessary words. Writers should use the minimum number of words necessary to express their ideas and information.

Simple, straightforward prose is mandatory for writing for the mass media. It has no substitute, and its absence will not be excused by readers or listeners.

A first cousin to simplicity is brevity. Writers should never use one more word than is necessary in their writing. They should be on the lookout for words, phrases, and sentences that do not add substantially to the content of what they are writing. They should also guard against those fancy phrases that draw attention to the writing and the writer—and take away from the content.

Eliminate jargon, clichés, and "bureaucratese." Jargon is the technical language that is used in specialized fields or among a small group of people. Scientists, sportswriters, and even students have their own jargon. Good writers, especially those for the mass media, should use words and phrases commonly understood by most people. It makes no sense to cut people off from receiving your ideas by using language that they cannot understand.

Clichés are overused words and phrases. They are phrases that have ceased to be meaningful and have become trite and tiresome. For example, "dire straits," "he's got his act together," "it's a small world," "par for the course" and "vast wasteland" have been used so much that they have lost their original luster. All of us have our favorite clichés; the trick is not to use them.

Bureaucratese is a general name for a serious misuse of the language. In order to make themselves or what they write sound more important than it is, many people try to lather their writing with unnecessary and imprecise phrasing. A speechwriter once handed President Franklin Roosevelt a draft of a speech with the following sentence: "We are endeavoring to construct a more inclusive society." Roosevelt changed it to say: "We are going to make a country in which no one is left out." Roosevelt's simple words carry far more weight than those of his speechwriter.

Isaac Asimov on writing

I try only to write clearly, and I have the very good fortune to think clearly so that the writing comes out as I think, in satisfactory shape.

© 1992 Jim Stovall

Once the football coach of a major state university was on a recruiting trip and heard over the radio that he had been fired. The next day, the athletic director at the school issued the following statement: "I regret the premature publication of the decision before appropriate notification could be made to all parties involved." The athletic director would not have sounded like such a fool if he had simply said, "I'm sorry we didn't get to tell him before the story got out."

Use familiar words rather than unfamiliar words or foreign phrases. William F. Buckley, the conservative newspaper columnist, tries to include at least one or two words that will send his readers scurrying to a dictionary. Readers expect this of Buckley and seem to accept it. Buckley is the exception, however. There are times when a writer must use a word that is not known by all of a mass audience, but those times are rare. Writers should not try to educate the masses by introducing them to new words. Such writing slows the reader down; it makes the reader think about the writing rather than the content; and it eventually drives the reader away.

Foreign phrases often have the same effect. They add little to the content and are often irritating to the reader. At times they may even be insulting, particularly when the writer does not bother to translate them.

Vary sentence type and length. There are four kinds of sentence structures: simple, complex, compound, and compound-complex. Using only one kind of sentence is boring. A good variety of types and lengths of sentences gives pace to writing. It allows the reader's mind to "breathe," to take in ideas and information in small doses.

Such variation also helps the writer. Writers often get so involved in what they are writing that they have trouble expressing their ideas clearly. They try to pack too much into one sentence or one paragraph. Breaking down complex and compound sentences into simple sentences, and then putting these sentences back into a variety of forms, often promotes clarity in writing.

One thing writers should not overuse is the inverted sentence. A good example of this kind of sentence is the previous sentence—and this sentence. The inverted sentence is not a good idea in writing for the mass media. Writers want to get ideas and information to readers quickly and efficiently.

Remember that nouns and verbs are the strongest words in the language. Sentences should be built around nouns and verbs; adjectives and adverbs, when they are used, should support the nouns and verbs. Relying on adjectives and adverbs, particularly in writing for the mass media, is a mistake.

Verbs are the most important words that a writer will use. A good verb denotes actions; a better verb denotes action and description. While adjectives and adverbs *modify* (that is, they limit), verbs *expand* the writing. They get the reader involved in the writing as no other part of speech does.

A good writer pays close attention to the verbs that he or she uses.

Transitions tie together what you have written. Unity means readers should be able to read through a piece of writing without stops or surprises. Introducing a new idea or piece of information without adequately tying it to other parts of a story is one way to stop a reader cold.

Writing for the mass media

Good writing can go anywhere. The good English theme has much in common with the good news story or the good letter to Mom or the informative label on a bottle of aspirin. All of these pieces of writing have different purposes and different audiences, and they express different ideas. But good writing is good writing.

Writing for the mass media differs from other forms of writing in several aspects:

Subject matter. Writers for the mass media must take on a wide variety of subjects, including news stories, feature stories, advertisements, letters, editorials, and so on.

Purpose. Writing for the mass media has three major purposes: to inform, entertain, and persuade.

Audience. Mass media writing is often directed to a wide audience, and this fact dictates not only the subject matter but the way in which something is written.

Circumstances of the writing. Writing for the mass media often takes place in the presence of others who are doing the same thing. The writing is frequently done under deadline pressure, and many times several people will have a hand in writing and editing a particular item for the mass media.

A few final thoughts

Here are a few final thoughts to keep in mind as the quest for good writing begins:

With the proper study and practice, anyone can become a better writer. Writing is not simply an inherent talent that some people have and others do not. There are steps that each of us can take to improve our writing, and this book will examine some of those steps and help you put them into practice.

Writing is a process. That is, the rules, techniques, and suggestions in this book must be mixed in with the individual's style, thoughts, and methods, and with the subject and form of the writing. They all should work together to produce writing that is good. The suggestions made in this book about achieving good writing are meant to help this process work.

Writing requires discipline. Most people give up writing as soon as they can because it is such hard work. It is physically, mentally, and emotionally demanding. The person who commits to writing must marshal all of his or her resources for the task.

Writing is building. Good writing doesn't happen all at once. It is formed, word by word, sentence by sentence, thought by thought. The writing process is often slow, tedious, and frustrating. But the product of this process—good writing—is well worth the effort.

Finally, reading about good writing is only the first step to learning about good writing. Reading good writing is the next step. If you are interested in learning to write well, in any form, you should read as much as possible—newspapers, magazines, books, and anything else you can get your hands on. Then there is the writing itself. This chapter tells you to "sit down and write." That is the only way to become a good writer.

Points for consideration and discussion

1. The author makes several strong points about what is and is not good writing. Did you find anything surprising or unusual about them? Do you agree with what he says about good writing?

2. Many teachers and philosophers believe the following: "Writing is thinking." How do you react to this statement?

3. Look up a passage from a book that you have read recently. What characteristics of good writing discussed in this chapter are exemplified in that passage? What characteristics of good writing are *not* present in that passage?

4. In the passage that you selected, make a list of the verbs. How many of them are linking verbs ("to be" verbs, such as is, was, were, etc.)? How many of them are active verbs? How many are passive?

5. The author says, "Good writing is good writing," no matter what form it's in. What does he mean by that? Do you agree?

Further reading

Brian S. Brooks, *Working with Words*. New York: St. Martin's Press, 1989.

Rudolf Flesch, *The Art of Readable Writing*. New York: Collier Books, 1949.

Jon Franklin. *Writing for Story : Craft Secrets of Dramatic Nonfiction by a Two-time Pulitzer Prize Winner*. New York: Atheneum, 1986.

H. W. Fowler, *A Dictionary of Modern English Usage,* (second edition, revised by Sir Ernest Gowers) Oxford: Oxford University Press, 1983.

Edwin Newman, *Strictly Speaking,* Indianapolis/New York: Bobbs-Merrill, 1974.

William Safire, *On Language,* New York: Avon Books, 1981.

William K. Zinsser. *On Writing Well,* 4th ed., New York: Perennial Library, 1990.

EXERCISES

The following section contains a variety of beginning writing exercises. You should follow your instructor's directions in completing them.

Autobiography

Write a 350-word summary of your life. Tell the most important things that have happened to you. Also talk about the things that interest you the most.

Letter to Mom

Write a letter to your mother, father, or some other close relative. The main part of your letter should be about the course that requires this assignment. Include some information about the professor for the course, what the course is about, the procedures for the class, the grading and attendance policies, and anything else you think is important. You will also want to give the name of your lab instructor. The letter should be at least 250 words long.

Describe your neighbor

Desribe the person sitting nearest to you. Be specific. Give the reader a lot of details about the person's physical appearance, including hair and eye color, height, shape of the face, the kind of clothes the person is wearing, and so on. Write at least 200 words.

An incident

Write about something that happened to you in the last week. It could be something dramatic, such as being in an automobile accident or meeting a famous person, or something common such as eating a meal or taking a ride on a bus. You should include some dialogue (quoting someone directly) in the description of this incident. Write 250 words.

Action

Decribe someone or a group of people doing something. It could be something like a couple of carpenters building a part of a house or your roommate trying to type a paper. Be sure to focus on the physical activity and on how people are doing it. Don't try to describe how the people feel or what they may think about what they are doing. Simply write about what you can see and hear. Write 350 words.

Instructions–1

Tell step-by-step how to do something. For example, tell how to change the oil in a car, use a tape recorder, or build a fire. Use simple terms and simple sentences so that anyone who can read could understand it. The following is an example of such a set of directions.

In order to drive a nail into a piece of wood, follow the steps below:
1. Be sure the wood is on a solid surface.
2. Check the nail you are using to make sure it is straight; if it is bent, discard it.
3. Hold the pointed end of the nail against the wood with the thumb and the first finger.
Etc.

The activity that you describe should have at least seven steps.

Instructions–2

Describe the procedure for tying a shoe in 100 or fewer words. You might approach the assignment this way: Write the procedure without regard to how many words you are using. Once you have finished the first draft, edit it to take out as many words as possible but still have it make sense. What does this tell you about the way you write?

Building

Describe the building in which this class is being held. Don't go outside and look at it but describe it from what you remember. Write at least 150 words.

Rewriting

Rewrite the letter below using simpler language. Make sure that you include all of the information contained in the original letter.

Dear Stockholder:

In accordance with company policies and the federal law, this letter is to inform you of the general annual meeting of the stockholders of this company which will be held on the 30th day of March of this year. The place of the meeting will be in the ballroom of the Waldorf Hotel, which is located at 323 Lexington Avenue, in New York. The beginning time of the meeting will be at nine o'clock in the morning on the 30th of March.

The agenda for this meeting includes a number of items and actions of great import to the company and its stockholders. The election of officers for the company's board of directors will take place beginning at approximately half past ten o'clock. This election follows the annual reports on the company's activities and financial position which will be presented by the president of the company and the chairman of the board of directors. Other items on the agenda include discussions of the company's operations in the foreign arena and the possibilities for investments in new areas of technology. Time will also be appropriated for discussions of general concerns of stockholders and for the answering of questions from stockholders directed to the company's officers. It is the sincere wish of the company's board of directors and officers that you will be able to attend this most important and hopefully informative meeting. The input of the company's stockholders is an important part of this company's operation and planning for the future.

Sincerely,
The Company President

2
Basic Tools of Writing

Writing is impossible in any form unless you know how to use the tools of writing. These tools are all the things a writer can use to present information and ideas—rules of grammar and punctuation, precise meanings for words, and proper spelling. The writer who knows these tools can write with authority. That writer can take on the forms of writing demanded by the mass media.

English is a basic tool of the writer. Like any other worker, the writer must know the tools of the trade thoroughly—their possibilities as well as their limitations. Knowing when and under what circumstances these tools can be properly used is vital. The writer who cannot coherently use the English language is like a carpenter who cannot saw a straight line. The products of such a writer or carpenter will not inspire confidence; nor will they be items people want to purchase.

Unlike the carpenter's hammer or saw, however, the English language is an extremely complex tool. It has many nuances and subtleties. People spend years mastering English. There are many rules for its usage and many arguments about the propriety of some of these rules.

One thing making English so complex is its dynamic nature. English is the closest thing the world has to an international language. It is spoken and understood by more than 300 million people in nearly every part of the globe. But no central control or authority governs its use. Consequently, the language is always changing. New words and expressions come into use as others fade. Old words take on new meanings. English is mixed with other languages. Spelling rules shift with differing usage. Humans are constantly discovering new phenomena needing description in the language. All this makes English a difficult but exciting tool.

Using the language effectively requires knowing the basic rules and conventions. Writers should know thoroughly the eight basic parts of speech (nouns, verbs, adjectives, adverbs, pronouns, conjunctions, interjections, and prepositions), and the basic unit of the English usage (the sentence) and its two parts (subject and predicate). They should not only have an eye for the language, but they should also have an ear for it. Writers should know when things that are technically correct sound wrong. Beyond that, they should be able to recognize—and hear—the confusing phrase, the unclear sentence, and the absence of transition. They must be able to spot the confusion and illogic that are the harbingers of misinformation, inaccuracy, and a failure to communicate. Like the carpenter, the writer should use the language to saw a straight line to the reader.

That straight line to the reader is one of the chief goals of the writer. The writer who does not use English correctly will annoy the reader and call the publication's credibility into question. A misspelled word will not destroy a publication, and an agreement error will not inspire calls for a repeal of the First Amendment, but too many such mistakes will convince the reader that a publication is not worth his or her time and money.

Grammar and punctuation

Sentences. A sentence is a group of words that contain a subject and a verb, and express a complete thought. "John ran to the store" is a complete sentence; it has a subject, *John*, and a verb, *ran*, and it expresses a complete thought. "After the rain stopped" is not a complete sentence; it does have a subject and a verb, but it does not express a complete thought. A phrase like "after the rain stopped" is called a dependent clause; it contains a subject and a verb but cannot stand alone. "John ran to the store" is an independent clause.

Structurally, there are four kinds of sentences: simple, complex, compound, and compound-complex. A simple sentence is one that has an independent clause and no dependent clauses, such as

John ran to the store.

A complex sentence is one which has an independent clause and a dependent clause.

John ran to the store after the rain had stopped.

Independent clause   **Dependent clause**

This is a complex sentence because it contains one of each kind of clause. A compound sentence is a sentence that contains two independent clauses, and these clauses should be separated by a comma and a coordinating conjunction.

John ran to the store, but he walked back.

Independent clause   **Independent clause**

**Comma and
coordinating conjunction**

The sentence above is a compound sentence because it contains two independent clauses; they are separated by a comma and the coordinating conjunction *but*. Another common coordinating conjunction is *and*. Sometimes a semicolon substitutes for the conjunction.

A compound-complex sentence is a sentence that contains two independent clauses and a dependent clause. The independent clauses should be separated by a comma and a coordinating conjunction, such as in the following sentence:

John ran to the store after the rain had stopped, but he walked back.

Independent clause   **Independent clause**

Dependent clause   **Comma and coordinating conjunction**

Here's a tip for recognizing the four different kinds of sentences. Look for the comma and coordinating conjunction. If a sentence does not have these two elements together, it is either a simple or a complex sentence. Then you need to look for a dependent clause. If there is one, it is a complex sentence; if not, it is a simple sentence. If the sentence does have a comma and coordinating conjunction together, it is either a compound or a compound-complex sentence. Again you need to look for the dependent clause. If it is there, the sentence is compound-complex; if it is not there, the sentence is a compound sentence.

There are four types of sentences: declarative, interrogative, imperative, and exclamatory. A *declarative* sentence is one which makes a statement. This is the most common type of sentence. An *interrogative* sentence is one which asks a question, and it is usually ended by a question mark (?). An *imperative* sentence is a command; it is usually ended by a period, but it may also end with an exclamation mark (!). An *exclamatory* sentence expresses some strong emotion (excitement, joy, fear, etc.) and usually ends with an exclamation mark.

Sentence fragments. Earlier we referred to sentences as groups of words that express a complete thought. Sometimes someone will write a group of words which does not express a complete thought. That is a sentence fragment. There are some situations in writing where using a sentence fragment may be appropriate. Generally writers for the mass media should write in complete sentences.

Parts of speech. English contains eight parts of speech: nouns, pronouns, adjectives, adverbs, verbs, conjunctions, prepositions, and interjections. You should be able to recognize any of those in any sentence.

Nouns are the names of objects or concepts.

Pronouns are substitutes for nouns, and they are among the most confusing parts of speech. There are two ways of looking at pronouns. One way is to decide what "person" they refer to; they may be first-, second-, or third-person pronouns. Another way of looking at pronouns is at a pronoun's case: subjective, objective, or possessive. Subjective case means that the pronoun can be used as the subject of a sentence; objective case means that it can be used as the object of a verb or a preposition; possessive case means that the pronoun is used as a modifier for a noun and indicates possession. On the next page is a chart containing cases and persons of pronouns.

Adjectives modify nouns; that is, they give some description to the noun or define it in some way.

Adverbs modify verbs, but they may also modify adjectives or other adverbs. Many adverbs end in -*ly*.

Verbs express action or state of being. We usually refer to verbs as being in a particular tense—or the time of the action. There are three basic tenses: past, present, and future. You should be able to recognize the tense of any verb in any sentence.

Conjunctions connect words, phrases, and clauses together. The most commonly used conjunctions are *and, but, so, or, and nor.*

Prepositions are words which go with nouns or pronouns to modify other nouns, pronouns, or verbs. Some common prepositions are *in, at, from, to, on,* and *with.*

Interjections are words that express strong emotion (*wow!*). When they are inserted into sentences, they should be set off by commas.

Punctuation. Commas (,), semicolons (;), periods (.), and colons (:) are among the most common forms of punctuation.

The comma is a mere blip on a page of type. No other punctuation mark, however, gives students more problems, raises so many questions among writers, and causes so much controversy among grammarians. Consequently, we need to give some added attention to the comma.

The comma is an extremely useful tool, and that is part of its problem. It is so useful that its uses are hard to prescribe.

For example, *Harbrace College Handbook* says that a comma should be used to separate items in a series, such as "red, white, and blue," including a comma before the conjunction (in this case, before *and*). Newspaper editors are afraid of using too many commas, so they have set up some rules against their use. Thus, the *Associated Press (AP) Stylebook* advises writers: "Use commas to separate elements in a series, but do not put a comma before the conjunction in a simple series." Using this rule, the example becomes "red, white and blue."

James J. Kilpatrick, the newspaper columnist and commentator on

Figure 2-1 Pronouns

The table of pronouns to the right represents one way that pronouns can be divided up and undersood. The mark of the careful and professional writer is that he or she knows how to use pronouns properly.

Personal Pronouns

		Subjective	Possessive	Objective
Singular				
	First person	I	my, mine	me
	Second person	you	your, yours	you
	Third person	he, she, it	his, her, hers, its	him, her, it
Plural				
	First person	we	our, ours	us
	Second person	you	you, yours	you
	Third person	they	their, theirs	them

Relative Pronouns

	Subjective	Possessive	Objective
Singular	who	whose	whom
Plural	who	whose	whom

grammar and usage, has advocated abolishing most rules for using commas, saying that there are too many exceptions for each of the rules to make them useful. A comma, he says, should simply be used whenever a pause is needed. That may be an adequate philosophy for the experienced writer, but for the student just learning the rules, the relevant questions are "When should I use a comma?" and "When is it wrong to use a comma?"

Webster's Seventh Collegiate Dictionary, in its grammar section, gives three general instances for using commas:

Commas used to set off items. These are commas used to set off parenthetical or independent words ("Inside, the building was dark and lonely. Nevertheless, the boys entered."); appositions and modifiers ("The man, who was nearly seven feet tall, was arrested. His reaction, silent and calm, was a surprise."); and transitional words ("On the other hand, the brothers held differing views.").

Commas used to separate items. These commas separate introductory clauses or phrases from other parts of the sentence ("After driving all night, they were exhausted."); items in a series ("The flag is red, white and blue"—if we use *AP* style); and parts of a compound sentence ("The sky is blue, and the grass is green.").

Commas used arbitrarily. Some instances in writing simply demand commas, such as large figures (*28,000*), dates, addresses, and inverted names (*Smith, John C.*).

Students trying to learn when to use commas should remember what the *AP Stylebook* has to say about punctuation in general: "Think of it (punctuation) as a courtesy to your readers, designed to help them understand a story." The comma that helps the reader is correctly placed.

Semicolons are used to separate independent clauses in the same sentence (see above) and to separate long items in a series ("Attending the dinner were John Smith, mayor of Tuscaloosa; Mary Johnson, president of the League of Women Voters; Joe Jones, vice-president of Jones Steel, Inc.; and Rhonda Jackson, head of the Committee for Better Government").

Colons are often used to link the latter part of a sentence to some previous part. For example: "The flag contains the following colors: red, white, and blue."

The period is most often used to end sentences, but it has other uses, such as ending abbreviations (Mr.). The question mark is used to end interrogative sentences, and the exclamation point ends sentences and expressions of excitement.

Agreement. Agreement refers to singular or plural references.

A singular subject takes a singular verb; plural subjects take plural verbs. In the sentence "The clock strikes on the hour," the subject is *clock*. A singular noun, *clock*, takes the singular verb, *strikes*. However, if the sentence were "The clocks strike on the hour," the plural subject, *clocks*, would take the plural verb, *strike*. All that is fairly simple, but what about a sentence like this: "The consent of both sets of parents are needed for a juvenile marriage." The subject and verb in this sentence are not in agreement. *Consent* is the subject, not *sets* or *parents*. Consequently, the verb should be *is*, not *are*.

Agreement is also a problem when you are using pronouns to refer to nouns. These nouns are called antecedents, and pronouns should always agree with their antecedents. In the sentence "The boys believed they could win," the antecedent *boys* agrees in number with the pronoun *they*. Often, however, the following mistake is made: "The team believed they could win." The antecedent *team* is a singular noun, and its pronoun should also be singular. The sentence should read, "The team believed it could win."

Active and passive voice

One of the most important grammatical tools that writers for the mass media should learn is recognition of the active and passive voice. Active and passive voice refer to the way in which verbs are used. If a verb is used in the active voice, the emphasis is on the subject as the doer or perpetrator of the action. Passive voice throws the action onto the object and often obscures the perpetrator of the action. It is formed by putting a helping verb such as "is" or "was" in front of the past tense of the verb. Look at the following examples:

Active: John throws the ball.
Passive: The ball is thrown by John.

Active: The president sent the legislation to Congress.
Passive: The legislation was sent to Congress by the president.

Active: The governor decided to veto the bill.
Passive: It was decided by the governor to veto the bill.

Generally, writers for the mass media try to use the active rather than the passive voice. The active voice is more direct and livelier. It is less cumbersome than the passive voice and gets the reader into the action of the words more quickly. When you edit your writing and find that you have written in the passive voice, you should ask, "Would this sentence be better if the verb were in the active voice?" Very often the answer will be yes.

Sometimes the answer will be no. When changing passive voice to active voice puts the wrong emphasis on the sentence, the passive voice should be used. Consider the following sentence, "The victims were rushed to a hospital by an ambulance." If we practiced strict adherence to the active voice, we would change that sentence to read, "An ambulance rushed the victims to a hospital." The important part of that sentence is the victims, not the ambulance, however. So, the use of the passive voice can be justified.

Take a look at the third set of examples above. In the passive voice sentence, the indefinite pronoun *it* is used with the passive voice verb. This usage is particularly insidious because it obscures those responsible for an action. This construction, *it* with a passive voice verb, is not acceptable in writing for the mass media.

Additional grammar problems

Besides the grammar problems we touched on in the previous sections, a few other problems recur, particularly for beginning students. Some of them are discussed next.

Dangling participles. A participial phrase at the beginning of a sentence should modify the sentence's subject and should be separated from it by a comma. One would not write, "After driving from Georgia to Texas, Tom's car finally gave out." The car didn't drive to Texas; it was driven. We must assume from this sentence that it was Tom who did the driving.

The apostrophe. The proper use of the apostrophe probably gives more users of English more problems than any other form of punctuation. The apostrophe can be used in a number of ways. First, we use apostrophes to form possessives, as in "Mary's hat" and "Tom's book." If a word ends in *s* or the plural of the noun is formed by adding *s*, the apostrophe generally goes after the final *s*, and no other letter is needed. For example, the possessive of the word *hostess* is *hostess'*. The plural possessive of the word *team* is *teams'*. The plural possessive of *child* is *children's*.

Even professionals have problems when the word *it* and an apostrophe come together. Is it *its, it's,* or *its'*? Here are some rules worth memorizing. *Its* (without the apostrophe) is the possessive of the pronoun *it,* as in *"its final score."* *It's* (with the apostrophe) is a contraction meaning *it is,* as in *"it's hard to tell."* *Its'* makes no sense because *it* has no plural form.

Appositive phrases and commas. Appositive phrases follow a noun and rename it. Such phrases are set off by commas in almost all cases. For example, in the sentence "Billy Braun, Tech's newest football star, was admitted to a local hospital yesterday," the phrase "Tech's newest football star" is the appositive to "Billy Braun." It is important to remember to put a second comma at the end of the appositive. This is easy to overlook if the appositive is extremely long. For example, the sentence "Job Thompson, the newly named Will Marcum State Junior College president who succeeded Byron Wilson has accepted the presidency of the Association of Junior College Administrators," needs a comma after Wilson.

Comma splices and run-on sentences. When two independent clauses are connected, they must be connected by two things: a comma and a conjunction. When two clauses are connected only by a comma, that is called a **comma splice** or a **run-on sentence.** For example, "The team won its final game, now they are the champs" is a comma splice or run-on sentence. The reader needs a conjunction to help separate the two sentences. Just as incorrect is the compound sentence with no comma before the conjunction: "The team won its final game and now they are the champs."

Commas between subject and verbs. Commas should be used to separate phrases and other elements in a sentence, but they should not be used solely to separate a subject from its verb. Obviously, you wouldn't write, "The boy, sat on the bench," but neither would you write, "The moment the train comes in, is when we will see her" or "Having no money, is a difficult thing."

That and which. One of the jobs of these two pronouns is to introduce dependent clauses. The trick is knowing which one to use. "Which" introduces non-essential clauses—clauses that are not necessary to the meaning of the sentence. In the sentence, "John wrecked his car, which he bought only last month," the clause "which he bought only last month" is not essential to the meaning of the sentence. "John wrecked his car" could stand alone as an understandable sentence. Non-essential clauses are usually set off from the rest of the sentence by commas.

That introduces an essential clause, one that is necessary to gain a proper understanding of the sentence. In the sentence, "Jane wanted the kind of computer that she had always used," the clause "that she had always used" is essential to understanding the sentence. The sentence would not make sense without it. Essential clauses are not set off by commas. When you are editing your copy, find all of the instances where you used *which* and determine whether or not you used it properly.

Spelling

We are living in an age of spelling rules. It was not always so. Centuries ago, when English was evolving as a written language, there were practically no rules of spelling. Writers spelled the way they thought words sounded, and that accounted for some wildly differing ways in which some words were spelled. As certain spellings were used more and more, they became generally accepted, although not universally so. By the eighteenth century, when the fathers of our modern dictionaries began their work, they not only had to decide among diverse spellings for words, but they also had to contend with generally accepted spellings that might not be the best or most efficient.

Since that time, movements to simplify the spelling of certain words have sprung up. These movements have targeted words that end in a silent *e*, such as *give, live, have,* and *bake,* and other such silent combinations, such as "-ought" (for example, *thought* should become *thot,* and *through* should become *thru*).

Despite the efforts of many people during the last two centuries, spelling changes have occurred very slowly. People learn to spell most of the words they use before they are ten years old, and they are not comfortable in changing what they have learned. It is not up to those in the mass media to lead the fight for most simplified spellings. (Several years ago a number of newspaper editors ran into some trouble on this very point. Thinking that the spelling of a number of words was clumsy and confusing , these editors arbitrarily changed the way these words were spelled in their newspapers. *Through* became *thru, thorough* became *thoro,* and *employee* turned into *employe.* Reader acceptance of these changes was less than complete, and many editors had to beat a hasty retreat.) Rather, people in the mass media should make sure that what they write conforms to the generally accepted rules of spelling and that the spellings they use do not distract or surprise the reader.

Spelling correctly involves three thought processes: applying phonics, memorizing some words, and knowing the rules that usually apply to most words. Writers should know how to do all three. Phonics can be learned, either in early years or later. One must memorize those words that are not spelled phonetically or do not follow spelling rules. However, most words can be spelled correctly without memorization because either rules or phonetics apply to the majority of English words. Some of the rules, with known exceptions, are explained in the following paragraphs.

1. With words of one syllable or words accented on the last syllable that end in a single consonant preceded by a single vowel, the final consonant is doubled before adding *ed* or a syllable beginning with a vowel—for example, *plan, planned; prefer, preferred; wit, witty; hot, hottest; swim, swimming; stop, stopped; bag, baggage; beg, beggar.*

There are a few exceptions. One illustrates the impact of accent. *Refer*

Figure 2-2
Samuel Johnson
Samuel Johnson (on the right of the picture) was an unlikely candidate to be a leading figure in the development of English, and yet he is rated as second only to Shakespeare in his contributions. After nine years of work, Johnson produced the *Dictionary of the English Language* in 1755. It was not the first attempt compiling, defining, and standardizing the spelling of the words in the English language, but it was to date the most elegant. The dictionary had 43,000 definitions and 114,000 quotations from all of English literature. Johnson's reputation was secured when he met a young Scottish lawyer, James Boswell, who became devoted to him. Boswell had a remarkable memory, and after Johnson died in 1784, Boswell wrote a two-volume biography of him that is still considered one of the greatest biographies in the English language.

JOHNSON AND BOSWELL AT THE MITRE.

becomes *reference*, without doubling the *r*, but the accent also changes away from the final syllable when the suffix is added.

There are other exceptions: words ending in *k, v, w, x,* and *y; benefit, benefited; chagrin, chagrined* (even though stress stays on the final syllable of the new word).

2. A final *e* is usually dropped on addition of a syllable beginning with a vowel: *come, coming; guide, guidance; cure, curable; judge, judging; plume, plumage; force, forcible; use, usage.* There are exceptions: *sale, saleable; mile, mileage; peace, peaceable; dye, dyeing.*

3. A final *e* is usually retained on addition of a syllable beginning with a consonant: *use, useless; late, lately; hate, hateful; move, movement; safe, safety; white, whiteness; pale, paleness; shame, shameful.* The case of *nine, ninety, nineteen,* but *ninth* is an exception. Other exceptions are *judge, judgment* and *argue, argument.*

4. Words ending in a double *e* retain both *e*'s before an added syllable: *free, freely, see, seeing, agree, agreement, agreeable.*

5. Words ending in a double consonant retain both consonants when one or more syllables are added: *ebb, ebbing; enroll; enrollment; full, fullness; dull, dullness; skill, skillful; odd, oddly; will, willful; stiff, stiffness.*

6. Compounds of *all, well,* and *full* drop one *l: always, almost welfare, welcome; fulfill and skillful.* (This is really a listing of exceptions to rule 5.) Exceptions include *fullness* and occasions when a word is hyphenated (as with *full-fledged*).

7. *I* before *e*, except after *c*, or when sounded like *a*, as in *neighbor* or *weigh: receive, deceive, relieve, believe.*

8. A final *y* preceded by a consonant is usually changed to *i* with the addition of an ending not beginning with *i*: *army, armies, spy, spies, and busy, business.* Some exceptions are *shy, shyness, pity, piteous* (but not *pitiful*). The *ay* endings are usually exceptions; for example—*play, played.*

9. This is really not a rule but just some information about a few tricky words, which must be described as exceedingly difficult. These must be memorized: *exceed, proceed,* and *succeed* all end with *-ceed*, but *supersede* ends with *-sede*. All others with this sound end in *-cede*. These include *precede, intercede, secede, concede, accede,* and *recede.*

Rule 9 tells you how to become a very good speller. Memorize the tricky words and the spelling "demons," and if you know both your rules and phonics, you can spell most of the rest.

You will also need to know some of the basic rules for forming plurals. Here are a few:

1. Most plurals for nouns are formed by simply adding *s* to the root word.

2. Nouns ending with *s, z, x, ch or sh* usually require an *es* ending to form the plural.

3. When a word ends with a consonant and then a *y*, the *y* is changed to *i* and an *es* is added (example: *army, armies*).

4. When a word ends in a vowel and a *y*, you can simply add an *s* for the plural (example: *bay, bays*).

5. Compound words without hyphens simply take an *s* on the end (*cupful, cupfuls*), but compound words with a hyphen take the *s* on the significant word (*son-in-law, sons-in-law*).

6. The *AP Stylebook* advises that *'s* should be used only in forming the plural of single letters (*A's, B's*) but not figures (1920s, 727s). Never use *'s* to form the plural of a word that is fully spelled out.

Computer aids

When the widespread use of word processors began in the late 1970s and early 1980s, they were little more than electronic typewriters that allowed writers to store documents and change them with ease. The software for these machines has grown increasingly sophisticated, and now they are becoming full-fledged partners in the writing process. Three major types of software are available to the writer: spelling dictionaries, stylebooks and grammar checkers.

Spelling dictionaries are large lists of words that reside in the computer's memory. In some software programs, they are activated while the document is being written and will check the spelling of words as the document is being created. In other programs, they can be activated whenever the writer wants to use them. They check spelling by matching the words in the document to the words in the list. When a word in the document does not match a word in the dictionary list, it is highlighted for the writer. Most spelling programs will then offer a set of alternative words for the writer. Writers can also "look up" words while they are writing; they can type a word and then ask the spelling program to check to see if it matches a word in the dictionary list.

The obvious shortcoming of these spelling programs is that they cannot understand the meaning of the words they are matching. Consequently, a writer can use the wrong word, and if it is spelled correctly, the spelling program will not find it. For example, if a writer makes a simple typographical error as in the sentence, "I am coming to you house tonight," the spelling program will not understand that the word *you* should be *your*. Because *you* is spelled correctly and matches a word in its list, it will skip over that error.

Stylebook programs work in much the same way. (Stylebooks and their importance are discussed in the next chapter.) Style guide programs can be installed on a computer, and when a writer has a question about a style rule, he or she can call up the program without leaving the document that is being produced. Some programs will automatically check a document for some style errors, but these checkers have some of the same shortcomings as spelling programs. They cannot catch all of the errors of meaning.

Grammar checking programs are the most sophisticated of all of these kinds of software. They not only check for certain kinds of grammatical and punctuation errors, but they also will measure the length of words, number of syllables in the words, and the number of words in sentences. They will tell writers when words and sentences are overly long according to some preset formulas. Some programs have built-in lists of jargon and clichés that will highlight such phrases for the writer. They will also point out the uses of the passive voice, giving writers an opportunity to change if they wish.

Although these programs have grown in sophistication—and are likely to become even more sophisticated—they cannot find all the errors in a document, and they cannot understand meanings or context. Many professionals and instructors argue that they should not be used at all because they allow writers to become lazy about checking their own work and dependent on these mechanical devices rather than their own knowledge and understanding of what they are writing. Those criticisms and fears are valid. Beginning writers should understand the very limited capacities of all of this software. No piece of software has been created that comes close to the ability of the mind to understand the subtleties and complexities of the English language.

Conclusion

This chapter had concentrated on the rules of writing, and it's likely many beginning writing students find a lengthy discussion of these rules boring, if not oppressive.

Serious students of writing, however, will remember through all this discussion why we should be concerned about the rules: In writing for the mass media, we are trying to transmit information and ideas to an audience of readers and listeners. Will bad grammar, misspelling, sloppy punctuation, and misuse of words help accomplish that goal? Will these mistakes tell the reader that the content of your communication is accurate and worthwhile— worthy of the audience's time and effort to understand it?

The answer, of course, is no. Good grammar, precise word usage, and correct spelling are a means to an end. That end is communicating with the reader or viewer.

Points for consideration and discussion

1.   The authors makes a strong case for knowing the rules of grammar, but some people do not think that this knowledge is very important. They believe that you can write well without knowing these rules. What do you think?

2.   The text says that there are some times when a sentence fragment might be appropriate. When would that be?

3.   What do you think are the most important rules for using a comma?

4.   Explain the difference between *its, it's,* and *its'*.

5.   Many of today's college students say they don't understand the rules of grammar because they didn't spend a lot of time with it in high school. What was your experience with grammar in high school?

6.   Make a list of words that you think should be spelled differently.

7.   Make a list of words that you often hear people misuing.

Further reading

Brian S. Brooks and James L. Pinson, *Working with Words.* New York: St. Martin's Press, 1989.

Bill Bryson, *The Mother Tongue: English and How it Got that Way.* New York: William Morrow and Co., 1990.

R. Thomas Berner, *Language Skills for Journalists,* Boston: Houghton Mifflin, 1979.

Theodore A. Cheney, *Getting The Words Right : How To Revise, Edit & Rewrite.* Cincinnati, OH: Writer's Digest Books, 1983.

John C. Hodges and Mary Whitten, *Harbrace College Handbook,* 7th ed., New York: Harcourt Brace Jovanovich, 1972.

Lauren Kessler and Duncan McDonald, *When Words Collide,* 2d ed., Belmont, CA: Wadsworth, 1988.

Lauren Kessler, *Mastering the Message: Media Writing with Substance and Style.* Belmont, CA: Wadsworth Pub. Co., 1989.

Floyd Watkins, William Dillingham, and Edwin Martin, *Practical English Handbook,* Boston: Houghton Mifflin, 1970.

EXERCISES

The following section contains a variety of beginning writing exercises. You should follow your instructor's directions in completing them.

2–1 Writing Skills

The following sentences were taken from newspapers and television broadcasts. Correct the errors you find either by copy-editing or by rewriting the sentences. Underline your corrections. Some of the sentences are correct, and you should write *correct* in the margin.

1. He is one of the greatest choreographers who has ever lived.

2. The general assumed what was then described as dictorial powers.

3. The couple has two children.

4. Inside the box was a man and a woman.

5. Absent from the meeting were the mayor and two councilmen.

6. Every fireman in the city, 250 in all were called out.

7. A total of 650 Eskimos was examined and tested.

8. Only two in four were urgent cases, a group that included cardiacs, asthmatics and those found unconscious.

9. The chairman stated that response to the committee's activities has convinced him that the money for renovation can be raised.

10. Business administration and journalism courses provide the student with good background for work in public relations.

11. Here comes the famous Kilgore College Rangerettes onto the field to perform at halftime.

12. Leading the United States' show of strength were Arthur Ashe and Clarke Graebner.

13. The investigation revealed that none of the team members were involved in illegal endorsements of sports clothing.

14. "There's two knocked out cold on the floor!" the sportscaster shouted.

15. Every one of us have asked that question sometime in our lives.

2–2 Writing Skills

Correct the following sentences.

1. The assistance of three lawyers, one an expert, and two advertising men (was, were) necessary.

2. A list of the semester's reading assignments (have, has) been posted on the bulletin board.

3. Around us in every direction (was, were) miles of empty desert.

4. The chancellor, as well as the provost and the dean, (was, were) going to camp.

5. Five members of the class, including John (was, were) going to camp.

6. There (was, were) two newspapers in town, but there (was, were) only one editorial policy.

7. Airplanes (was, were) Randall's chief interest in life.

8. Randall's chief interest in life (was, were) airplanes.

9. Neither had finished (their, his) job.

10. Maybe some day each person will have (his or her, their) own helicopter for commuting to the city.

11. I have always maintained that a person should mind (his or her, their) own business.

12. After basic training, almost everyone is sent to different schools, according to (his or her, their) ability.

13. Neither of the two nephews (live, lives) in Montana.

14. Neither had finished (their, his or her) job.

2–3 Writing Skills

Do whatever is necessary to correct the following sentences.

1. Their rival forces meanwhile prepared to meet Wednesday to patch up peace.

2. Pasadena California is the site of the Rose Bowl.

3. It was O. J. Simpson (who, whom) the coach praised so highly.

4. The tomb of the pharaoh had (laid, lain) buried in the desert for centuries.

5. I heard the train whistle at the crossing that was going to Denver.

6. She borrowed an egg from a neighbor that was rotten.

7. For a year we almost heard nothing from our former neighbors.

8. There was a canary in a cage that never sang.

9. We hope that you will notify us if you can attend the banquet on the enclosed post card.

10. Come here Mary and help us.

11. I know she (swum, swims) the channel regularly in this weather.

12. The children looked forward to celebrating Christmas for several weeks.

13. After setting foot on the uninhabited island of Europe, off Africa, to direct the filming of the sea turtles, a hurricane whirled across the Indian ocean and hit the island.

14. He ran swiftly the dog in front of him and plunged into the forest.

15. The casings had (tore, torn) (loose, lose) from their bearings.

2–4 Punctuation

Insert the correct punctuation in the following sentences.

1. In fact I hope to leave tomorrow

2. My friends we have no alternative

3. He said "the story has been told

4. Our failures not our successes will be remembered

5. Sandburg the biographer of Lincoln was awarded the Pulitzer Prize

6. My companions were James White M.D. and Rufus Black Ph.d.

7. William the Conqueror invaded England in 1066

8. My son James is sick

9. The work is on the whole very satisfactory

10. He was inducted into the army at Fort Oglethorpe Georgia on Sept 30, 1942

11. Please send all communications to 750 Third Ave New York New York 10017

12. Pearl Harbor Hawaii was bombed on December 7 1941

13. Manuscripts should be mailed to the Managing Editor 109 Parrington Hall University of Washington Seattle Washington

14. "We believe" he replied "that you are correct"

15. We believe however that you should go.

2–5 Punctuation

In the following sentences, insert the correct punctuation.

1. I subscribe to the *New Yorker Harper's Magazine* and the *Reporter*

2. Seven legislators from the southern part of the state changed their votes and with their help the bill was passed.

3. Do you like your steak rare medium or well done?

4. A tape recorder gives very accurate reproduction and it has the great advantage that it can be used at home as well as at the studio.

5. The gun went off and everyone jumped

6. The new cars are certainly more powerful but it is doubtful that they are any safer

7. Light entered the room through cracks in the walls through holes in the roof and through one small window.

8. Hundreds of church bells ringing loudly after years of silence announced the end of the war

9. The book was lying where I left it

10. The advisor who is never in his office makes registration difficult

11. Some years ago I lived in a section of town where almost everyone was a Republican

12. Hearne was still disclaiming with great eloquence but no one in the crowd was listening

13. I bought a large bath towel

14. We were sitting before the fire in the big room at Twins Farms and Lewis had rudely retired behind the newspaper

15. The ranchmen rode with their families into the little town and encouraged their sons to demonstrate their skill with broken horses

2–6 Clauses

In the following sentences, underline the independent clause and circle the subordinate (dependent) clause.

1. They agreed to open negotiations when both sides ceased fire.

2. If he had known, he would never have said that.

3. Since the current was swift, he could not swim to shore.

4. The horse came up to the first jump, when he stumbled and threw Jean off.

5. This is called the cryptozoite stage, after which the plasmodia break out of the liver cells and float about in the blood stream.

6. An especially big wave rolled in, when I finally managed to get my line unsnagged.

7. While walking past the building, the night watchman noticed the door was unlocked.

8. Harkey's injured knee has failed to heal completely; therefore, he may see little action against Notre Dame on Saturday.

9. The Ace Manufacturing Company, where I used to work, went bankrupt.

10. This last semester, if it has done nothing else, has given me confidence in myself.

Write five correct sentences containing independent and subordinate clauses.

1.

2.

3.

4.

5.

2–7 Word Choice

In the following sentences, fill in the blank with one of the words that appears in parentheses.

1. _____ are good reasons why _____ about to sell _____ house.(there, their, they're)

2. _____ not _____ late _____ give the cat milk.(its, it's, to, too)

3. If _____ going home, take _____ books with you. (your, you're)

4. Do you know _____ the _____ is pleasant _____ ?(whether, weather, there, their, they're)

5. They _____ known for a long time that you would _____ gone if you had heard _____ the game in time. (have, of, 've)

6. Where _____ are many opinions, most people feel justifed in holding on to _____ own; and while there are several scientific explanations for stubborness, _____ be few changes unless we can convince men that they ought to be more open-minded. (there, their, they're, there'll)

7. My _____ objection to the _____ of that school is that he is a man of no _____(principal, principle)

8. Not until _____ will you be able to tell whether you have more _____ you need. (than, then)

9. If _____ strap is _____ , you may _____ your books. (lose, loose, you're, your)

10. Not even in the _____ would I _____ the table before eating _____ (desert, dessert)

11. "_____ going to punch _____ nose?" (whose, who's)

12. We _____ the ruling without protest, although we _____all those over 45. (except, accept)

13. His speech _____ the audience greatly. (affected, effected)

14. _____ 50,000 people attend the opening game of the World Series. (Over, More than)

15. He was always one to do things _____ .(different, differently)

2–8 Pronouns and Verbs

In the following sentences, underline the correct pronoun or verb.

1. He is the player (who, whom) probably will play shortstop.

2. Is this the person (who, whom) you want?

3. Each of the three quarterbacks (is, are) good runners.

4. Both Baylor and Arkansas (has, have) won six games and lost two.

5. Either of the two players (are, is) eligible.

6. Each of the members (was, were) in (his, their) seat(s) when the session began.

7. (Who, Whom), then, would the tax hurt?

8. Do you know to (who, whom) that notebook belongs?

9. (Who, Whom) is going with the reporter to get a picture of the crash?

10. He declared that everybody must play (his, their) part.

11. This story is between you and (I, me).

12. No matter how you look at it, it was (I, she, her) (who, whom) they opposed.

13. Bryan is the kind of man (whom, who) always thinks before he acts.

14. This is the only one of the typewriters that (is, are) working.

15. Everyone was on (their, his or her) best behavior.

2–9 Verbs

In the following sentences, underline the correct form of the verb.

1. What (lays, lies) in the future for Alaska?

2. He had been (lain, laid) on a stretcher.

3. "(Lay, Lie) down and be quiet for an hour," he ordered.

4. The six-year-old boy was just (setting, sitting) there in the ruins, trying not to cry.

5. The Ohio State football team (sat, set) back and enjoyed the movie of its game with Michigan.

6. The men worked all night (raising, rising) a monument in spite of the (raising, rising) tide of the river.

7. After lunch she had (laid, lain) down for a nap.

8. The hard tackling by the Georgia Bulldogs had really (began, begun) to tell.

9. Suddenly a cloud of dust (rises, raises) in the west.

10. Had the tight end simply (fell, fallen) on the ball, he would have (catched, caught) it.

11. Spillane (led, lead) you to believe that the butler was the murderer.

12. Chris Gilbert had (proved, proven) to be the outstanding player.

13. He said that he could (loose, lose) his fortune, but he had (chose, chosen) to gamble all he had.

14. The Smiths (use, used) to live in San Francisco.

15. If Martin hadn't (drown, drowned), he surely would have been (hanged, hung).

2–10 Brevity

Edit all unnecessary words from the expressions below.

a bald-headed man

a pregnant Cuban woman

returned back home

skirted around obstacles

wearing a happy smile on her face

set a new record

a near approximation

throughout the entire day

cannot possibly be

assembled crowd of people

his other alternative

was engaged in studying

red-colored cloth

in the year 1962

at the hour of noon

2–11 Brevity

Edit all unnecessary words from the expressions below.

wore a white goatee on his chin

throughout the length and width of the entire nation

was positively identified

appeared to be ill

a dead body was found

in the city of Los Angeles

cost the sum of ten dollars

broke an existing rule

for the month of May

for a short space of time

an old pioneer

the present incumbent

will draw to a close

at the corner of Sixth and Elm streets

for the purpose of shocking

3
Style and the Stylebook

Much about writing for the mass media revolves around **style**. This *style* is not that of a particular writer, such as Ernest Hemingway's style or William Faulker's style, but rather the conventions or assumptions underlying the writing and the generally accepted rules of writing and usage for a particular medium. This chapter discusses both the conventions and the rules.

The ABC's of media writing are accuracy, brevity, and clarity. The most important of these is accuracy.

Accuracy

The chief goal of any writer for the mass media is accuracy. A writer will spend much energy in "getting it right." That is, the writer will make every reasonable attempt to ensure that everything in the writing is factually correct and that the language and style the writer uses correctly present that information.

Accuracy is important to the writer for a number of reasons. First, our society puts much stock in truth and honesty, and most people in our society have come to expect that the mass media will take reasonable steps to be accurate in the information they present. There is a great tendency for mass audiences to believe what they see and read in the mass media, and this tendency translates into a responsibility that those who work in the mass media must fulfill.

A very practical reason for an emphasis on accuracy is that people will not watch or subscribe to media they believe to be inaccurate. A newspaper, television station, advertising agency, or public relations department that does not tell the truth will not be trusted by the people it is trying to serve and ultimately will not be effective.

The most compelling reason for a strong emphasis on accuracy, however, comes not from the audience but from the person who works in the mass media. Few people, if any, want to be false in what they do or want their life's work to be looked upon as a charade. Consequently, they feel a moral need to do the best they can; in the mass media professions, that means trying to produce accurate and honest information.

How can a writer for the mass media be accurate? What are the steps that will ensure that the information presented in the writing is correct? These next two chapters will discuss practical measures about gathering information and writing news. Thinking about accuracy begins here by making the following observations.

Writers for the mass media should have an open mind. They should be receptive to new ideas and to various points of view. They should listen to those with whom they may disagree as well as agree. They will not put everything they read and hear in their writing, but the more they know, the better judgments they can make about the accuracy of what they write.

Following closely on this characteristic is that writers for the mass media should read widely. Reading, even in the age of video, is still the best way for a person to prepare himself or herself as a writer.

Writers for the mass media should pay attention to the details of what and how they write. The previous chapter discussed the importance of using the language correctly. That discussion continues in this chapter about style. Individually, many of the points made in each of these chapters are small ones, but as a whole, they are important for the writer's effort to achieve accuracy. Accuracy may be thought of as a large building made up of many small bricks. The writer is the bricklayer and must pay attention to each of the bricks as they are put down.

Clarity

Clarity must be one of the chief goals of a writer for the mass media. Facts that are unclear are of little use to the reader. The English language is extremely versatile, but that versatility can lead to confusion when the language is in the hands of amateurs. Writers must be experts in the language and in the proper and clear structuring of a story. Writers must be on constant guard against writing or story structures that could be confusing to the reader.

The pursuit of clarity is a state of mind for the writer. Everything the writer does must promote the clarity of the copy. After a piece of copy is written, a writer must look at it with a fresh mind—one that is unencumbered with too much knowledge of the subject. The writer must, like the reader, approach a story as one who was not there and did not see it happen and who has not talked with anyone about it. This approach is doubly difficult for the writer who has followed one of the first rules of good writing—knowing the subject thoroughly. Writing clearly and editing for clarity demand a rare degree of mental discipline on the part of the writer.

The opposite of clarity is confusion. Confusion can infiltrate a story in many ways, and it is the writer's responsibility to eliminate this confusion. The chief source of confusion is often the writer who does not understand what he or she is writing about. Writers who do not understand their subjects are likely to write a story that other people cannot understand.

Clear writing is an art, but it is also a skill. Expressing thoughts, ideas, and facts in a clear way is one of the most difficult jobs a writer has—even though the product may read as if the clarity were easily accomplished. The mind moves much faster than we can write or even type; thoughts can be easily jumbled and so can writing. The key to clear writing is understanding the subject. When a writer can express thoughts about a subject in clear terms, then that understanding has been achieved.

The following are some tips for helping writers and editors achieve clarity in their writing:

Keep it simple. Many people believe that they can demonstrate their intelligence by using complex terms (like *terminology*). Their language, they feel, will show others that they have mastered a difficult subject or that they speak or write with authority. Consequently, they use big words and complex sentences to express the simplest ideas.

The problem with this attitude is that people forget their original purpose for writing—to communicate ideas. Any writing that draws attention to itself, and thus draws attention away from the content, is ineffective. Writing, especially for the mass media, should be as simple and straightforward as possible. Reporters and editors should use simple terms and sentence structures. They should avoid piling adjectives and phrases on top of one another. They should do this, not in order to talk down to their readers, but to transmit ideas and facts as efficiently as possible.

Avoid all kinds of jargon—even your own. Jargon is specialized language which almost all groups in society develop. Students, baseball managers, doctors, and gardeners use words that have special meaning for them and no one else. Journalists are not doing their jobs if they simply record jargon, however accurately, and give it back to the reader. Today's journalists must be translators. They must understand the jargon of different groups they cover but must be intelligent enough not to use it in their stories. Writers, too, must keep a watch out for the jargon that can slip into stories. Phrases like "viable alternative," "optimum care," and "personnel costs" must be made to mean something by journalists. They cannot simply thrust them on the reader and believe that they have done their job adequately.

Be specific. Journalists must set the stage of the story for their readers. They must make sure that their readers understand what is going on, when it is happening, where it is happening, and how it is taking place. Reporters and editors cannot assume that readers know very much about the stories they write and edit. They cannot get by with telling readers that it was a "large crowd" or a "long line" or a "beautiful landscape." Stories are built on facts—little facts and big facts. Sometimes it is the little facts that will make the difference in whether or not a reader understands a story.

Readers who have not seen what reporters have seen will not know what reporters are talking about. One aspect of this problem occurs with the use of *the*, especially by less experienced reporters. For example, a lead paragraph may begin in the following way, "City council approved funds for purchasing the new computer system for the finance department at its meeting Tuesday night." A reader is likely to ask, "What new computer system?" While covering the story, the reporter kept hearing everyone talk about "the new computer system," so that's what appeared in the story. Writers particularly need to watch for this kind of assumption and to make sure that readers are not left behind by the assumptions a writer makes.

Check the time sequence. Most news stories will not be written in chronological order, but readers should have some idea of the narrative sequence of the events in a story. When the time sequence is not clear, readers may become confused and misunderstand the content of the story.

Transitions. Transitions, as we have mentioned before, are necessary for smooth, graceful, and clear writing. Each sentence in a story should logically follow the previous sentence or should relate to it in some way. New information in a story should be connected to information already introduced. Readers who suddenly come upon new information or a new subject in a story without the proper transition will be jolted and confused. The following first paragraphs of a story by a beginning writing student about the high costs of weddings illustrates the point about transitions:

```
      The nervous young man drops to one knee,
 blushes and asks that all-important question.
      What about all the planning involved in a
 wedding, from  reserving the church to choos-
 ing the honeymoon site? June and July are the
 traditional months for making the
 big  decision, according to Milton Jefferson
 of the Sparkling Jewelry Store.
      Jefferson said most engagements last from
 seven to 16  months.
      A woman sometimes receives a ring that has
 been passed  down through her fiancé's family
 for generations, or maybe her boyfriend has
 bought an estate ring.
```

The first paragraph assumes that the reader will know what "that all-important question" is. This assumption might be acceptable if the second paragraph followed the lead properly, but it does not. Instead, it plunges the reader into the subject of planning a wedding; the reader has no indication from the lead that this is coming next—and what happened to "that all-important question?"

In a similar manner, the second sentence of the second paragraph introduces yet another new subject to the reader, again without the proper transition. The reader is taken from a question about planning to the traditionally popular months for weddings, with no connection being made between them. In addition, the attribution forces the reader to make another transition. The reader must say, "The man is a jewelry store owner. Jewelry stores sell wedding rings. The jewelry store owner,then, is an authority about when weddings occur."

The third paragraph introduces yet another new subject—the length of engagements. Again, the reader has no transition—merely bombardment by one fact after another.

The fourth paragraph talks about how prospective brides attain their wedding rings. What has this information got to do with what has been said? The writer has left it to the reader to figure it all out. The writer has said, "My story is about weddings. Therefore, anything I put in my story about weddings is okay."

Good writers need to develop a mental discipline that prevents this kind of thing from happening. They must read their own copy with cold and glaring eyes, never assuming that a reader will take the time and effort to "figure out" what the writer has written.

Brevity

"Brevity is the soul of wit," according to Polonius, Shakespeare's ill-fated character in *Hamlet*. Polonius was, in reality, one of Shakespeare's most verbose personalities. Words came tumbling out of his mouth. He went on and on. He was not only verbose; he was boring. Polonius was one of those people you try to avoid at parties. He talked too much.

Writers can do the same thing. They can use too many words, piling phrase upon phrase and letting the sentences run on far after their thoughts have run out. They put too many words in the way of what really needs to be said.

Writers need to recognize when they are being long-winded. They should remove the well-turned phrase that is unnecessary and eliminate that which has already been stated. The process can go too far, of course. Accuracy and clarity should never be sacrificed for brevity's sake, but brevity should be another major goal in the mind of the writer.

The following are some tips for achieving brevity:

Get to the point. What is the story about? What does the story need to tell the reader? A writer needs to be able to answer these questions in the simplest terms possible. Answering these questions is sometimes the hardest part of writing or editing, but once that is done, the writing or editing job can become much easier.

Watch for redundancies and repetitions. A redundancy uses too many words to express an idea. Redundancies in the language abound: Easter Sunday (Easter is always on Sunday); component parts (parts are components); advance notice (what other kind is there?). Redundancies show a lack of disciplined thinking. They slip into writing unnoticed, but their presence can make the most important stories seem silly.

Repetitions repeat words or phrases more than is necessary for the reader to understand what is meant. Repetition is also an indication that the editor was not concentrating on the story. Sometimes facts need to be repeated for clarity's sake, but this is not often the case.

Cut out the unnecessary words. There may be words in a story that simply add nothing to its meaning. These words are hard to pin down, but a sharp-eyed writer can spot them. They are words like *really, very,* and *actually.* They are simply phrase-makers, but they do not tell the reader much.

Finally, when you have run out of things to write about, stop writing.

Journalistic conventions

A strong sense of professionalism has developed in journalism during the 300 years of its history in America. With this professionalism has come a powerful tradition of conventions in journalistic writing. Like rules of style, these conventions are known to trained journalists and used by them to communicate things about their stories to readers. Most readers do not think about what these conventions are when they read the newspaper, yet most regular readers of newspapers know these conventions and what they indicate about the judgments made by editors and reporters.

The conventions include both the basic structures of the stories and the individual ordering of facts and even words within sentences that regularly are used in certain types of stories.

Inverted pyramid. The inverted pyramid is the structure most commonly used for the modern American news story. For the writer, the inverted pyramid structure means two things. First, information should be presented in the order of its importance, with the most important facts coming at the beginning. Second, a story should be written so that if it needs to be cut, it may be cut from the bottom without loss of essential facts or coherence. The inverted pyramid is certainly not the only acceptable structure for the presentation of news, but its use is so widespread that if it is not used, the facts of a story must dictate the alternate form used by the writer. Chapter 5 will discuss writing with the inverted structure more fully.

Many in and out of journalism believe that the inverted pyramid structure has lost its usefulness and that journalists should develop and use other structures. One of the objections to the inverted pyramid is the argument that in the age of instant communication through television and other means, the inverted pyramid is no longer necessary for readers of the written word. They are likely to know what the news is because they have seen it or heard it in some other medium.

Another objection to the inverted pyramid is that it restricts the creativity of the writer. Many writers argue that stories are more readable and even more accurate if they take some other form, particularly a narrative or chronological form.

Because of its emphasis on presenting information from most important to least important, the inverted pyramid structure often prevents writers from putting dramatic endings onto their stories. This characteristic is another reasons why many writers and editors object to its use. They argue that the inverted pyramid washes the drama out of a story.

These and other objections to the inverted pyramid are forcing those in the mass media to rethink their reliance on the form as the sole structure for news stories. Still, the inverted pyramid remains useful for many types of stories and will continue to be one of the chief ways in which information is presented to the reader.

Types of stories. The news values discussed in the next chapter make it incumbent upon reporters and editors to cover and give importance to certain types of stories. These kinds of stories are handled so often that a set of standard practices governing how they are written has been established. For instance, the disaster story must always tell early in the story if anyone was killed or injured. Newspapers develop their own styles for handling obituaries, and some even dictate the form in which the standard obituary is written. For instance, the *New York Times* has a set two-sentence lead for an obituary: "John Smith, a Brooklyn real estate dealer, died at a local hospital yesterday after a short illness. He was 55 years old." Other types of routine stories are those concerning government actions, the courts, crime, holidays, and weather. These stories have standard forms in many newspapers and other publications.

Balance and fairness. One of the basic tenets of American journalism is fairness. Journalists should attempt to give all people involved in a news story a chance to tell their sides of it. If an accusation is made by a news source concerning another person, that person should be given a chance to answer in the same story. Journalists should not take sides in a controversy and should take care not to even appear to take sides.

Writing and editing a balanced story means more than just making sure a controversial situation or issue is covered fairly. In a larger sense, balance means that journalists should understand the relative importance of the events they cover and should not write stories that overplay or underplay that importance. Journalists are often charged with "blowing things out of proportion," and sometimes the charge is a valid one. They should make sure that they are not being used by news sources and being put in a position of creating news rather than letting it occur and then covering it.

The concepts of balance and fairness sometimes come under the name of **objectivity,** a term you are likely to hear often in the world of the mass media. Objectivity means that a news reporter, editor, and publication could and should report only what they know and can find out. They should be scrupulously "fair" to all sides of a story, although "fair" has many different meanings. In being objective, news people should not inject themselves or their opinions into a report. Objectivity assumes not only that journalists should do all of these things but that they could.

Many inside and outside the profession have come to believe that journalists cannot achieve the standards set by objectivity and that attempts to do so actually hurt their performance. Objectivity, they argue, demands that journalists suspend their judgment in ways that would prevent them from fully informing their readers and viewers. Journalists must always decide what stories to cover, whom to use as sources, and what information to include and exclude in their reports. The very fact that these decisions must be made flies in the face of an ideal standard of objectivity.

The impersonal reporter. Closely associated with the concepts of balance and fairness is the concept of the impersonal reporter. Reporters should be invisible in their writing. Reporters should not only set aside their own views and opinions, but they should avoid direct contact with the reader through the use of first-person (*I, we, me, our, my, us*) or second-person (*you, your*) pronouns outside of direct quotes.

Reporters and editors inherently state their opinions about the news in deciding what events they write about, how they write about them, and where they place those stories in the paper. No journalist can claim to be a completely unbiased and objective observer and deliverer of information. Yet stating opinions directly and plainly is generally not an acceptable practice. Even for reporters to include themselves with readers is not a good idea. For example, the following lead is not acceptable because of its use of a first-person pronoun: "The Chief Justice of the Supreme Court said yesterday our legal system is in serious trouble." There may be someone reading this story who makes no claim to the United States' legal system, and the reporter should write for that person as well as for all who do.

Journalism in this era is beginning to see cracks in the armor of the impersonal reporter. More personal references are showing up in news stories, and reporters are acknowledging their own involvement in news events. One recent example of this occurred during the Persian Gulf War in 1991 when Peter Arnett of the Cable News Network was allowed to remain in Iraq and to send live reports from there while American bombers were destroying many parts of the country. Arnett's unique position was part of the story itself, and both he and CNN recognized that in their reporting of the war. Readers and viewers often realize that reporters are involved in the stories they cover, and news organizations feel they should honestly state what that involvement is.

Reliance on official sources. Much of the information printed in a newspaper comes from what we might call "official" sources. These sources are those who are thought to have expertise on the subject, not those who may merely have opinions about the subject. An example of this reliance might be found in a story about inflation. A journalist writing a story about inflation would probably use information from government reports and the studies and opinions of respected economists and influential politicians. These would be the "official" sources, and they would have a large amount of credibility with the reader. An "unofficial" source might be a homemaker, who would certainly have an opinion about the effects, causes, and cures of inflation, but who would not have information that would be credible in the mass media.

The use of official sources has come under scrutiny and some criticism. Studies of sources used by journalists show that the sources themselves are relatively few in number, thus limiting the range of information and opinion that is presented to the reader. Another objection to the use of official sources is that too few people affected by events are quoted. The example of the inflation story in the previous paragraph is a good example. The unofficial source of the homemaker or the hourly wage earner is often ignored. Finally, media critics object to official sources because they are likely to be white and male. Relatively few women and members of other ethnic and racial groups make it into the realms of official sources.

Attribution and quotes. Journalists should make it clear to readers where information has been obtained. All but the most obvious and commonly known facts in a story should be attributed. Writers should make sure that the attributions are helpful to the reader's understanding of the story and that they do not get in the way of the flow of the story.

A number of journalistic conventions have grown up around the use of indirect and direct quotations. First, except in the rarest instances, all quotes must be attributed. The exception is the case where there is no doubt about the source of the quote. Even then, editors should be careful.

Second, using quotation marks around a word or group of words means that someone has spoken or written those exact words. A writer must not put words inside quotation marks that have not been used by the source. Sometimes a writer is tempted to say, "I know my source said that, but I am sure she meant something else, so I'm going to change the quote to what was meant rather than what was said." This is a dangerous practice at best. In this situation, the best course for the writer is to get in touch with the source and ask about the quote in question. Most of the time, people's exact words will accurately express their meaning.

Finally, should incorrect grammar and slang, profane or offensive language appear in a direct quotation? Most publication have policies in place for the use of profane or offensive language. The question of bad grammar plagues journalists. Journalists have a commitment to accuracy, which dictates that they should use the exact words that there sources use. Quoting someone using bad grammar can make that person appear unnecessarily foolish and can distract from the real meaning of the story. Most professionals believe that if a source is used to being quoted, grammatical mistakes should be included in the statements they make. The grammatical mistakes of those who are not used to talking with journalists should be changed, however. Neither practice should be followed in every instance. Writers and editors should make a decision together when these situations come up.

These conventions are important to observe if journalists are to gain the respect of their readers and colleagues. Conventions should not be looked upon as arbitrary rules that must be followed at the expense of accuracy and clarity. Rather, they are a set of sound practices that are extremely useful to journalists in the process of deciding what to write and how to write it.

Journalistic style

English is an extremely diverse language; it gives the user many ways of saying the same thing. For instance, 8:00, eight o'clock, 8 A.M., eight a.m., and eight in the morning may all correctly refer to the same thing; a reference may be to the president, the U.S. president, the president of the United States, and so on. All of these references are technically correct, but which one should a journalist use? And does it really matter?

The answer to the first question is governed by journalistic style. Style is a special case of English correctness which a publication adopts. It does so in order to promote consistency among its writers and to reduce confusion among its readers. Once a style is adopted, a writer won't have to wonder about the way to refer to such things as time.

Journalistic style may be divided into two types of style: **professional conventions** and **rules of usage**. Professional conventions have evolved during years of journalistic endeavor and are now taught through professional training in universities and professional workshops. The rules of usage have been collected into stylebooks published by wire services, news organizations, syndicates, universities, and individual print and broadcast news operations. Some of these stylebooks have had widespread acceptance and influence. Others have remained relatively local and result in unique style rules accepted by reporters and editors working for individual news organizations.

For example, a publication may follow *The Associated Press Stylebook* and *United Press International Stylebook* and say that *AM* and *PM* should be lowercase with periods: a.m. and p.m. The writer will know that a reference to the president of the United States is always simply "president," lowercased, except when referring to a specific person, such as President Clinton.

Likewise, the reader will not be confused by multiple references to the same item. Unconsciously, the reader will expect the style that the publication uses. Consequently, if the reader is very familiar with a college newspaper and that paper always refers to its own institution as "the University," uppercase, the reader will know what that means.

Similarly, a reporter may follow the usual convention in newspaper writing and write the sequence of time, date, and place of a meeting despite the fact that it may seem more logical to report the date before reporting the time.

Having a logical, consistent style is like fine-tuning a color television. Before the tuning, the colors may be there and the picture may be reasonably visible. Eventually, however, the off-colors and the blurry images will play on the viewer's mind so that he or she will become dissatisfied and disinterested. That could cause the viewer to stop watching altogether. In the same way, consistent style fine-tunes a publication so that reading it is easier for a reader and offers few distractions from the content.

Beyond that, the question may still remain: Does style really matter? The answer is an emphatic "yes!" Many young writers think of consistent style as a repressive force hampering their creativity. It isn't. Style is not a rigid set of rules established to restrict the creative forces in the writer. Style imposes a discipline in writing that should run through all the activities of a journalist. It implies that the journalist is precise not only with writing but also with facts and with thought. Consistent style is the hallmark of a professional.

Adherence to a consistent style is also important to society. As Thomas W. Lippman write in the preface to *The Washington Post Deskbook on Style,* "A newspaper is part of a society's record of itself. Each day's edition lives on in libraries and electronic archives, to be consulted again and again by the scholars and journalists of the future. The newspaper is thus the repository of the language, and we have a responsibility to treat the language with respect. The rules of grammar, punctuation, capitalization, spelling, and usage set down here are our way of trying to meet that responsibility."

Editors are the governors of the style of a publication. It is their job to see that style rules are consistently and reasonably applied. If exceptions are allowed, they should be for specific and logical reasons and should not be at the whim of a writer. Editors and writers should remember that consistent style is one way of telling readers that everything in the publication is certified as accurate.

Stylebooks

Stylebooks are a fact of life for writers for the mass media. Any area of writing, from newspapers to advertising agencies to public relations firms, will require the use of some form of stylebook. Stylebooks deal primarily with three things, the first and foremost being **consistency.** The main reason for the existence of any stylebook is to promote consistency in writing. To do this, a stylebook establishes the **rules of writing** for a publication. These are often arbitrary rules, such as using *a.m.* instead of *AM* to refer to morning times and spelling certain numbers out while using figures for others. These rules also eliminate inconsistencies in spelling, such as mandating that the Southeast Asia country be spelled Vietnam rather than Viet-Nam. Stylebooks also deal with **usage,** particularly when dictionaries assign a variety of meanings to a word. A good stylebook will say when a word should be properly and consistently used. Beyond that, a good stylebook helps a writer find the precise words he or she needs.

This chapter refers mostly to *The Associated Press Stylebook and Libel Manual* because that is the most commonly used reference for writers in the mass media. The first AP stylebook appeared in 1953, growing out of demands from newspaper editors who subscribed to the Associated Press wire service. Many of these editors wanted to make their local copy consistent with the copy they were receiving and running from the AP. Many of these same newspapers also subscribed to the nation's other major wire service, United Press International, and they wanted the wire services to use a consistent style. Consequently, AP and UPI got together and came up with a common stylebook in 1960. These first stylebooks were simply small handbooks that dealt mainly with the rules of writing. During the next decade, newspaper editors saw the need for a book that would also deal with usage, so in 1975 a committee of editors from AP and UPI again got together and put together a comprehensive stylebook that is in use today.

A number of other publications have produced comprehensive stylebooks. Two of the most influential are *The New York Times Manual of Style* and *The Los Angeles Times Stylebook*. Each contains many local references and has become the major style reference for writers on those publications. Most publications, however, have small stylebooks that deal with local style questions and preferences and rely on a larger reference, such as *The AP Stylebook and Libel Manual*, to answer broader questions. Any publication, even college newspapers and yearbooks, should have its own stylebook because there are always local questions a major reference will not answer. For instance, how should students be identified? One college newspaper stylebook says that students should be identified by class rank and major, as in "Mary Smith, a junior in journalism"; a stylebook for another student newspaper says that students should be identified by major and hometown, as in "Mary Smith, a journalism major from Midville." It doesn't take much imagination to come up with a number of style problems like this one that need to be answered by a local stylebook.

Students should be aware of two other major style references. One is *A Manual of Style* by the University of Chicago Press. This book is the chief reference for something known as the "Chicago style," and the Chicago style is used in most books. It contains a number of major differences from the *AP Stylebook*. For instance, Chicago style mandates that numbers one through one hundred be spelled out, while AP style says that numbers one through nine should be spelled out. Chicago style began as a single proofreader's sheet in 1891 and was first published for those not working with the University of Chicago Press in 1906. Today it is more than 500 pages long and deals extensively with footnotes, referencing, and many other style problems that arise when books are produced.

Another important style reference is the *Style Manual* of the U.S. Government Printing Office. This is the style guide for all government publications and is particularly good in dealing with governmental material and foreign languages.

Are stylebooks necessary? That question is argued, even among seasoned journalists. Most come down on the side of using stylebooks, but usually with reservations. Roy Copperud, author of *A Dictionary of Usage and Style*, criticizes those who use style rules arbitrarily or who enforce style rules that make no sense. "Meditation and prayer lead to the conviction that the best style is the one which governs least." Style rules should not inhibit creativity or initiative in writing. They should promote readability. Style, as *The United Press International Stylebook* points out, is the "intangible ingredient that distinguishes outstanding writing from mediocrity."

The Associated Press Stylebook

A number of years ago, the two major U.S. wire services negotiated an agreement on the basic rules of style found in their two stylebooks. As a result, the AP and UPI now publish stylebooks that are in fundamental agreement on the basic rules of style. This agreement has resulted in widespread adoption of these rules by newspapers around the United States. Since the Associated Press has published its stylebook in a form commonly available to students in universities around the country, we shall refer to that stylebook in this section of our discussion. Keep in mind that this style is now held in common with UPI and is accepted by many newspapers nationwide.

Most publications base their style on that found in *The Associated Press Stylebook*. Here are some representative problem areas and some advice generally taken from the *The Associated Press Stylebook*.

Capitalization. Unnecessary capitalization, like unnecessary punctuation, should be avoided because it slows reading and makes the sentence look uninviting. Some examples: Main Street, but Main and Market streets; Mayor John Smith, but John Smith, mayor of Jonesville; Steve Barber, executive director of the State Press Association. (Note lowercase title after name, but uppercase for State Press Association, a formal name and therefore a proper noun.)

Abbreviation. The trend is away from alphabet soup in body copy and in headlines, but some abbreviations help conserve space and help to simplify information. For example: West Main Street, but 20 W. Main St. The only titles for which abbreviations are called for (all before the name) are Dr., Gov., Lt. Gov., Mr., Mrs., Rep., the Rev., Sen., and most military ranks. Standing alone, all of these are spelled out and are lowercased. Check the stylebook for others.

Punctuation. Especially helpful are the sections of the stylebook dealing with the comma, hyphen, period, colon and semicolon, dash, ellipsis, restrictive and nonrestrictive elements, apostrophe, and quotation marks.

Numerals. Spell out whole numbers below ten, and use figures for ten and above. This rule applies to numbers used in a series or individually. Don't begin sentences with numerals, as a rule, but if you must, spell them out.

Spelling. In journalism a word has but one spelling. Alternate spellings and variants are incorrect (because of the requirement of style consistency). Make it *adviser,* not *advisor; employee,* not *employe; totaled,* not *totalled; traveled,* not *travelled; kidnapped,* not *kidnaped; judgment,* not *judgement; television,* not *TV,* when used as a noun; *under way,* not *underway; percent,* not *per cent; afterward, toward, upward, forward* (no *'s); vs.,* not *versus* or *vs; vice president,* not *vice-president.* Check the stylebook or a dictionary for others.

Usage. *Comprise* means to contain, not to make up. "The region comprises five states," not "five states comprise the region" and not "the region is comprised of five states." *Affect* means to influence, not to carry out. *Effect* means a result when it's a noun and means to carry out when it's a verb. *Controller* and *comptroller* are both pronounced "controller" and mean virtually the same thing, though *comptroller* is generally the more accurate word for denoting government financial officers, and *controller* is better for denoting business financial officers. *Hopefully* does not mean it is hoped, we hope, maybe, or perhaps —it means in a hopeful manner: "Hopefully, editors will study the English language" is not acceptable usage of the word. Good editors use fad expressions because readers do, but they do not use them as crutches, and they should know when they are using them.

Ages. Use numerals always: a 2-month-old baby; he was 80; the youth, 18, and the girl, 6, were rescued.

Dates. Feb. 6 (current calendar year); in February 1978 (no comma); last February.

Dimensions. He is 5 feet 9 inches tall; the 5-foot 9-inch woman; 5-foot-9 woman; a 7-footer; the car left a skid mark 8 inches wide and 17 feet long; the rug is 10 by 12. The storm brought 1 1/2 inches of rain (spell out fractions less than one).

Language sensitivity

Writers must understand that language has the ability to offend and demean. Readers and viewers of the mass media are a broad and diverse group, and those who would communicate with them should be aware of language sensitivities of some of the people within that group. While some people have gone to extremes in identifying supposedly offensive language, there are terms and attitudes in writing that should legitimately be questioned and changed. The current state of public discourse demands it.

Writers have not always paid attention to such sensitivities. Phrases such as "all men are created equal" and "these are the times that try men's souls" drew no criticism for their inherent sexism when they were first published, largely because women were not allowed to be a major part of the public debate. We may accept those phrases now because we understand the context in which they were written, but we would not approve of them if they were written in our age.

Writers for the mass media should examine their work closely to make sure that they have treated people fairly and equally, that they have not lapsed into easy or commonly accepted stereotypes, that they have not used phrases or descriptions that demean, and that they have included everyone in their articles who is germain to the subject. The following are a few areas in which writers should take special care:

Sexist pronouns. It is no longer acceptable to use the pronoun *he* when the referent may be a man or woman. "A student should always do his homework" should be "A student should always do his or her homework." In some instances, rewriting the sentence using plurals is easier: "Students should always do their homework." Sometimes a sentence can be rewritten so that it does not require any pronoun. "Students should always do homework that is assigned."

Titles. Many titles that had sexist connotations, such as "mailman" and "fireman" are being phased out of the language, becoming "mail carrier" and "firefighter." (In these two cases, not only are the terms gender neutral, but they are much more descriptive.) Writers need to be aware, however, that some gender-based titles are still common, and they should look for more acceptable alternatives.

Descriptions. "All people are described equal." That awkward take-off on the Thomas Jefferson phase should be an abiding principle of the modern writer for the mass media. One of the classic areas in which this has not been done has been references to women's appearance and attire. Sometimes such references are important to an article, but often they are not. They are included gratuitously and as such are offensive.

Racial descriptions and references may not be necessary. Richard Arrington is the mayor of Birmingham, Alabama. To describe him as "Richard Arrington, the black mayor of Birmingham" is not necessary unless it is important to the understanding of a story to know his race. The test here is to ask the questions, "What if Richard Arrington were white? Would it be important to know that?"

Stereotypes. Our society abounds in stereotypes, and not all are based on race. We describe women who stay at home as women who "don't work." We refer to a "Jewish mother" as someone with certain hectoring characteristics, not remembering that not all Jewish women who have children have those characteristics. We write about "southern bigots," forgetting that bigots can live anywhere in the country. An older woman who has never married is called a "spinster," when she may never have spun anything in her life. We should constantly question these blanket references and phrases—and more importantly, our attitudes that give rise to these descriptions.

Illness and disability. American society is taking some steps, by private initiative as well as by law, to open itself to people who have various handicaps, disabilities, or limitations. One of the things that Americans should learn as this happens is that identifying people by these limitations is in itself unfair and inaccurate. To say that a person "has a handicap" is different from saying that a person is "handicapped." The way in which these limitations are referred to can also be disabling. For instance, to describe someone as a "reformed alcoholic" is neither complimentary nor benign; "reformed" implies that the person did something wrong and now the problem is solved. A person who is an alcoholic but who no longer drinks is "recovering." To say that someone has a "defect," such as a "birth defect," is to demean by implication (i.e., the person is defective). It would be better to say a person "was born with a hearing loss."

These are just a few of the areas in which writers need to maintain great sensitivity and to continue close examination of their work. Constantly questioning what you have written and making reasonable changes is not just the mark of a good writer; it is a sign of an intelligent and sensitive person.

Conclusion

This chapter attempts to introduce you to the concept of "style" and what it means to those who work in the mass media. Conforming to the rules and conventions of the medium in which you are working is the mark of a true professional. Strict adherence to the details of style shows that you care about what you write.

Points for consideration and discussion

1. How has this chapter changed your thinking about the meaning of "style" and its use in writing for the mass media?

2. What are some of the reasons why there is such a strong emphasis on accuracy in writing for the mass media? How does adherence to a consistent style contribute to goal of accuracy for a journalist?

3. Find a piece of writing in which you think that writer used big words instead of simple ones. Rewrite it using the simpler language. Now compare the two pieces of writing. Which is better?

4. Some people say that a consistent style restricts creativitiy, while others say it enhances creativity. What are the arguments on both sides of this question.

5. The concept of objectivity is a controversial one in the field of journalism. Why do you think it causes so much controversy?

Further reading

The Associated Press Stylebook and Libel Manual. Rev. ed., New York: The Associated Press, 1987.

Theodore Bernstein, *The Careful Writer, A Modern Guide to English Usage.* New York: Atheneum, 1973.

Theodore Bernstein, *Watch Your Language.* Manhasset, NY: Channel Press, 1958.

Roy Copperud, *A Dictionary of Usage and Style.* New York: Hawthorne Books, 1964.

Thomas W. Lippman, *The Washington Post Deskbook on Style.* New York: McGraw Hill, 1989.

A Manual of Style. Chicago: University of Chicago Press, 1982.

The New York Times Manual of Style and Usage. Rev. ed. by Lewis Jordan. Chicago: Quadrangle Books, 1976.

Lawrence C. Soley. *The News Shapers: The Sources Who Explain the News.* New York: Praeger, 1992.

William Strunk and E.B. White. *The Elements of Style.* Rev. ed. New York: Macmillan, 1972.

U.S. Government Printing Office Style Manual. Rev. Ed. Washington, DC: Government Printing Office, 1973.

EXERCISES

The following section contains a variety of style exercises. You should follow your instructor's directions in completing them.

3–1 Using the stylebook

Correct the following items so that they conform with AP style.

1. The defense department is about to propose a new missele system.

2. F.C.C., hitch-hiker, three dollars, 4 million

3. The three most important people in his life are his wife, son, and mother.

4. part-time, 10 year old child, 5 PM, 5300

5. The cardinals won the last game of the world series, 7 to 5.

6. spring (season), fall (season), south (point on compass), south (region)

7. November 15, the last day of Feb., Mar. 16

8. 13 people travelled to Austin, Tex. for the rally.

9. He had ten cents left in his pocket.

10. home-made, well-known, Italian-American, questionaire

3–2 Using the stylebook

Correct the following items so that they conform with AP style.

1. The U.S. is sometimes not the best market for U.S. products.

2. Circle the correct form:

   upward, upwards

   British (Labour, Labor) Party

   Riverside (Ave., Avenue)

   cupsful, cupfuls

   eying, eyeing

3. The Republican differed from the democrat many times during the debate.

4. Dr. John Smith and Dr. Mary Wilson preformed the operations.

5. Circle the correct form:

   donut, doughnut

   pants suit, pantsuit

   plow, plough

   U.S. Weather Bureau, National Weather Service

6. He said he was neither a Communist or a member of the Communist Party.

7. After her surgery, she had to wear a Pacemaker.

8. "What a hair-brained scheme!" she exclaimed.

9. preempt, speed-up (noun), 55 miles per hour, hookey

10. The underworld, or mafia, was responsible for the murder.

3–3 Using the stylebook

Correct the following items so that they conform with AP style.

1. He was charged with trafficing in drugs.

2. The Rev. Billy Graham said God was alive and His will would triumph.

3. pianoes, nation-wide, P.T.A., Viet-nam war

4. The flag, which Frances Scott Key saw, has been preserved.

5. life-like, outfielder, inter-racial, IOU's (plural)

6. The train will arrive at twelve noon on Tues.

7. The US Census Bureau defines the south as a seventeen-state region.

8. The judged ruled that because of his oral skills he had entered into a verbal contract.

9. She had an afternoon snack of some oreo cookies and cake.

10. harrass, accomodate, weird, likeable

3–4 Using the stylebook

Correct the following items so that they conform with AP style.

1. His solution turned out to be the most equal of the two.

2. Ga. Sec. of State George Smith testified at the Congressional hearing.

3. tis, the Gay 1890's, a South America country, 1492 A.D.

4. Write the plurals for the following words: Eskimo,_____ ;
    chili, _____ ; memorandum, _____ ; ski,
    _____

5. The ballif opened the court by saying, "Oyes, oyes, oyes!"

6. He spread out his palate and went to sleep.

7. carry-over (adj.), nitty-gritty, nit-picking, know-how

8. What do the following abbreviations stand for?

    USIA _____

    GOP_____

    EST _____

    TVA _____

    Are any of these abbreviations acceptable for first reference? _____

9. The pan had a teflon surface.

10. He was graduated from a teacher's college in the north.

3–5 Using the stylebook

Correct the following items so that they conform with AP style.

1. Write the plurals for the following words: referendum, _____;
   court martial, _____; 1920, _____;
   dead end, _____.

2. Daylight savings time begins on the last Sun. in April.

3. He made the Dean's List after Dean Smith talked to him.

4. The game, that was scheduled for to-night, was rained out.

5. He said the car would go further on premium gas.

6. The movie which starred Sam Jones received an r rating.

7. He had run the gauntlet of criticism and abuse for his views.

8. The woman who the article referred to was a German Jewess.

9. judgement, naval orange, resistible, self-defense

10. He played semi-pro baseball for 3 years.

3-6 Using the stylebook

Correct the following story so that it conforms to AP style. The story contains other errors besides style errors that you will need to correct. Use the proper editing marks.

Baseball game

The Bay City Bluebirds rallied from a 3-run defict last night to defeat the Carmel Cardinals 6-3 and win the Western Tri-state division championship.

The bluebirds are now assured a place int eh Tri-state playoffs which begin next week. Their opponent will be determined tonight in a game between the Santa Ana Gnerals and the Redwood Knights.

The cardinals led the bluebirds for most of the game, and they hasa 3-0 lead in the eighth inniny.

In the bluebird hafl of the eighth, Tim Story, the first baseman, walked and stole second. Left fielder Biff Carbosi was walked intensionally, and both runner moved up a base on a wild pitch by cardinal started ronnie Miller. Miller was then relieved by Chuck Nelson.

Bluebird secondbaseman Carbo Garbey lined Nelson's first pitch into deep centefield, scoring both baserunners. Two pitches later, Garbey stole home to tie the game.

Nelson got the next 2 hitters out, but then Carey Clark, the bluebird catcher, homered to put the bluebirds ahead. The bluebirds added two more runs in the ninth to insure their victory.

3–7 Using the stylebook

Correct the following story so that it conforms to AP style. The story contains other errors besides style errors that you will need to correct. Use the proper editing marks.

Survey

Over half of the nation's high school principles favor some sort of corporal punishment for students who are discipline problems, according to a survey conducted by the American Education Association (A.E.A.)

The survey found that 53% of the principals in the U.S. felt teachers and administrators should have the option of using corporal punishment on students who were discipline problems. 29% of the principals disagreed, saying teachers and administrators should not have this option.

AEA president Virginia Howell said the survey showed that administrators are concerned with discipline and ""want as many options avaiable as possible.

Classroom Discipline, she ssaid, is a continuing problem for many teahers and principals. "The disciplien problem gets in the way of effective teaching, and its not fair to the students who are there to learn." she said.

Miss Howell said the results of the survey indicated that many people are not becoming teachers today because they do'nt want to deal with "the disciplien problems their hearing about in the schools."

3–8 Using the stylebook

Correct the following story so that it conforms to AP style. Use the proper editing marks.

Guilty verdict

A jury found a Midville man guilty of Second-Degree Manslaughter after an hour's worth of deliberations on Tuesday.

Johnny Gene Garber was convicted at the end of a 3-day trial which featured his mother testifying against him. He was charged in the death of a thirty-nine year old brickmason, Gardner Jackson, of Number Twelve, Ninth Street in Jonesville.

Mr. Garber stood sliently as the jury read the verdict. The Presiding Judge, Jonas T. McMillan, set a sentencing hearing for next Monday at eight o'clock in the morning.

Garber was charged with being druck while driving down highway 69 last March. His car served out of control and ran head on into a car driven by Mr. Jackson, who had been attending services at the Midville Baptist church.

During the trial, the Prosecution Attory, Able Sasson, called Garber's mother, Mrs. Minnie Lee Garber, to testify that her son had been drinking heavily at there home that evening before the accident occured.

Garber could recieve a sentence of two to five years in prison for the crime he committed.

3–9 Using the stylebook

Correct the following story so that it conforms to AP style. The story contains other errors besides style errors that you will need to correct. Use the proper editing marks.

City council

The city council passed an ordinance last night requireing people convicted of their second drunk charge to serve a minimum of thirty days in jail and to have their driver's license suspended for six months.

The ordinance was passed by a vote of five to three.

Councilman Clarissa Atwell sponsored the change in the law which wil take effect on December 31st of this year.

"I think this new law will save the lives of a lot of people, Miss Atwell said.

The council chamber was filled to overflowing with people interested in the law. Many of the people there were members of Mothers Against Drunk Driving (M.A.D.D.)

One Councilamn who voted against law, Les Honeycutt, said he felt the laws against drunk driving were strong enough and that they needed to be inforced for rigidly. His comments received hoots and jeers from the crowd, and at one point the council president, Harley Sanders, trhreatened to have some of the audience removed and evicted.

3–10 Using the stylebook

Correct the following story so that it conforms to AP style. Use the proper editing marks.

Power failure

Power was cut off to nearly a 3rd of the residents of Midville, last night, after a violent storm ripped through the city around six o'clock.

Police chief Robert Dye said that power was restored to most homes within about two hours, but "a substantial number of people," had to go without power for most of the night.

Chief Dye said that many of the city's traffic lights were knocked out by the storm, and traffick problems developed on several of the more busy streets.

Chief dye says that everything should be back to normal today.

A Power company official said that more than 1500 homes were without electricity for some part of the night. They said that crews worked throughout the entire night to get people's power turned on.

The storm dumped over 2 inches of rain on the city in about 30 minutes. The power failure was due to lighting hitting one of the power companys substations in the Western part of the city.

4
The News Story

When President George Bush ordered American and allied bombers to begin raids on Baghdad on Jan. 16, 1991, Americans were getting off from work and watching their evening news programs. A vast number of Americans abandoned other activities and gathered in front of their television sets. By the time the president spoke to the nation later that evening, the audience had grown to about 90 million, more than had watched the funeral of John F. Kennedy in 1963 and quite possibly the largest television audience in history.

The next day the *New York Times* sold 1.2 million copies, 82,000 more than usual. The *Boston Globe* printed an extra 130,000 copies that day, while the circulation of the *Miami Herald* increased 90,000. (Similarly, on the day after Bill Clinton was elected president in November 1992, *USA Today* sold 2.6 million copies, about 30 percent more than normal.)

News is one of the elements that holds a society of diverse and scattered people together. The fact that a group of individuals share the same information—and that the information is current—allows the group to operate as a community. If we were a society of hermits, or if we dealt with only the small group of people we have physical contact with, news might not matter so much. Our business and interests extend far beyond our group of acquaintances, however, and one of the ways we establish relationships with those beyond this group is to understand that we share the same current information.

This centrality of news makes the news story a fundamental form of writing for the mass media. Those who would write for the mass media in any form should first understand and master the news story format. Writing for the mass media is one of the most important jobs in our society. The people who do this job have a tremendous impact on the shape and direction of the community. They tell us about ourselves. They establish a bond between the individual members of the society and the community and nation as a whole. They must be honest, talented, and dedicated. The job is too important and too difficult for people of lesser qualities.

This chapter discusses the news story as it is most commonly defined and understood by the industries of the mass media. The focus here will be on what goes into making the news story. Here we should think of news and information in a broad way. News is not only something that appears in a newspaper or on television; it is also information that appears in a company's newsletter or employee magazine. Advertising is also a form of news in that it delivers information about a product or service.

The writer for the mass media has two jobs. The first is gathering information; the second is putting that information into the form appropriate for the medium in which he or she is working. This chapter will concentrate on that first job. An understanding of defining news and gathering information is essential to the writing process.

News values

News is built on traditional **news values** that beginning students need to understand. These news values are the basis on which journalists decide whether or not an event is news. There are millions of "events" that occur in our society every day. Only those few events that editors select and that have at least one of the following criteria can be classified as news.

Impact. Events that affect people's lives are classified as news. The event itself might involve only a few people, but the consequences may be wide-ranging. For example, if Congress passes a bill to raise taxes or if a researcher discovers a cure for a form of cancer, both actions will affect larger numbers of people. They have impact, and they would be considered news.

Timeliness. Timeliness is a value common to almost all news stories. It refers to the recency of an event. Without the element of timeliness, most events cannot be considered news. For example, a trial that occurred last year is not news; a trial that is going on right now may be news. How much time has to elapse before an event can no longer be considered news? No one answer to that question applies to every case. Most events that are more than a day to a day-and-a-half old are not thought to be news. (Look in today's newspaper and see if you can find a news story about an event that occurred two days ago.)

Prominence. Prominent people, sometimes even when they are doing trivial things, make news. The president of the United States is a prime example. Whenever he takes a trip—even for purely personal and private reasons—his movements are covered in great detail by the news media. The president is a prominent and important person. Anything he does is likely to have an impact on the country, and people are very interested in his actions. The president is not the only example of a prominent person who often makes news. Movie stars, famous politicians, advocates of social causes—all of these people make news simply because they are very well known.

Proximity. Events that occur close to home are more likely to be news than the same events that occur elsewhere. For example, a car wreck killing two people that happens on a road in your home county is more likely to be reported in the local news media than the same kind of wreck which occurs 1,000 miles away. We are interested in the things that happen around us. If we know a place where something goes on, we are more likely to picture that event and have a feeling for it and for the people involved.

Conflict. When people disagree, when they fight, when they have arguments—that's news, particularly if one of the other news values, such as prominence, is involved. Conflict is one of the journalist's favorite news values because it generally ensures that there is an interesting story to write. One of the reasons that trial stories are so popular with newspaper readers and television watchers is that the central drama involves conflict—two competing forces, each vying to defeat the other.

The bizarre or unusual. A rare event is sometimes considered news. There is an adage in journalism that goes, "When a dog bites a man, that's not news; when a man bites a dog, now that's news." These events, though they may have relatively little importance or involve obscure people, are interesting to readers and enliven a publication. For example, it's not news when someone's driver's license is revoked (unless that someone is a prominent person); it is news, however, when a state department of transportation revokes the license of a person called "the worst driver in the state" because he had twenty-two accidents in the last two years.

Currency. Issues that have current interest often have news value, and events surrounding those issues can sometimes be considered news. For example, a panel discussion of doctors may be held in your community. Normally, such a discussion might not provoke much interest from journalists. If the discussion topic were "The Latest Cancer-fighting Drugs," the news value of the event would change, and there would likely be a number of newspaper, radio, and television journalists covering it. Issues that have the value of currency come and go, but there are always many such issues being discussed by the public.

A news writer and editor must make decisions about events based on these news values. News values are also used in deciding the kind of information needed for a story and in helping the writer structure the story so that the most important and interesting information gets to the reader in the most efficient manner.

Gathering the news: Five Ws and One H

A journalist gathering information or writing a story tries to answer six basic questions for the reader:

Who. Who are the important people related to the story? Is everyone included so that the story can be accurately and adequately told? Is everyone properly identified?

What. What is the major action or event of the story? What are the actions or events of lesser importance? A journalist ought to be able to state the major action of the story in one sentence, and this should be the theme of the story.

When. When did the event occur? Readers of news stories should have a clear idea of when the story takes place. The when element is rarely the best way to begin a story because it is not often the most important piece of information a journalist has to tell a reader, but it should come early in the story and should be clearly stated.

Where. Where did the event occur? Journalists cannot assume that readers will know or be able to figure out where an event takes place. The location or locations of the event or action should be clearly written.

Why and How. The reader deserves explanation about events. If a story is about something bizarre or unusual, the writer should offer some explanation, so that the questions the event raises in the reader's mind are answered. The writer also needs to set the events or actions in a story in the proper context. Reference should be made to previous events or actions if they help to explain things to the reader.

Sources of information

Where does the information in a news story come from? A news reporter has three fundamental sources of information: people, records (any information that is written or stored so others may find it), and personal observation.

Most information in most news stories comes from **personal sources**—that is, people. A news reporter is likely to spend most of his or her nonwriting time talking to people either face to face or over the telephone. In fact, many would argue that the more people the reporter talks to, the better a story is likely to be because of the variety of information and views the reporter can obtain.

Here are some examples of paragraphs from news stories in which the information comes from personal sources:

> According to the theater owner, Martin Miller, about 340 attended the first-night showing of the controversial film.

> Although he attended the inauguration, the congressman said he disapproved of the amount of money spent on the event.

> "I'm against that proposal because it's unfair to the middle class," the senator said.

The first two of the examples are indirect quotations or paraphrases; the third is a direct quotation. The next chapter discusses more fully the handling of direct and indirect quotations.

Interviewing is when a reporter talks to a source. This is a skill that must be carefully cultivated if the reporter is to be effective. A reporter tries to determine what information the source has and would be willing to share. Then the reporter attempts to ask the kind of questions that would elicit this information. The next section in this chapter discusses these interviewing skills.

To make this job easier, reporters will develop sources among the people whom they contact regularly; that is, the reporters will find people who have information and are willing to talk with the reporter about it. Reporters soon realize that many people can provide them with information and sometimes that information can come from surprising sources. For instance, most reporters who are assigned to a beat—a term in journalism meaning a place or topic a reporter must write regularly about—learn that secretaries, rather than their bosses, are the best sources of information. Secretaries often know what is happening before their bosses do. Consequently, many reporters get to know the secretaries on their beats very well. As reporters and sources deal with each other, they should develop a relationship of mutual understanding. Reporters find out whom they can trust among their sources, and sources realize that the information they give to reporters will be used wisely.

One general rule governs the relationships that reporters have with their sources—reporters should always identify themselves clearly to their sources. Sources should know before they talk to reporters that the information they give may be used in a news story. Sources should have the opportunity not to talk with news reporters if they do not want to.

Attribution in a news story means telling readers where information comes from. Attribution phrases are those such as "he said," "she said," and "according to officials." Most of the major information in a news story needs to have some attribution, particularly information that comes from personal sources.

The second major source of information for the news reporter is **observation.** Whenever possible, news reporters like to attend the events they are writing about. They like to see for themselves what happens, even though they rarely write from a first-person point of view. Here are some examples of news reports that have used observational sources:

> The anti-abortion rally drew people from many areas of the Midwest. Cars in the parking lot bore license tages from Missouri to West Virginia.

> Bailey High's Sam Love kicked a 14-yard field goal in the first period, and Mateo Central's Jack Mayo had a 34-yarder in the second period to account for the second-lowest scoring first half in the history of the championship game.

> The packed courtroom listened in a hushed silence as the defendant took the witness stand and began to tell her story.

In each of these cases, it is clear that the reporters attended the events they described. One indication of this is the lack of attribution in each of these paragraphs.

The third major source of information available to news reporters is records, or **stored sources.** This type of information includes any books, reports, articles, press releases, documents, and computer information to which a reporter has access. Here are some examples of reporters using stored sources:

> Furillo, who died Sunday, played right field for the Brooklyn and Los Angeles Dodgers from 1946 through 1960. He won the NL batting title with a .344 average in 1953, when he missed the last few weeks of the season because of a broken hand he sustained during a fight with manager Leo Durocher.

A City Social Services Department report estimated that more than 10,000 people were "without permanent or temporary shelter" in the city last year.

A statement issued by the new administration said that foreign policy problems would be high on the president's agenda.

Stored sources are located in many places—government documents, company records, books, magazines, and so on. A news reporter should be familiar with the holdings of the local public library because that can be a major source of stored information.

One of the most important types of stored information is that found in on-line or electronic information services. Such services provide subscribers with fingertip access to a wide range of information, such as newspapers, magazines, television transcripts, governmental reports, legal opinions, encyclopedias, library card catalogues and many other sources. These services come through telephone lines from central data banks and tie in to personal computers. People who work with information, particularly those in the mass media, are relying more and more heavily on these on-line data bases.

In most cases, information that comes from stored sources—like that which comes from personal sources—should be attributed. In two of the foregoing examples, the attribution is clear. Occasionally, as in the first example, the information may either be common knowledge or be available in many references so that telling the reader the source is not that important.

Interviewing

Interviewing ranks at the top of the most important activities a mass media professional can engage in. Talking with people is the chief way we have of gathering current information about almost any topic. Within the daily press, more information is collected through interviews than by any other method.

News stories use two kinds of quoted material—direct quotations and indirect quotations. Direct quotations are those words that the source has used to express an idea; those words should be surrounded by quotation marks.

"I believe the tax reform proposal that the Congress is debating would wreck our economic recovery," the president said.

Indirect quotations, or paraphrases, express what the source said but use different words from those the source used.

The president expressed his opposition to the tax reform proposal currently before Congress, saying it would hurt the nation's economic recovery.

A paraphrase may use some of the exact words of the source, and the writer may want to put those inside quotation marks.

```
     The president expressed his opposition to
the tax reform proposal currently before Con-
gress, saying it would "wreck our economic
recovery."
```

The qualities of the "good" interview (from the standpoint of the journalist) mirror the qualities of any good conversation. The participants quickly reach an understanding about why they are talking with one another.

They exchange views and information. They learn something about one another. They share nonverbal gestures, such as smiles or frowns.

Yet, interviewing for the journalist is not just having a good conversation. The journalist's purpose in an interview is to gain information and material for an article that will be dissemminated to others. Because of that purpose, a journalist needs to develop interviewing skills that include not only proper conduct during the face-to-face conversation but also proper preparation and follow-up. This section outlines briefly some of the steps a journalist should take in having successful interviews.

The first step in interviewing is deciding, sometimes simultaneously, what information is needed and who would be the best source for that information. A journalist should have a fairly clear idea of what information it will take to make a good article. Developing that kind of clear idea takes some experience, but it is certainly within the grasp of the beginning reporter. The information that a reporter needs will often dictate who the best source is to provide that information, but the selection of the source may depend on other factors as well. For instance, the best source for certain information might not be available or might be hesitant to talk with a journalist. These are situations in which journalists might have to find other sources of information.

The second step to a successful interview is preparing for the conversation. This preparation may include doing research on the topic of the interview or on the person to be interviewed. In general, the more the journalist knows about both, the more successful the interview is likely to be. In the world of daily journalism, time and deadline pressure may not permit much preparation. In such instances, the journalist must draw upon his or her experience and the cooperativeness of the source.

Another part of the preparation phase of the interview is figuring out what questions to ask. The questions, of course, will depend on the information that is needed, but they will also depend on the willingness of the source to give information. Information that is simple and not necessarily controversial can usually be gained from clear, straightforward, and efficient questions, as in the following exchange:

```
Reporter: Can you tell me how the wreck occurred?
Police officer: Well, the witnesses said it wasn't rain-
          ing but the roads were pretty wet from a thunder-
          storm that had just come through the area. The
          car traveling in the westbound lane put its
          brakes on for some reason and the car skidded out
          of control and into the eastbound lane.
Reporter: Why did the car brake?
Police officer: We're not sure. Maybe an animal ran
          across the road. Sometimes at night, especially
```

in wet conditions, you think you see things that
aren't there and you hit the brakes.
Reporter: What happened when the car skidded?
Police officer: It skidded about fifty feet and slammed
into a car in the eastbound lane. A third car,
also traveling eastbound, then crashed into those
cars. Fortunately for everyone else, those were
the only three cars involved in the wreck.
Reporter: Was anyone hurt?
Police officer: Yeah, two people were hurt pretty bad,
and two others were injured. Everyone was alive
when we got them to the hospital. You'll have to
check with the hospital to see how they are doing. . . .

This short exchange has given the reporter a lot of information (though certainly not everything) that can be included in a story. Chances are the reporter did not have much time to prepare for this interview. But the reporter understands news values and story construction well enough to ask relevant and productive questions.

Sometimes the information a reporter seeks is much more controversial and the source is not as adept or as willing to give the information. Journalists should be sensitive and empathetic with their sources, but they should also remember their professional responsibilities. They should also remember that there are different ways of asking questions and different types of questions to be asked. Here are a few:

Closed-end questions: These usually require very short answers or the question itself may contain a choice of answers from which the respondent will choose. How often do you travel out of town? Do you feel good or bad about the way things turned out?

Open-ended questions: Sometimes an interviewer will want to give a subject the chance to say anything he or she wants. Open-ended questions allow this to happen. What do you think is the most important issue facing the city council now? When you think about a person who is homeless, what picture comes into your mind?

Hypothetical questions: These are questions that set up a situation or condition and ask the interviewee to respond to it. They are sometimes known as "what if" questions. If someone came to you and asked your help in finding a job, what would you tell that person?

Agree-disagree questions: As the name implies, these questions ask respondents to express agreement or disagreement with a statement or action. Some people say Congressmen should be prevented from serving more than two terms. Do you agree or disagree with that?

Probes: These are questions that follow up on something the interviewee has said. They can be neutral (Can you tell me more about that?), provocative (Are you saying you will never do that?), or challenging (I think a lot of people will find difficult to believe.). The purpose of a probe is to get the interviewee to give more information about what he or she has just said.

Personal questions: These questions have to do with the personal life of a subject. They may be very relevant to the article that the journalist must do, but the questions need to be approached carefully. Most experienced interviewers agree that such questions should be left until the middle or end of the interview, giving the respondent a chance to establish some trust in the interviewer.

One of the most important products of planning an interview is for the journalist to have a list of questions that will be asked when the interview takes place. Because interviews are not always predictable, it may not be feasible or necessary to ask every question—and it may be that unplanned questions arise—but a journalist should always have some kind of a plan for the interview session.

The next step in the interview process is to establish contact with the source and to set up some mutually agreeable time and place to conduct the interview. When a reporter is working near a daily deadline, he or she may insist that the interview be conducted immediately on the phone. In other instances, however, a source should be told who wants to conduct the interview, for what publication it will be conducted, and what information in general the reporter needs. The reporter should be flexible about the time and the place of the interview so that it is as convenient for the source as possible.

The interview itself is the most important part of the process. A reporter should keep in mind why the interview is taking place—to obtain certain information—but should also remain open to possibilities other than those that had been planned. If a source decides to offer some new or surprising information, the reporter should be able to evaluate the worth of the information and handle it appropriately. Most of the time, however, a reporter's planning will pay off with an efficient and productive interview. The following are a number of things that an interviewer should keep in mind about an interviewing situation:

• Control the situation. Keep the conversation on track by remembering what you came for and what information you need to get from the source. Refer to your notes or questions.

• Normally, the first few questions will set the tone for the interview, so the reporter should think carefully about how the interview should be structured. If there are difficult questions that the reporter needs to ask—questions that would make the source uncomfortable—they are usually not the questions that should be asked first. Those questions will be easier to ask and answer later in the interview when the reporter and source have established some rapport.

Ernest Hemingway on interviewing and observing

When people talk, listen completely. Don't be thinking what you're going to say. Most people never listen. Nor do they observe. You should be able to go into a room and when you come out know everything that you saw there and not only that. If that room gave you any feeling, you should know exactly what it was that gave you that feeling.

© 1992 Jim Stovall

- Take notes. Do so as unobtrusively as possible, but if you are there as a journalist, the source will expect you to do this. Write down the key words and phrases that the source uses if you cannot get every word. Concentrate on what is being said so you can reconstruct an accurate quote later. Even during the interview session you should begin thinking about what information and direct quotations you will use in your article.
- If you don't understand what a source has said, ask that the quote be repeated. Read back what you have written to make sure that you have it right. If you don't understand a word or phrase that the source has used, ask about it. It is better that you show your ignorance to the source than to thousands of readers or viewers when you do your story.
- If a source attacks or criticizes you, try to respond as little as possible. Remember that you are there to get information, not to defend yourself.
- Use a tape recorder only if you have the permission of the source. Ask the source's permission before you turn it on. If the source is reluctant, you might say, "This will help me make sure I get everything you say correctly." If the source will not permit the use of the tape recorder, do not use it.
- Even if you use a tape recorder, always take notes. A tape recorder may not work, or the tape may be bad. Any number of things can happen.
- Sometime during the interview, take note of something other than what is being said such as gestures or other physical details of the source, pictures or awards on the wall, or other objects in the room. You may see something you want to ask about or something you will want to use in your article.
- Always be courteous and professional.

As soon as possible after the interview, you should go over your notes and listen to your tape recording. Many reporters will listen to a tape and fill in their notes. If there is no tape, it is a good idea to read your notes carefully and fill in parts of the interview that you may want to use in your article.

If possible, a reporter should check important information that the source has given with another source to verify it. Many reporters have been taken in by sources who sounded as if they knew exactly what they were talking about, and these reporters have looked foolish in print or on the air.

Finally, a reporter should never hesitate to call a source back for more information or for clarification of information or discrepancies. These callbacks show that a reporter is serious about producing an accurate report, and sources who are honest will not mind helping the reporter in this effort.

Using quotations

Learning proper newswriting form means understanding how to use quoted material properly. A good news story usually has a mixture of direct and indirect quotations, and a news writer must have a good sense of when to use a direct or an indirect quotation.

Most news stories will use more indirect quotations than direct quotations. An indirect quotation may contain one or a few of the same words that a speaker has used but will also have words that the speaker did not use.

Indirect quotations should maintain the meaning of what the speaker has said but use fewer words than the speaker has used. Competent writers quickly learn that most people use more words than necessary to say what they have to say. They can paraphrase what people say and be more efficient than the speakers themselves. And as a news writer, you will find that you can get more information into your story if you use indirect quotes.

If that is the case, why worry about using direct quotations at all? Why not just use indirect quotations all of the time?

Direct quotations can be used by the skillful writer to bring a story to life, to show that the people in the story are real, and to enhance the story's readability. Occasionally, people will say something in a memorable or colorful way, and that should be preserved by the writer. Think about some of the famous direct quotations in American history:

"Give me liberty or give me death." (Patrick Henry)
"Read my lips. No new taxes." (George Bush)
"We have nothing to fear but fear itself." (Franklin Roosevelt)
"Four score and seven years ago. . . ." (Abraham Lincoln)

Another reason for using a direct quote is that some quotations simply cannot be paraphrased. They are too vivid and colorful and they capture a feeling better than a writer could. For instance, when Bo Jackson was playing college football, he was once stopped from making a game-winning touchdown near the end of the game. The opposing lineback who made the hit on Jackson was asked about the play after the game. Still high from his accomplishment, he said, "I waxed the dude!" That quotation would be impossible to paraphrase.

If you are going to use direct quotations in your stories—and you should—you should follow some basic rules.

Use the exact words of the speaker. Anything that is within quotation marks should be something the speaker actually said. The words should be the speaker's, not the writer's.

Use direct quotations sparingly. Good writers will let people speak, but they won't let them ramble on. Most news writers avoid putting one direct quote after another in a story. You should never pile one direct quote onto another in paragraph after paragraph of a story. The writer who does that is not a writer but a stenographer.

Use direct quotations to supplement and clarify the information presented in the indirect quotes. In a news story, a direct quote is rarely used to present new or important information to the reader. It is most commonly used to follow up information that has already been presented.

Knowing how to deal with direct and indirect quotations is one of the most important skills that a newswriter can acquire. It takes some practice to paraphrase accurately and to select the direct quotations that should be used in a story. The key to both is to listen—listen carefully so that you understand what the speaker is saying and so that you remember the exact words that the speaker has used.

The correct sequence for a direct quote and its attribution is DIRECT QUOTE, SPEAKER, VERB. This sequence is generally used in news stories because it follows the inverted pyramid philosophy of putting the most important information first. Usually, what has been said is the most important element a journalist has; who said it, assuming that person has already been identified in the story, is the second most important element; the fact that it was said is the third most important element.

One of the common faults among many writers is the inverted attribution—putting the verb ahead of the subject.

```
"I do not choose to run," said the president.
```

There is no good reason for writing this way, and it violates one of the basic structures of English sentence: Subjects come before verbs. Remember, one of the major goals of the journalist is to make the writing of a story unobtrusive and the content of the story dominant. Sticking with basic English forms is one of the ways the journalist can do this.

One additional note: Use the past tense of verbs in news stories unless the action is continuing at the time of publication or unless it will happen in the future. Writing

```
"I do not choose to run," the president says.
```

is inaccurate unless the president goes around continually saying it. Chances are that it was said only once. It happened in the past, and that's the way it should be written. Although you would probably be able to find many examples of the use of the present tense in many publications, it is inaccurate when it is referring to things that have happened and to action that has been completed.

The importance of accuracy

The overriding goal of the writer for the mass media is accuracy. The attempt to be accurate must govern all of the actions of the writer, from the way he or she gathers information to the language that is used to convey that information. Previous chapters have discussed the necessity of using the language precisely and about the attention that a writer must give to the format, style, and usage in writing. These efforts are important because ultimately they help increase the accuracy of the writing that is produced.

This attention to precise writing should be preceded by an attention to the details of reporting. Developing good habits in gathering information will pay off for the reporter in many ways. The following are some of the areas of reporting that deserve the special effort of a reporter.

Spell names correctly. One of the most important possessions a person has is his or her name. The misspelling of a name is more likely to offend someone than almost any other mistake. Consequently, news reporters should take special care to make sure they have the correct spelling for the names they use in their stories. They should never assume they can spell a name correctly. For instance, "John Smith" may really be

```
John Smithe
John Smythe
John Smyth
Jon Smith
```

The person whose name you are spelling is the best source for the correct spelling, and you should never be afraid or embarrassed to ask. In fact, asking specifically often demonstrates that you are trying to be careful and increases the confidence that source has in you.

Checking with the person may not always be possible, however. In that case, telephone directories and city directories are generally reliable sources for correctly spelled names. The people who put these directories together are professionals and understand that they are creating a resource that will be checked by others. Police reports, printed programs and other such material are not reliable sources, and they should not be used for name checking.

Quote your sources correctly. This chapter has already discussed gathering and using quoted material, and more discussion will follow in the next chapter. The point here is to make sure you get it right. Many people who are used as sources in news reports complain about being "misquoted" or "quoted out of context." Often that is a way for the source to back away from what he or she has said after it has been printed or broadcast. On the other hand, news reporters do make mistakes, and it is their responsibility—not that of the source—to make sure they have heard and understood what the source has said. The simplest solution to not understanding what the source has said is to ask. Make sure you know not only what words the source has used but the meaning that the source has given to them.

Get information from more than one source if possible. As a general rule, news stories are better if reporters get information from more than one source. Different people know various things about a situation, or they may have differing viewpoints about it. The more people a news reporter talks to about a story, and the more records that he or she checks, the more likely he or she will be to understand the story fully.

Make sure that the numbers in a story add up correctly. Numbers don't have to throw journalists, but they often do. For instance, consider this paragraph about a student election that appeared in a college newspaper:

```
Officials said a total of 5,865 ballots
were cast, representing a 34.2 percent turn-
out. Smith defeated Jones by receiving 3,077
votes to Jones' 2,385, a margin of 393 votes.
```

The reporter should have done two things with this story. He or she should have added up to the totals for the two candidates to make sure that total matched the total number of ballots cast. If the numbers did not match, the news reporter should have found out why. Second, the story says that "officials" said there was a 34.2 percent turnout. The reporter should have gotten the figures that these officials used and done his or her own calculations. It may be that the 34.2 figure is correct. The reporter should have made sure.

Conclusion

This chapter has given you some idea of what a news story is and of how a news reporter gathers information to put into a news story. Once the news-gathering process is finished, it's time for the news gatherer to become the news writer. The next chapter will help you begin that process.

Points for consideration and discussion

1. The author says that writing for the mass media is "one of the most important jobs in our society." Do you agree or disagree?

2. Look at three news stories in your local newspaper. What news values are present in each of them?

3. One of the criticisms of the news media that many people make is that journalists emphasize "bad news" rather than "good news." What do you think that people mean by that? Do you agree? Do the news values listed in this chapter mean that journalists are more likely to look for "bad news" than "good news"?

4. The author says that secretaries are often good sources of information. Can you think of other job categories that would make good sources for journalists?

5. Why is it important for a journalist to get information from more than one source?

Further reading

John Joseph Brady, *The Craft of Interviewing.* Cincinnati, OH: Writer's Digest, 1976.

Fred Fedler, *Reporting for the Print Media*, 3d ed., New York: Harcourt Brace Jovanovich, 1984.

Julian Harriss, Kelly Leiter, and Stanley Johnson, *The Complete Reporter,* 4th ed., New York: Macmillan, 1981.

Ralph S. Izard, Hugh M. Culbertson, and Donald A. Lambert, *Fundamentals of News Reporting,* 4th ed., Dubuque, IA: Kendall/Hunt, 1983.

George M. Killenberg and Rob Anderson, *Before the Story: Interviewing and Communication Skills for Journalists.* New York: St. Martin's Press, 1989.

Bruce D. Itule and Douglas A. Anderson, *News Writing and Reporting for Today's Media,* New York: Random House, 1987.

Ken Metzler, *Creative Interviewing,* Englewood Cliffs, NJ: Prentice Hall, 1977.

EXERCISES

Answer the questions below about the following five news stories.

1. What are the news values that are present in each of the stories?

2. List the *who, what, when, where, why,* and *how* elements of each story.

3. Which of the three major types of sources of information are used in these stories?

4. List the sources specifically mentioned in each story. How do you think that the reporters were able to get this information?

5. Based on your limited knowledge about the events, analyze each of the stories for accuracy. Are there points in the story that might not be accurate? If you were the editor, what would you question? What would you want the reporter to double-check?

Story No. 1–Death penalty

CHILLICOTHE, Mo.—A jury has recommended a 69-year-old woman be sentenced to death for the murders of four transient farm workers whose bodies were found buried in northwestern Missouri last year.

Jurors in Livingston County Circuit Court deliberated more than three hours before making the recommendation Tuesday night in the case of Faye Copeland, who the jury had convicted Saturday of five counts of first-degree murder.

The jury of eight women and four men recommended Copeland be sentenced to life in prison without parole on the fifth murder conviction.

Circuit Judge E. Richard Webber must decide whether to accept the jury's recommendations or to sentence Copeland to life in prison. He ordered a pre-sentence investigation.

If sentenced to death, Copeland will become the oldest person on Missouri's death row.

Copeland's attorney, public defender David Miller, has said he will file a motion for a new trial. Miller said he would appeal the court's refusal to allow a psychologist to testify about "battered-wife syndrome."

Miller had argued Faye Copeland was dominated by her 74-year-old husband, Ray, who is awaiting trial on the same charges, and had only a minor role in the crimes.

Ray Copeland's trial is scheduled to begin Jan. 24 but the court first must determine whether he is mentally competent to assist in his own defense. His attorneys contend Ray Copeland suffers from senile dementia, including an organic brain disorder.

The bodies of the victims were found last year in shallow graves in barns or dumped in wells on farms in Livingston County where Ray Copeland had worked. Investigators said the victims had been shot to death. No bodies were found on the couple's farm near Mooresville, about 65 miles northeast of Kansas City.

The Copelands originally were arrested on charges of conspiracy in an alleged fraudulent cattle-buying conspiracy.

Authorities contended the couple hired the transients to work as cattle buyers, then killed and buried them. Prosecutors said the Copelands netted $32,000 by reselling the cattle. The fraud charges were dismissed after the murder charges were filed.

Story No. 2–Mob grave

NEW YORK—Federal agents and state police continued digging up a suspected secret mob grave Monday, where the remains of at least three people were found buried in a garage behind a locksmith shop, officials said.

The owner of the shop, convicted bank robber Richard Joseph Beedle Sr., 58, appeared in U.S. District Court in New Haven and was ordered held without bond, said U.S. Attorney Stanley A. Twardy Jr.

The bones of three and perhaps four people believed to be victims of warfare within the Patriarca organized crime family in the Hartford, Conn.–Springfield, Mass., area were found in a garage behind Beedle's home, Twardy said.

Beedle was charged with being an accessory after the fact of a murder committed in aid of racketeering, which is punishable by up to 10 years in federal prison and a $250,000 fine, Twardy said.

Arrested on the same charge Monday was Salvatore "Butch" D'Aquila Jr. of Middletown, 48, who operates Central News, a newspaper and variety store on Main Street in Middletown, Twardy said.

D'Aquila has past convictions on state gambling and fraud charges, said Twardy.

FBI agents discovered the mass grave in a garage behind Beedle's home in Hamden on Friday after searching for weeks with the cooperation of another suspect convicted on racketeering charges.

Jack Johns, a reputed organized crime figure arrested in March in a roundup of the Providence, R.I.–based Patriarca family, told authorities that bodies had been buried in Hamden, but he could not remember the address, Twardy said.

Johns rode through the New Haven suburb with FBI agents and spotted the house Friday, Twardy said.

Beedle was arrested and federal and state investigators with a search warrant and picks and shovels dug up the remains over the weekend.

Beedle, who operated Dick's Locksmith Shop in Hamden, was convicted in a 1970 bank robbery in Allentown, Pa., and was long associated with organized crime, New Haven police said.

The grave had been disturbed earlier in an apparent attempt to remove the remains and no other fragments were found in the search which continued Monday, Twardy said.

Twardy said he could not comment on the possible identities of the victims,but a published report said one of those buried in Hamden may be William Grant,an East Hartford restaurant owner who vanished in 1988.

Story No. 3–Hostage

CHARLESTOWN, W. Va.—A teenager described as a "good guy" who "wouldn't hurt anybody" took a teacher and about 15 students hostage at gunpoint Monday in a high school classroom, gradually releasing his captives until the standoff ended more than eight hours later.

The suspect, Eli Dean, 18, did not fire a shot during the siege, and no injuries were reported.

By mid afternoon, Dean, who recently was suspended from school for pranks, had released all but five students from a classroom at Charlestown High School, and early in the evening released four more hostages, state police Sgt. Martin Jenkins said.

The siege ended about 7:30 p.m. EST when Dean surrendered and released the last student, he said.

The youth was armed with a pistol, believed to be a .44-caliber revolver taken from his stepfather's room, Jenkins said, but no shots were fired throughout the ordeal in Charlestown, a community of about 500 people about 15 miles north of Louisville, Ky.

Dean, twice suspended from the school in the last two weeks for setting off a fire alarm and breaking a window, went to the school to speak to Melody Money,43, a teacher who had counseled him about previous trouble at the school, the state police sergeant said.

Dean walked into Money's classroom about 11:10 a.m. and brandished the revolver in front of her and about 15 students, Jenkins said.

The suspect was persuaded to release most of his captives soon after the siege began, but state police could not give an exact count of the number of hostages freed.

Dean continued holding six students and Money until about 2 p.m., when a freshman, Stacy Medelli, were allowed to leave, followed soon by the teacher, Jenkins said.

Dean made no demands throughout the stand off.

A fellow student, Amanda Garr, said she believed the young gunman was "upset" at the recent suspensions, but expressed astonishment at his reaction.

"Eli, to me, is the best guy anybody could ever ask for," Garr said. "Something got in him and he's gone crazy about about. He's a very good guy. He wouldn't hurt anybody."

Garr said she and other students at first thought there had been a bomb threat when the school was evacuated and a police SWAT team moved into place, but later "we found out it was Eli and everybody started crying."

The youth's parents and stepfather, Rocky Williams, were called to the school to help police negotiators. Williams said he believes Dean took his .44-caliber revolver from their home.

Story No. 4–Crash

LISBON, Portugal (AP) — An American charter jet filled with Italian tourists slammed into a fog-covered mountain in the Azores today and exploded, and all 144 people on board were feared dead, officials and news reports said.

Maria della Versesi, a spokeswoman at the Italian Embassy in Lisbon, said all 137 passengers were Italian and the seven crew members were American. She did not release any names. The aircraft belonged to the U.S. airline Independent Air Corp., based in Smyrna, Tenn.

The flight originated in Bergamo, Italy, and was to have proceeded to Puerto Plata in the Dominican Republic, and Montego Bay in Jamaica, after making a refueling stop in the Azores.

The Portuguese news agency LUSA quoted an official from the Azores Civil Protection Service as saying about 50 bodies had been recovered and it appeared all on board died. LUSA also quoted an unidentified member of a local flying club as saying all the passengers and crew had been killed.

Afonso Pimentel, a LUSA reporter based in the Azores, said the Boeing 707 was preparing to land at Santa Maria airport when it crashed into Pico Alto, a fog-covered, 1,794-foot-high mountain, and burst into flames. LUSA quoted the civil protection official, who was not identified, as saying the pilot asked the airport to clear a runway for an emergency landing.

The Civil Protection Service is a state body that provides rescue services and assistance in civilian emergencies. A.L. Pittman, president of Independent Air Corp., said in an interview in Smyrna that the 15-year-old company makes 400 to 500 charter flights a year, mostly in the Caribbean and Europe.

Pittman, who declined to identify the seven American crew members, said the 20-year-old jetliner that crashed had a relatively low number of flight hours and no history of trouble. Pittman said the airplane, one of two Boeing 707s owned by the company, had 12,500 cycles, or takeoffs and landings, and less than 50,000 hours in the air.

Story No. 5–3-pointer

ENTERPRISE, Ala. (AP)—Gwen Smith's favorite shot is the 3-pointer.

Last week, the 5-foot-10 senior guard at Coffee Springs High School in Geneva County hit 11 of the long-range shots to set a new national high school record.

Bruce Howard, record book editor for the National Federation of State High School Associations in Kansas City, Mo., said Wednesday the previous girls' record of 10 3-pointers in a game was held jointly by players in Louisiana and Florida.

Smith, who connected on 11 of 16 3-pointers in the 75-32 victory over G.W. Long last Friday night, said she spends a lot of time at practice working on her outside shooting.

"One thing that helps me is the 3-point drill," said Smith, who scored a career-high 52 points in the game. "In each practice, we shoot about 20 each, and my favorite shot is the 3-pointer."

"She had a good night," Coffee Springs Coach Trey Holladay told the *Enterprise Ledger.* "She plays well on defense and plays down low. But on offense she plays guard because she can handle the ball and shoot so well."

The old state record for 3-pointers was held by Katrina Davidson of Buckhorn, who hit nine last year in toe Class 5A playoffs.

Interview plan–1

Plan an interview with the mayor of your city. First, you will need to decide the central reason why you want the interview. It could be that there is some issue facing the city currently that you will want to build your story around. If no such issue exists, you may want to talk to the mayor about what it is like to be mayor—duties, responsibilities, daily schedule, etc. Or you may want to do a personality profile on the mayor, asking about family, friends, recreation, etc.

Once you have decided what the interview is to be about, what background research will you have to do? How will you go about getting the information you need? Be specific about what information you will need and where you can get it.

Finally, formulate a list of tentative questions that you will want to ask the mayor during the interview. This list of questions should be in the approximate order of how you would like to ask the questions.

Interview–2

Plan an interview with the president of your college or university. Go through the same steps outlined in the exercise above in planning this interview.

Paraphrasing

Rewrite the following using a combination of direct quotations and paraphrases:

Martin Goldsmith, general manager of the local public radio station: "Our goal in this year's fundraising effort is to raise $100,000, which will be about 15 percent more than we raised last year. The money we are seeking—this $100,000—will go toward our programming efforts. We spent about $130,000 buying programs each year for the station, and those costs are going up each year. There is a lot that our audience would like to have on the station, and this is the way for them to help pay for it."

Tom Nelson, president of the citywide Parent-Teachers Association: "Our major concern this year will be security in the schools, particularly in the high schools. We will be working with school officials on ways we can help create a safer environment for the education of our children. A number of incidents in the past year have been very disturbing to many parents. We are going to try to provide a way for those parents to make a real difference in their local schools."

Marilyn Wall, president of the Walls Tire Co., a locally owned tire manufacturer: "The current year has been a good one for our company and its employees. Our orders were up about 20 percent over last year, and we were able to recall many of the employees that we had had to lay off during the past three years. In addition, we have expanded out workforce to add about 20 new jobs in various parts of the factory."

Marsha Moss, director of the local symphony orchestra: "The response of the audience to last night's concert was particularly gratifying. They seemed to enjoy everything that we put on the program. I can tell you that playing before an audience like that is a lot more fun than playing to a bunch of critics. It's good to know that people appreciate the many hours of hard work that this orchestra puts into each concert that we do."

5
Writing for Print

The person who writes for the mass media always works at two jobs: gathering information and putting that information into an acceptable form—that is, writing. Having the proper information—all the relevant facts of a story, the people involved, the times and dates, quotations, etc.—is vital to the writing process, but it is only the beginning. There comes a time when the information gathering must cease and the writing must begin.

The ability to write well requires that the writer have a thorough knowledge and understanding of the subject about which he or she is writing. In addition, the writer must understand the basic structure of the news story and the conventions or customs of news writing in order to complete the process.

This chapter focuses on putting information into a form appropriate for the print media. Many writing forms populate the print media, but the most common are the news story and the feature story. These forms are found in newspapers, magazines, newsletters and many other publications. Mastering these two forms will give the person beginning to write for the mass media a good foundation on which to build in learning to write in other forms and for other media.

Characteristics of news stories

All good pieces of writing have one thing in common—a unifying theme. A central idea should govern every book, magazine article, advertisement, or news story that anyone tries to create. The idea of a central theme is important for writers who are learning the different forms of writing for the mass media and particularly those learning to write a news story. Faced with a mass of information, facts, ideas, quotations, and the like, the news writer can use the central idea to help sort out what should be included in the article and how the various pieces of information should be presented to the reader.

The central idea will usually be expressed early in the story, normally in the first paragraph. This paragraph, called the lead, will set the tone and direction for the story. Lead paragraphs will be examined in more detail later in this chapter, but their importance is noted here. A strong lead that sets forth the central idea of the story will help to unify the writing for the reader.

Transitions. The central idea should be carried through the rest of the story, and the information the story presents should be used to develop and amplify it. Technically, the relationship between various pieces of information and the central theme are accomplished with the use of transitions. Transitions are a way of tying the information together and tipping the reader off as to what may come next. Readers should not be surprised by a brand new subject in the middle of a news story.

If news stories were written chronologically, writers could use chronological transitions, such as *then, after that, meanwhile, next,* etc. News stories do not often follow such chronological patterns, however, so the transitions must be more subtle. In news stories, transitions most often come through repeated references to people, things, or events in the story. The figure below demonstrates the way transitions within a news story help to tie the various pieces of information together.

Attribution. Another characteristic of news stories is the use of attribution. Attribution simply means telling readers where the information in a story

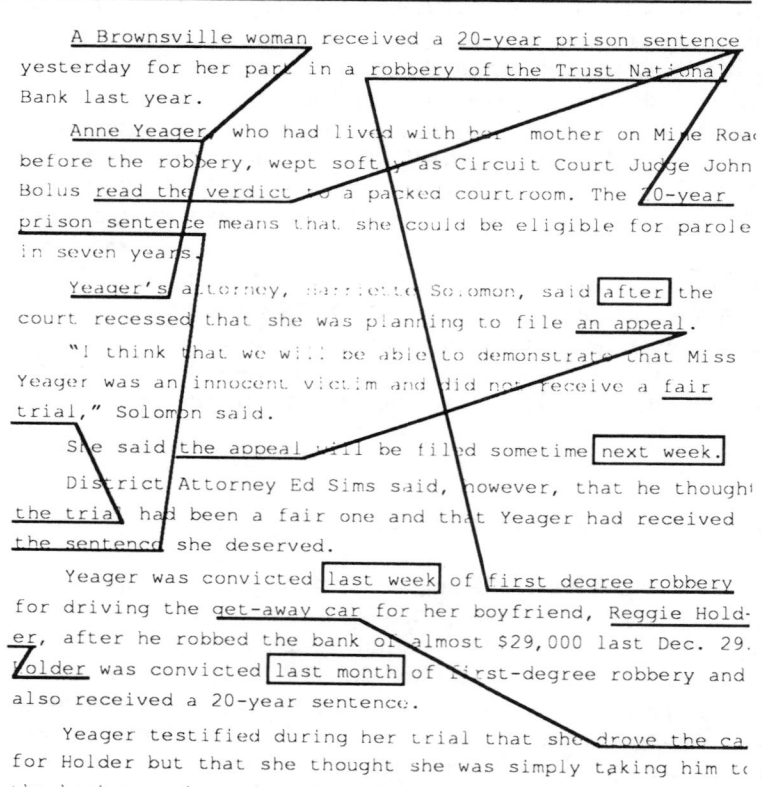

Figure 5-1 Transitions

While each new sentence in a news story should introduce some new information, the story should follow a logical sequence so that the reader is not surprised or shocked. One of the best transitional devices is the use of references, words that refer to things mentioned previously in the story. Some of the referents in this story are marked and tied together with diagonal lines. Another good transitional device is the use of words that refer to the time sequence of the story. Some of those words are boxed in the story below. Finally, in the sixth paragraph, the word *however* ties that paragraph to the information in the previous two paragraphs.

comes from. Attribution is important because it establishes the news report's credibility. Readers are more likely to believe that the publication is trying to be accurate in its reporting if they know clearly the source of the information. News reports in which the information is properly attributed reflect the professionalism of the publication and its reporters.

Another reason for attributing information in a story is to allow the reader to assess the information by assessing its source. Some sources are more credible than others. By telling the reader where information comes from, the news reporter is letting the reader make up his or her mind as to whether the information can be believed.

Beginning news writers sometimes have trouble with attribution because it can occasionally be awkward to work into a sentence. In most cases, however, the attribution can be included in a natural or unobtrusive way. Look at these examples:

```
The mayor said the city is facing a bud-
get crisis.

According to the police report, the car
skidded 50 feet before stopping.

The grand jury's report will be announced
tomorrow, the prosecutor said.
```

Most of the major facts in a news story should be attributed to some source (unless they come from an eyewitness account by the reporter), but information that is common knowledge to most readers usually does not have to be attributed. For instance, in the sentence, "A heavy cloud of smog hung over the city today, National Weather Service officials said," the attribution is unnecessary and even silly. As in many other aspects of writing, a balance should be struck. Too much attribution will get in the way of a story; too little attribution will harm the credibility of the story and confuse the reader. The good writer wants neither of these things to happen.

Many writers, particularly beginning journalists, complain that the word *said* is used too much in news stories. It is a colorless word which does not add much to the life of the copy. With this thought in mind, many writers begin the tortuous search for adequate substitutes for *said*. Surely, they think, the English language can come up with at least a few good words to use in its place.

While English does have many words that can describe the way words are spoken, there is no word that does the job the way *said* does it. *Said* is a neutral word. It simply connotes that words have been spoken; it doesn't say anything about the way in which they were spoken. Consequently, it is the kind of word that journalists ought to be using. Another point in the word's favor is that *said* is fairly unobtrusive in a news story. Even if used repeatedly, it does not jump out at the reader and get in the way of the information that is being transmitted.

Trying to find substitutes for the word *said* is a dangerous game for the beginning journalist. While there are many words that might be used in its place, writers should remember that they must use words for their exact meaning, not simply for variety's sake. Too often writers misuse these substitutes and create erroneous impressions about what was said. Another danger in the search for substitutes for *said* is that most substitutes are not neutral. If used, they make a statement about how the journalist feels about what was said. For instance, a person accused of a crime may "say" that he is innocent, or he may "claim" that he is innocent. That second verb carries a more negative or doubtful connotation, one which the journalist should not be implying.

Figure 5-2 Verbs of attribution
While few verbs are as versatile as *said* for use in attribution, there are occasions when a writer will need to use something different. At left are some of the most commonly used verbs of attribution. These verbs should be used only when they serve the specific purpose of the writer.

Said is a word that connotes only the fact that words were spoken or written. It says nothing about the way the words were spoken, the circumstances of the utterance, or the attitude of the speaker. The word is a modest one, never calling attention to itself. It can be used repeatedly without disruption to the writing. Consequently, there are few real substitutes for *said*. There are words you can use in its place, however, when it is proper for you to do so.

Explain means that more facts are being added to make something more understandable. It can be a neutral synonym for *said*, but it must be used in the right context. It is incorrect to write: "Bill Clinton is our current president," he explained. It would be correct to use *explain* as the verb of attribution for the following sentence: "The presidency is the nation's most important office," he explained.

Point out means to call attention to a matter of fact. A speaker can point out that grass is green, but a journalist should not write: "The majority leader pointed out that the president was tough in standing up to the communists." That statement is opinion, not fact.

State should be used for formal speeches or announcements such as the State of the Union address in January. It is incorrect to write: "Smith stated that the party would begin at 8 p.m."

Declare, like *state*, implies formality.

Add indicates more facts or comment about the same subject or an afterthought, a comment less important than what has been said before. It is incorrect to write: "She said she was unable to finish her paper. 'My typewriter was broken,' she added."

Revealed and **disclosed** are suitable only when referring to something that previously was unknown or concealed.

Relate means to pass along facts. It implies an absence of opinion on the part of the speaker.

Exclaim means to cry out in surprise or sudden emotion. It can easily be overused, so writers should be careful. It is usually written with an exclamation point. It is incorrect to use it in the following way: "The meeting will be at 3 p.m.," she exclaimed.

Short sentences, short paragraphs. News stories use short sentences and short paragraphs. Remember that the newswriter is trying to get information to the reader as quickly as possible. That is accomplished more easily if the writer uses short sentences. They are easier for the reader to digest.

Unlike other forms of expository writing, the news story does not require that a writer fully develop paragraphs. Paragraph length usually should be kept to three sentences or less and to less than 100 words. Again, the goal is getting information to readers, not fully developing an idea. Another reason for short paragraphs is that the width of a column of type in a newspaper is so narrow that a long paragraph is difficult and daunting for the reader.

Third person. News stories are usually written in the third person. A writer should not intrude into a story by using first person pronouns (unless they are part of a direct quotation from one of the story's sources). Even if a writer witnesses an event, he or she should not tell the story from the point of view of the first person.

WRONG: From where I was sitting, it looked like the umpire made the wrong call.
RIGHT: The manager protested the call by the umpire.

WRONG: The principal said enrollment at our school has gone down.
RIGHT: The principal said enrollment at Central High has gone down.

By the same token, news stories rarely directly address the reader by using the second-person pronoun *you*. Occasionally, lead paragraphs are questions directed at the reader, but this device can be overused quickly, and it is best avoided when you are beginning to learn newswriting.

Personal opinions—or what journalists call "editorializing"—should be kept out of news stories. News reporters should report only what they see and hear. How they feel about that information is not relevant to the news story. They should present the information and let the readers make up their own minds about it.

An attitude for accuracy. The chief goal of a journalist is accuracy. It is a central part of the writing process. Journalists expend many efforts in making certain that all of the information he or she has is correct. Achieving accuracy is not just a matter of techniques of reporting and writing but a state of mind that the journalist should foster. A journalist should never be satisfied with false information or with information about which he or she has doubts. The journalist should make whatever effort it takes to alleviate those doubts and to clear up any discrepancies.

This attitude should extend not only to the major information that a journalist has but to the smallest bits of a story. Making sure that dates and identifications are correct, that numbers in a story add up properly, that locations are correct—all of these things are part of a journalist's job. Journalists should take special care with the names of people to make sure they are spelled correctly.

Journalists strive for accuracy because they realize that their readers and viewers trust them and expect their reports to be accurate. If those reports are not accurate, journalists will lose that trust and eventually lose their readers.

The inverted pyramid

Once a writer has gathered the information necessary to begin a story, he or she must decide on the structure of the story. The goal of a proper structure is to get information to the reader quickly and to allow the reader to move through the story easily. The reader must be able to see the relationships between the various pieces of information that the reporter has gathered.

The most common structure for writing news stories is called the inverted pyramid. The daily newspaper contains many stories. Most stories must be written so that readers can get the most information in the least time. The inverted pyramid structure concentrates the most interesting and important information at the top of the story so that readers can get the information they need or want and then go on to another story if they choose. Headlines and leads should be written to describe what the story contains as succinctly and as interestingly as possible.

The lead, or first paragraph, is the focal point of the basic news story. It is a simple statement of the point of the entire story. It should be written as simply as possible and should contain as many of the five Ws as can be easily understood. Lead paragraphs are discussed more fully in the next section of this chapter.

The body of the inverted pyramid story adds detail to information that has been introduced in the lead and the first two or three paragraphs. The body should provide more information, supporting evidence, context, and illumination in the form of more details, direct and indirect quotes, and other description.

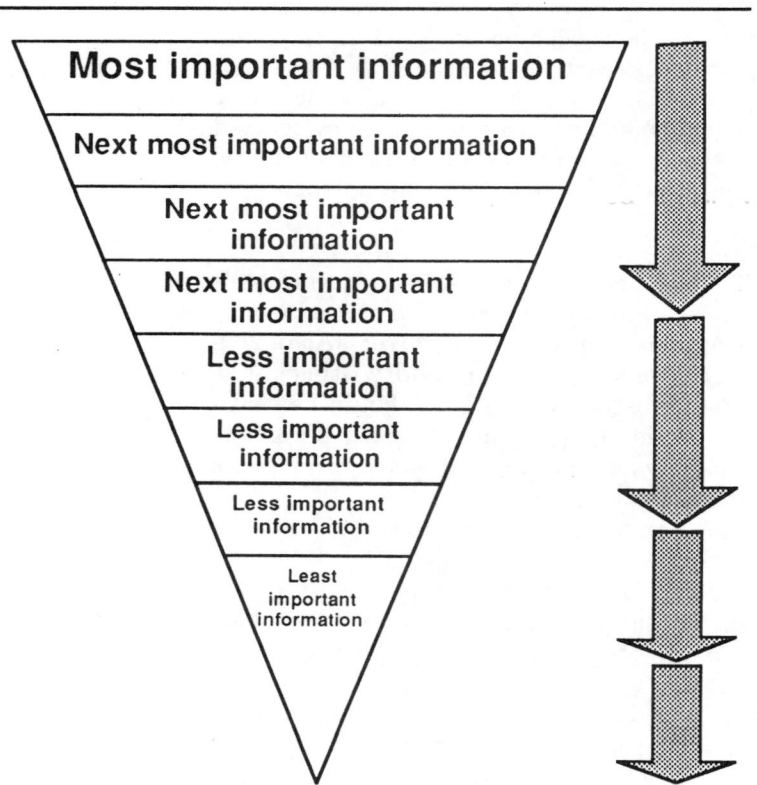

Figure 5-3 Inverted pyramid
Most news stories are structured in the inverted pyramid form; that is, they begin with the most important information, and the information is presented in descending order of importance. To write in this way, the writer must use some judgment about what information is the most important and the most interesting to the reader and what information the reader should have in order to understand the story.

The major concept of the inverted pyramid structure is to put the most important and latest information toward the top of the story. As the story continues, the writer should be using information of less importance. There are two reasons for writing a story this way. One is what we have already talked about: Putting the most important information at the top allows a reader to decide quickly whether or not to stick with the story.

The inverted pyramid also organizes the information in such a way that the reader can be efficient. Not every reader will read all of every story in a newspaper. In fact, one of the strengths of a newspaper is that it offers a wide variety of information that will appeal to many people. The inverted pyramid structure for news stories allows the readers to get as much of the most important information in that story as quickly as possible; it also allows the readers to stop reading and go on to something else when they have satisfied themselves with that story.

This process would not be possible if all stories were written chronologically. Very often, what happens at or near the end of the story is the most important or interesting thing to the reader. Readers are not accustomed to wading through a lot of less important or less interesting information to get to these parts. Consider a story that begins with the following paragraphs:

> The City Council opened its meeting last night with a prayer from the Rev. Jonathan Fowler, pastor of the Canterbury Episcopal Church.
>
> The minutes of the previous meeting were read and accepted without changes.
>
> Mayor H.L. Johnson then called for a report from the city budget director, Hiram Lewis, who said that property tax collections were running behind what had been expected when the budget was adopted last year.
>
> "If property tax collections continue at this rate, the city will be facing a major deficit," he said.
>
> When Councilmember Fred Greenburg asked what that meant, Lewis replied that the city would have to borrow money or cut back on some of its services.
>
> Johnson then proposed that the council raise the property tax rate by 5 percent for most property owners. The new rates would go into effect next year and would last for only one year, he said. This increase would allow the city to continue operating without any cutbacks in service.
>
> Council member Marge Allen objected to the increase, saying the citizens of her district already had too many taxes to pay. She also said that an increase in the property tax would discourage industries from locating in the city. . . .

Think about the reader of that story who is a property owner in the city. Most likely, that person is asking, "Are my taxes going up?" The reader should not have to wait for six or more paragraphs to find out the answer to that question. Instead, the answer should come immediately in the first paragraph:

```
          The City Council voted against raising
property taxes 5 percent last night, despite
warning from officials that the city faces a
cutback in services unless it gets more mon-
ey.
```

Another reason for the inverted pyramid structure is a technical one. When stories are prepared for printing, they are set in type and laid out on a page. An editor must decide how to fit stories together on a page. Sometimes stories will be longer than the space allotted for them. If this is the case, an editor will try to cut a story from the bottom, knowing that if the story is written properly, none of the essential facts will be lost.

The inverted pyramid structure demands that the writer make judgments about the importance of the information that he or she has gathered—judgments based on the news values discussed earlier in this chapter.

The inverted pyramid structure, though it is the most common, is not the only type of story structure that can be used in news writing. There are several others, which we will discuss in the next few paragraphs. These structures are not rigid. If one style alone won't do, a writer should search for combinations of styles which will best fit the information and ideas he or she is trying to organize.

The lead paragraph

The most important part of the news story is the first, or lead (pronounced LEED), paragraph. The lead should tell the reader the most important information in the story. It should be written so that the reader will be interested in going further into the story. Let's go back to the example of the city council story in the previous section. A lead on that story might simply say:

```
          The City Council voted against raising
property taxes last night.
```

This lead gives the most important information in this story, but it should also invite the reader to continue reading, as the following lead does:

```
          The City Council voted against raising
property taxes 5 percent last night, despite
warning from officials that the city faces a
cutback in services unless it gets more mon-
ey.
```

This lead tells the reader the following: There was a debate about this matter, and it has some consequences that you might be interested in.

An otherwise good story will not be read by many people if the lead is dull or confusing. The lead is the first part of the story a reader will come in contact with after the headline, and if the lead does not hold the reader's interest and attention, little else will.

In writing the lead, a reporter must make a judgment on what to put in a lead based on the news values discussed in the previous chapter. The writer must get information to the reader quickly, but also accurately and interestingly. Accuracy, speed, and entertainment are finely balanced in a good lead paragraph.

Leads on news stories generally contain at least four of the five Ws and H that were discussed in the previous chapter. Those four elements are who, what, where and when. A lead paragraph may emphasize any one of these elements, depending on the facts that are available to the reporter, but usually all four of these questions are answered in the lead. Sometimes the lead will contain or emphasize the why and the how of a story, but such stories are unusual.

Lead paragraphs should say neither too much nor too little. One of the mistakes that beginning news writers often make is that of trying to put too much in a lead. A lead should not be crowded with information; rather, it should tell enough to answer the reader's major questions about a story and to do so in an interesting way. If a lead tries to tell the reader too much, it can be boring or confusing.

Leads can come in a wide variety of forms and styles. While journalistic conventions restrict what writers can do in some ways, there is still plenty of room for creativity. The following types of leads and examples demonstrate some of the ways writers can approach a story.

The straight news lead is a just-the-facts approach. It delivers information quickly and concisely to the reader, and does not try to dress up the information. For instance:

```
    Two people were killed and four were in-
jured today when a truck collided with a pas-
senger car on Interstate 59 near the Cotton-
dale exit.
```

This straight news approach is the most common type of news lead and lends itself to most of the stories a reporter will have to cover. Because of this, a couple of technical rules have been developed for this kind of story. Such leads should be one sentence long, and they should contain about thirty words (a maximum of thirty-three words). It is particularly important for the beginning writer to master this one-sentence, thirty-word approach because of the discipline of thinking that it requires. A writer must learn that words cannot be wasted, particularly at the beginning of the story.

The summary lead is one in which there may be more than one major fact to be covered. Again, the one-sentence, thirty-word approach should be used even though such an approach may require even more effort on the part of the writer. For example:

```
    A tanker-trailer truck carrying dangerous
chemicals crashed on Interstate 59 today,
killing one person, injuring four others, and
forcing the evacuation of several hundred
people from their homes.
```

The emphasis in this kind of lead is on outlining the full story for the readers in a brief paragraph. Writers using summary leads need to take care that they do not crowd their leads with too much detail but also that they do not generalize too much. A balance should be achieved between including enough detail to make the story interesting and enough general material to avoid confusing the reader.

Up to this point, we have been dealing with **straight** leads for the most part. Straight leads give the who, what, when, where, and why elements of the story to the reader in a straightforward, no-frills fashion. Other types of leads exist, however, and the good news writer should be aware of when they can be used most effectively.

The **blind** lead is a lead in which none of the people in the story are named. The two previous examples are blind leads. This kind of lead is common when the people in the story are not well known. In the last lead about the accident, we assume that none of the people involved in the accident are well known. If one of the people hurt was the mayor of the city, we would not want to write a blind lead. We would want to mention his name in the lead.

The **direct address** lead is one in which the writer speaks directly to the reader. The main characteristic of this lead is the word *you*, present or implied.

```
     If gardening is your hobby, you'll need to
know about Tom Smith.

     If you're a property owner in the city, the
City Council is about to take at least $50
more from you each year.
```

The direct address lead is a good way of getting the reader's attention, but it should be used sparingly. It is also important to follow up a direct address lead quickly in the second and third paragraphs with information about the lead. By implication, the direct address lead promises the reader some immediate information.

The **question** lead attempts to draw the reader into the story by asking a question.

```
     Do you really want to know how hot dogs are
made?

     Why doesn't the president tell Congress how
he stands on the pay increase issue?
```

The question lead has some of the same advantages and disadvantages as the direct address lead. It is a good way of getting the attention of the reader. On the other hand, it can easily be overused. It, too, promises to give the reader some immediate information, and the writer should make good on that promise.

The direct address and the question lead also imply that the story has some compelling information for the reader. That's why writers should be careful to use them only when that is the case. Otherwise, the reader will likely be disappointed.

The **direct quote** lead uses a direct quotation to introduce the story and to gain the reader's attention. The direct quote, of course, should be something that one of the participants in the story said, and it should be compelling and informative enough to serve as the lead.

```
    "A city that cares!"
    That's  what  mayoral  candidate  George
Bramble promised today as he hit the campaign
    trail in. . . .
```

Any of these leads can be used when a writer feels that the facts of a story warrant their use. Writers should be careful, however, not to use one of these leads simply for the sake of using something different and not to use them when a story does not lend itself to their use.

Developing the story

The inverted pyramid requires that writers make judgments not only about what should be at the beginning of the story but also about the relative importance of all of the information they present in the story. In other words, writers must decide what the most important information is for the lead, but they must also decide what the second and third most important pieces of information are. Developing the story in a logical and coherent way requires much skill and practice.

If the lead paragraph is the most important part of the news story, the second paragraph is the second most important part of the story. In some ways, it is almost as important as the lead but for different reasons.

A lead paragraph cannot contain all of the information in a news story. If it is written well, it will inform the reader, but it will also raise certain questions in the reader's mind about the story. Chief among the roles of the second (and succeeding) paragraphs is to answer these questions. The writer does this by providing additional information about the story. The writer must decide what information is most important and what will help the reader to understand the story.

One method that writers use to make these judgments is to put themselves in the place of the reader and ask, "If I were a reader of this story, what would I want to know next?" For instance, a lead might say

```
    Authorities are searching for a state pris-
on inmate who escaped from a work crew at the
Kidder Correctional Facility yesterday.
```

That lead gives some information about the story, but it also raises a number of questions, such as:

Who was the inmate?

Why was he in prison?

How long had he been there and how long was his sentence?

How did he escape?

Where is the search for him taking place?

Is the inmate dangerous?

What does he look like?

How have the prison officials explained his escape?

These are just a few of the questions that could be asked about this story. The writer must answer these questions in a logical and coherent manner that will result in a unified and interesting story. The order in which these questions are answered will depend on the specific information that the writer has to work with.

The writer will probably want to give the name of the inmate quickly and the circumstances of the escape. Beyond that, the type of information the writer has will dictate the order in which the questions are answered. For instance, the second paragraph might go something like this:

```
Billy Wayne Hodge, 22, who was convicted
two years ago for armed robbery, walked away
from his work crew yesterday afternoon at
about 3 p.m., according to prison officials.
The crew was picking up trash along Highway
69 about four miles from the prison at the
time of the escape.
```

This paragraph answers some of the questions but leaves others unanswered. Even though a second paragraph can be longer than the lead, it still cannot answer all of the questions a lead can raise. Now the writer will have to decide what questions he or she will answer in the third paragraph. Again, those decisions will be based on the kind of information the writer has. The writer might want to say something about the search for the prisoner. For instance:

```
Sheriff Will Harper said last night that he
thought the prisoner was still in the thick
woods in the area of the escape. He said dep-
uties would patrol the area tonight and a
full-scale search would begin early today.
```

Or the writer may expand on the circumstances of the escape:

```
"It appears that one of our guards wasn't
watching the prisoners as closely as he
should have been," Sam Mayer, the prison war-
den, said: "There were 15 men in the work
crew and only two guards."
```

Either choice might be correct, depending on the circumstances of the story and the writer's preference. Still, the writer has not answered all of the questions raised by the lead, but the story is becoming more complete.

The following is another example of the way in which a story can be developed:

An automobile accident occurs on a busy street in your city. Three cars are involved. The driver of one of the cars is arrested for drinking and driving. One person is killed and another is seriously injured. The accident occurred during the afternoon rush and tied up traffic for more than an hour.

A reporter covering that accident would get all of the information listed above plus other details. Of all of these facts, however, which one would you say is the most important? Which one would rank as the second most important fact? the third?

Death and personal injury are usually considered the most important facts in a story such as this one. The fact that one person was killed and another seriously injured would be the most important thing that the reporter would have to tell the readers.

The reporter would then have to decide what the second most important fact was. It could be that the arrest of one of the drivers would be second in the mind of the reporter, especially since drinking and driving is in the news a lot these days. Or it might be that the reporter would think that traffic being tied up for so long on a busy street was the second most important fact; a lot of people (and possibly many readers) would have been affected by the traffic jam. A reporter would have to decide about this, and about the other information he or she would gather.

If the fact that one person was killed and another seriously injured is the most important fact, the reporter will want to use that fact to start the lead. But what else will be in the lead? Think about the "what," "when," and "where" or the story. If we put all those things together in one sentence, it might come out like this:

> One person was killed and another seriously
> injured in a three-car accident Tuesday af-
> ternoon during rush hour on Chester Street.

What do you think? Is this the best lead that could be written for a story like this one, or can you think of a better approach to this story? (One of the most noticeable problems about the way it is written is that it uses the passive voice—something we try to avoid in writing for the mass media.)

This paragraph above is a serviceable lead, but there may be more that can be done with it. Adding a few more details, such as more identification of the person who was killed, might make it more interesting for the reader. Then we might have the following lead:

> A Centerville man is dead and another per-
> son seriously injured after a rush hour col-
> lision on Chester Street on Tuesday after-
> noon.

Or if we wanted to take a different tack and try to work in the fact that one of the drivers was arrested, the lead might read like this:

> One person is dead and another seriously
> injured after a three-car accident on Chester
> Street on Tuesday, and police later arrested
> one of the drivers involved in the collision.

As you can tell from this one example, there are many approaches to even the simplest story. Note some things about each of these examples, however. All of them begin with the most important information—the fact that one person was killed and another injured. All of these are one sentence long and contain thirty words or less. And all use simple, straightforward language to give the reader information. The writer does not try to bowl the reader over with fancy words or phrasing but rather tries to keep the language as simple as possible.

Now for the second and third paragraphs of the story. The reporter would want to give the name and identification of the accident victims and would want to relate a few more details about the events surrounding the accident. A second or third paragraph for this story might read this way:

> George Smith, 2629 Silver St., was killed when the car he was driving crashed into a telephone pole after being hit by another car. His wife, Sylvia Smith, was also injured in the accident and is in serious condition in General Hospital, according to hospital officials.
>
> Police said they arrested Sam Johnson, 30 Pine Ave., and charged him with driving under the influence of alcohol in connection with the accident.
>
> Sgt. Roland Langley, the officer who investigated the accident, said the car Johnson was driving swerved across the road and hit the Smith vehicle, driving it into a telephone pole. A third car was also hit, but no one in that car was injured.

At this point, the writer might want to make the story even more interesting by adding some direct quotations from the news sources.

> "A number of witnesses said they saw Johnson's vehicle swerving all over the road, and it appears that he was going pretty fast, too," Langley said.
>
> The police measured 60-foot skid marks made by the Johnson vehicle, Langley added.
>
> A spokesman for the City Jail said Johnson was being held pending other charges that might be lodged against him. A bail hearing for Johnson was set for today.

So far, the story has concentrated on the accident. Now, however, the writer might return to the victims and give more details about them.

> Hospital officials said Smith suffered head injuries, and he died shortly after he arrived at the hospital. Mrs. Smith also suffered injuries to her head and neck and has three broken ribs and a broken arm.
>
> The third car in the accident was driven by Lester Matson, 406 Altus Drive. Matson said Johnson's car smashed into his after it had hit the Smith's car.
>
> "There was simply nothing I could do to get out of the way," he said. "I saw this car up ahead, swerving all around the road, but there were cars all around me, and I couldn't go anywhere." Matson was not hurt, but he said his car was damaged in the accident.

The two examples in this section should give you some idea as to how a news story is developed. That development is based on a series of decisions that the writer must make about the information he or she has. Even with simple stories, these decisions are rarely simple ones. They require that the writer understand the news story structure as well as the facts of a particular story.

How should a news story end? A writer should stop writing when all of the logical questions have been answered and when all of the interesting information has been presented in the story. A writer should not be concerned with concluding or summarizing a story, particularly when he or she is beginning to learn how to write news. Instead, the writer should make sure that the reader can understand and be satisfied with what is written.

Figure 5-4 News story critique

On the right is a news story written in a typical inverted pyramid structure. This story demonstrates a number of points that we have made about newswriting in this chapter. We have pointed some of them out on the right. See if you can find others.

The lead summarizes the story and gives the latest and most important information to the reader.

Note that FBI is not spelled out, even on first reference. Acording the the *AP Stylebook,* FBI is so well known that it does not need to be spelled out on first reference.

The second paragraph builds on the lead paragraph with additional information. By the end of the second paragraph, the reader has most of the major information of this story.

Note the use of the direct quotes in the third and fifth paragraphs. They reinforce information that has been presented previously. The direct quotes also add life to the story; they let the readers know that this story is about real people.

The last paragraph gives the reader some background information on this story. We can assume that the information has already been published, but this paragraph informs the readers who haven't heard about this incident and reminds those who have.

FBI questions two about park death

The FBI has begun questioning two of its most wanted fugitives about the unsolved death of a Memphis woman in the Great Smoky Mountains National Park.

An FBI spokesman, however, was careful not to declare Howard Williams, 44, or his wife, Sarah, 36, suspects in the death of Gladys Roslyn. Roslyn's skeletal remains were found by hikers in the park more than two years ago.

"At this point, they are being regarded as material witnesses, and that's about all that we can say about the case," Larry Tims, assistant special agent in charge of the local FBI office, said Tuesday.

Clark Summerford, a lawyer for the couple, confirmed that the FBI is seeking information from them about the woman's death, but he, too, emphasized that the FBI was not about to charge them with any additional crimes.

"As far as I know, the FBI has no evidence directly linking the Williamses with this woman's death," Summerford said.

The Williamses were captured last week after more than a decade on the run. They were spotted by a local truck driver who said he had seen them on "America's Most Wanted," a television show that features stories about fugitives from justice. The Williamses escaped from a Massachusetts jail more than 10 years ago, after they had been convicted of armed robbery of a bank in Salem, Mass.

Other story structures

The inverted pyramid story structure is not the only form that writers of news and information can use. Sometimes the facts, the publication, or the situation will dictate that a different form be used to present ideas and information. Beginning news writers should first master the inverted pyramid form, but they should also be able to use a different story structure when the situation calls for it. The following is a brief summary of some of the various story structures that are used in writing for print:

Narrative. As the name suggests, this form uses traditional storytelling techniques, particularly a chronological approach. Instead of a summary lead paragraph, the story begins at the beginning. Events are then related in the order in which they occurred.

The narrative structure demands a strong, interesting lead paragraph to draw the readers into the story, just as the inverted pyramid structure does. It also requires the writer to relate everything to a central theme and to weave the events together so that they have a unity for the reader. Finally, readers must come away from a narrative story with a strong sense of the sequence in which events occur and an understanding of why this sequence is important.

Eyewitness accounts. This approach to news writing can occur in two ways. One is when the reporter is present at the events. This type of eyewitness report requires that the reporter get away from the impersonal account in which most news is written. It opens up possibilities for the reporter to describe sights, sounds, and smells that might be left out of most news stories.

Another type of eyewitness account is for a reporter to collaborate with an eyewitness to an event to produce an on-the-scene story about the event. This approach requires more than just interviewing an eyewitness. It means that the reporter should talk with the subject long enough to understand not only what the subject saw and heard but how the subject felt about the event. Be-

Violent storm crashes city

A violent thunder and wind storm ripped through the city Tuesday afternoon, downing trees and power lines and causing personal injuries and property damage.

The storm hit about 3 p.m. and took approximately 45 minutes to sweep through the city.

While most of the city felt the storm, the most damaging high winds and sheets of rain were confined to the Hillsdale area west of downtown.

Arthur Major, 227 W. Hill St., was struck by a falling limb and taken to Community Hospital during the storm. He suffered severe head injuries and was in serious but stable condition on Tuesday evening.

Hospital officials said five other people were injured in car accidents caused by the storm. All were treated and released by emergency room doctors.

The storm downed power lines throughout the city. West Point Power Co. officials said at one time during the afternoon about 30,000 city residents were without electricity. They said power was restored to every part of the city except the Hillsdale area by 9 p.m.

Figure 5-5
News story structure
Inverted pyramid
The story on the left is written in the inverted pyramid style. Compare this one to the stories in Figures 5-6 (page 117) and 5-7 (page 118), which are about the same event but written in a narrative and eyewitness style.

fore this approach is used, the reporter and the subject should agree on their collaboration. Normally, a reporter will draft an account of the event using the words of the eyewitness as much as possible and writing from that person's point of view. The eyewitness will then review the draft and suggest changes. This process of drafting and reviewing will continue until the article is ready for publication. An eyewitness should always see the final draft before it is published.

Bullet. This structure is useful when several things happen at an event that are not closely related to one another but the event itself needs to be covered in one story. It uses a summary lead to tell the reader what the story is about in general and then a series of short paragraphs—called bullets, and thus the name—summarizing the different events or points that the story will cover. This establishes the structure of the story. Each bullet is then expanded with several paragraphs of explanation. In this structure, the news writer does not have to be closely concerned with transitions or with trying to tie the different parts of the story together for the reader.

Micro-macro. This structure, used most prominently by the *Wall Street Journal* in its lead articles on page 1 each day, works well when the topic of the story is a large event that affects many people. It begins by focusing on some person or situation that has been affected by the event. This "micro" beginning reflects or demonstrates the larger issue or problem. After describing the person or situation, the story then expands to the larger problem (the "macro") with a transition paragraph that explains what the story is about. This transition paragraph often uses facts and figures that summarize the issue. The subsequent paragraphs continue to discuss the larger issue, although they may refer to the situation presented at the beginning. The story will return to the beginning situa--

Figure 5-6
News story structure
Bullet
The story on the right is written in the bullet style. The story begins with a summary lead paragraph and then quickly summarizes several pieces of information in the next few paragraphs. Compare this one to the stories in Figures 5-5 (page 116) and 5-7 (page 118), which are about the same event but written in an inverted pyramid and eyewitness style.

Violent storm crashes city

A violent thunder and wind storm ripped through the city Tuesday afternoon, downing trees and power lines and causing personal injuries and property damage.

The storm caused the following injuries, disruptions and damage:

• One man was seriously injured when a tree limb hit him on the head; five others received minor injuries because of car accidents caused by the storm;

• Some 30,000 West Point Power Co. customers were without electricity for part of the evening Tuesday; power has been restored in most areas;

• Several homes and businesses in the Hillsdale area were seriously damaged by the strong winds;

• Traffic signals were out in much of the western part of the city immediately after the storm, but all have been restored.

Arthur Major, 227 W. Hill St., was struck by a falling limb and taken to Community Hospital during the storm. He suffered severe head injuries and was in serious but stable condition on Tuesday evening.

Hospital officials said five other people were injured in car accidents caused by the storm. All were treated and released by emergency room doctors. . . .

tion for some type of resolution or ending. These stories take time to develop because the reporter must become familiar enough with the large problem and the small situation to write about both accurately. A lead story in the *Wall Street Journal* can take as much as three or four months to research and write.

These are just a few of the different approaches that news writers can take to their stories. All of these structures demand that writers adhere to the basic characteristics of good news writing: a goal of accuracy, a knowledge of the language, and an adherence to the rules of style.

Editing and rewriting

Benjamin Franklin would tell the following story:

John Thompson, a hatter, was about to open his first shop. He made a sign to put in front of his business that read, "John Thompson, hatter, makes and sells hats for ready money." He was proud of his sign and showed it to his friends. One friend said it was a fine sign, but the word "hatter" was unnecessary because the sign also said "makes and sells hats." Another friend said "makes" could be dropped. Yet another friend said the phrase "for ready money" could be eliminated because it could be assumed that people would pay money for the hats. The word "sells" could also be dropped, another friend pointed out, because it could also be assumed. With all these suggestions, Thompson remade the sign to read, "John Thompson, hatter." Then a friend suggested that a picture of a hat could replace the word, "hatter." The sign was redone again, hung outside the shop, and Thompson had a long and prosperous business.

All writers need an editor. The nature of writing is that first drafts are rarely satisfactory. They do not often accomplish what the authors intend.

Editing and rewriting are integral parts of the writing process. A writer who finishes an initial draft has the responsibility to try to improve it, and most writers readily recognize this necessity.

In writing for the mass media, editing and rewriting in some form are usually part of the production process. News organizations employ

---

Violent storm crashes city

By Guy Hibbs

I have lived in this city for nearly 20 years, and I've never seen anything like it.

The storm that blew through this city yesterday was the noisiest, most violent roaring of Mother Nature in my memory. Others who have lived here longer than I have have told me the same thing.

Normally, I'm in the office of the *Daily News* at 3 p.m., usually putting the finishing touches on the day's work and thinking about the evening at home.

But yesterday, when the storm hit, I happened to be driving back to the office from an interview that I conducted for a Sunday feature story.

As I was driving by the Hillsdale shopping center – later to be one of the hardest hit areas – I looked at the sky and noticed a line of thick, dark clouds marching from east to west across the sky. The wind was picking up.

A bad storm, I thought, but nothing too unusual.

Within minutes, I knew I had misjudged the elements. . . .

Figure 5-7
News story structure
Eyewitness account
The story on the left is written as an eyewitness account. Here the writer centers the story around himself and his experiences. Compare this one to the stories in Figures 5-5 (page 116) and 5-6 (page 117), which are about the same event but written in an inverted pyramid and narrative style.

people to edit copy just as they employ reporters to write it. These copy editors, many of whom have experience as news reporters, develop an expertise in the techniques of copy editing. They can edit under deadline pressure, just as writers must learn to write under those same pressures.

The first responsibility for editing lies with the writer. A writer should develop a good understanding of the purpose and techniques of copy editing. The writer should also acquire good editing habits that, when put to use, will improve what has been written.

Two general types of editing can occur: copy editing and rewriting. Copy editing involves various techniques and operations that change and improve copy but do not alter its basic structure and approach. Rewriting, just as its name implies, means rewording large portions of the copy and reexamining it structure. Rewriting produces a different piece of copy, and its purpose is to make it more suitable for the medium in which it is to be used. Both copy editing and rewriting should be done when the copy demands it, but the amount of time available for these activities will often dictate how much can be done.

Walt Whitman on writing & rewriting

Write short; to the point; stop when you have done . . . . Read it over, abridge, and correct it until you get it into the shortest space possible.

© 1993 Jim Stovall

Given that time is not often available to rewrite completely every piece of copy, the following are some of the things that writers should look for first in articles they have drafted:

Spelling, grammar, and style mistakes. No mistakes are more embarrassing or more harmful to the writer than spelling and grammar mistakes. Such mistakes tag the writer as unprofessional or ignorant of the basic tools of the language. These are the mistakes that a writer should look for first. They should look up any words they are not sure about, and they should use every means possible to verify that the proper names in their stories are spelled correctly.

Style mistakes can also be painfully embarrassing to a writer. Ignorance of style rules for a particular medium will signal to other professionals that the writer does not understand the importance of consistency in writing and does not care to learn.

Verbs. The quickest way to improve writing is to improve the verbs. If possible, verbs should be active and descriptive. A writer should look at every instance where he or she has used the passive voice (see page 18) and consider whether or not the passage should be changed to the active voice.

Writing that is laden with linking verbs is probably not going to sound very interesting. These verbs (*is, are, was, were*) are useful and necessary at times, but they lack the power that active, descriptive verbs have. Changing linking verbs to descriptive verbs will inject life into a piece of writing.

Wordiness. Some writers delight in finding passages in their own writing that use too many words. They recognize that wordiness—using too many words to say something—is one of the major and consistent problems in writing. Most writing has this problem. Just as the man in Benjamin Franklin's story, every writer could use friends who are good editors to improve copy.

In examining your own writing, look at the parts that were difficult for you to write initially. You may have gotten something down to express the idea or information, but chances are you could improve it on a second reading. This improvement will usually involve cutting down on the number of words it takes to express the thought.

Answering all the questions. Writing for the mass media will raise questions in the minds of the readers. Writers must make sure that they answer all of the logical questions that their articles create. For example, an article may say that three people were hurt in an automobile accident and may give the name of the person hurt seriously enough to remain in the hospital. A natural question from this information would be, who are the other two people? Or, an article may mention that a coastal storm is the second worst such storm in the history of the state. What was the worst storm? The article should tell the reader at some point.

An article that does not answer all of the logical questions often means that reporters have not done a complete job in gathering information about the subject. It is not unusual for a reporter to discover in the editing process that he or she must find out more if the article is to be complete.

Internal consistency. An article should make

A new law that gives prosecutors additional power to halt the distribution of movies they believe are obscene prompted videotape rental stories in Decatur to pull nearly 2,000 adult films off their shelves.

Rewrite

Owners of videotape rental stores in Decatur have pulled nearly 2,000 tapes off the shelves because of a new law that gives prosecutors more power to halt the sale of obscene materials.

Several steps are being taken to prevent a repeat of the error that caused an ambulance answering a heart attack call to be sent to the wrong street last week, the Emergency 911 board of directors was told Tuesday.

Rewrite

Emergency 911 is taking several steps to make sure that ambulances are sent to the correct addresses, according to testimony before the E–911 board.

Civilian unemployment, rising at the fastest clip in more than three years, jumped to 5.3 percent last month, the government said Friday in a report that was taken as the strongest evidence yet of an economic slowdown.

Rewrite

Unemployment is up to 5.3 percent, the steepest rise in three years, according to a government report, and many economists believe that is the strongest sign yet of an economic slowdown.

Figure 5-8 Rewriting Leads

The lead paragraph is the most important part of a news story. It should present the reader with the most important information in the story. It should be long enough to give the reader a good idea about what is in the story, but short enough to let the reader get through it quickly.

In other words, leads are not easy to write. Quite often, it takes more than one try to write a good lead. On the left are some lead paragraphs as they appeared in print. The writers and editors who produced them did not have the time or make the effort to rewrite them. Below each lead are rewritten versions that are considerable improvements over the first efforts.

sense for the reasonable and sensible reader. Figures should add up properly, and times and dates should be logical. Even though most news stories are not written chronologically, a reader should have a good idea of the time sequence of a story. Confusion in the writing often indicates confusion on the part of the writer—and it almost guarantees confusion for the reader.

Looking for the writing problems listed above constitute the beginning of good copy editing. Given enough time, writers should not stop with these problems. They should judge their copy on its emphasis, tone, and structure. All of these factors need to be correct for writing to be at its best. The best writers avoid falling in love with their copy. In fact, the best writers are among their own worst critics. Good writers are always trying to improve their writing, using whatever means are necessary. A willingness to copy edit and rewrite are two such means that writers should never shy away from.

Feature styles

Dividing feature stories from news stories is misleading. The two actually have a great deal in common. The difference is in emphasis. The styles commonly used for feature stories assume that the reader has more time to read. They still require a central theme. The writer must be able to summarize the point of the story. But the writing may require that the reader go further in order to fully understand the point of the story. Of course, that means the writer must sustain interest for a longer period of time.

Feature writing is a way for both readers and writers to get away from the relevant facts-only approach of most news stories. Feature stories generally contain more detail and description. They go beyond most news stories by trying to discover the interesting or important side of an event that may not be covered by the six basic news values.

Feature stories are also a way of humanizing the news, of breathing life into a publication. Most features center around people and their activities and interests. A good way for a feature writer to approach the job is to believe that every person is worth at least one good feature story.

Feature stories not only vary in content but also vary in structure. The following is a brief discussion of some of the structures a feature writer may use. Feature stories have no single structure that is used most of the time. Feature writers are freer to adapt whatever structure is suitable to the story they are trying to tell.

Anecdotal features. This style usually begins with a story of some kind and usually will follow with a statement of facts to support the point of the story. Quotations, anecdotes, and facts then weave in and out of one another throughout the story. The trick is to keep the quotes and the anecdotes relevant to the point of focus and to keep the story interesting without making it trite.

Suspended interest features. This style is often used for producing some special effect. Usually it is used for a short story with a punch line. But sometimes it is drawn out into a much longer story. In either case, the style requires the writer to lead readers through a series of paragraphs that may raise questions in the minds of the reader while at the same time keeping readers interested in solving the puzzle. At the end, the story is resolved in an unexpected way.

The question and answer. This is a simple style used for a specific effect. An explanatory paragraph usually starts the story. Then the interviewer's questions are followed by the interviewee's answers word for word. Using this style requires articulate participants in the interview. Sometimes, however, it makes clear how inarticulate an interviewee is about a topic. In any case, it is effective for showing the reader an unfiltered view of the interviewee's use of language.

Characteristics of feature writing

To the reader, the feature story seems to exhibit a more relaxed style of writing than a news story. It may be easier to read than a news story, and because of its content it may be more entertaining. Feature writers, however, work just as hard and are just as disciplined as news writers. They may work under a slightly different set of rules than news writers, but the goals of a feature writer are essentially the same ones that a news writer has: to tell a story accurately and to write well.

The main thing that sets feature stories apart from news stories is the greater amount of detail and description features contain. This difference is the backbone of a good feature story. While the news story writer wishes to transmit a basic set of facts to the reader as quickly as possible, the feature writer tries to enhance those facts with details and description so that the reader will be able to see a more complete picture of an event or a person. For instance, while the news writer might refer to "a desk" in a news story, the feature writer will want to go beyond that simple reference by telling the reader something more—"a mahogany desk" or "a dark mahogany desk." Or better yet, the writer might rely on verbs to enhance the descriptions of the subject: "A large, soft executive chair enveloped him as he sat behind a dark mahogany desk."

The three major kinds of descriptions that should be contained in a feature story are description of actions, description of people, and description of places. All of these are important to a good feature story, but the description that makes for the strongest writing is generally the description of action. Telling about events, telling what has happened, telling what people are doing—these things make compelling reading. Descriptions of this type help readers to see a story, not just read about it. In addition, feature writers should make sure that readers see the people in their stories, just as the writers themselves have seen the people. Feature writers also need to describe adequately the places where the stories occur. Readers need an idea of the surroundings of a story to draw a complete picture of the story in their minds.

A couple of tips will help writers attain more vivid descriptions in their stories. One is the reliance on nouns and verbs. Beginning writers sometimes feel that they should use as many adjectives and adverbs as possible to enhance their writing, and in doing so, they rely on dull and overused nouns and verbs. That approach is a wrong turn on the road to producing lively, descriptive writing. A second tip for writers is to remember the five senses. Often writers simply describe the way things look, and they forget about the way things sound, feel, taste, or smell. Incorporating the five senses into a story will help make a description come alive for a reader.

Feature stories often contain more quotations and even dialogue than news stories. Newswriters use direct quotations to enhance and illuminate the facts they are trying to present. Feature writers go beyond this by using quotations to say something about the people who are in their stories. Quoted material is generally used much more freely in feature stories, although, as in news stories, dumping a load of quotes on a reader without a break often puts too heavy a burden on the reader. Dialogue and dialect are other devices a feature writer may use if the story calls for them.

One of the charms of feature writing for many writers is that they can put more of themselves into a story. Unlike news stories, in which writers stay out of sight as much as they can, feature writers are somewhat freer to inject themselves and their opinions into a story. While feature writers have a little more latitude in this regard, they must use this latitude wisely and make sure that a feature story does not become a story about themselves rather than about the subject they are trying to cover.

Parts of a feature story

Feature stories generally have four parts: a lead, an engine paragraph, a body, and an ending. Each needs special handling by the writer.

As in a news story, the lead of a feature story is its most important part. Feature writers are not bound by the one sentence, thirty-word lead paragraph structure that newswriters must often follow. A lead in a feature story may be several sentences or paragraphs long. From the beginning sentence, however, the feature writer must capture the reader's attention and give the reader some information of substance—or at least promise some information of substance. A newswriter can depend on the story's subject to compel the reader's interest. A feature writer must sell the reader on the subject in the first few words or sentences.

A good lead uses the first words or sentences of a story to build interest in the story's subject, but the reader must soon discover some benefit for reading the story. That's why the writer should build a lead toward

Figure 5-9 Feature Articles ——————

Below are the beginnings of two feature articles. Take a close look at each of them. Any feature story can be approached and written in a variety of ways. Note the approach of each. What are the attention-getting devices? What are the sources of information in each article? Do you have any changes that you would suggest for any of these articles?

She spends most of her day in her six-by-ten-foot cell, reading her Bible, writing a letter occasionally, and walking back and forth a little. She rarely speaks to other inmates at the Miranda State Women's Prison even when she has the chance. She prefers to keep to herself.

"All my life I've been around other people. I never had any privacy," she says. "That's the one good thing about being in this place all alone."

"This place" for Wendy Hoffman is Death Row, an isolated corner of the third floor of one of Miranda's cellblocks. She's "all alone" because she is currently the only woman in the state living under a death sentence.

Hoffman has been there for six months now, ever since the end of her celebrated trial in Molene. There she was convicted of shooting 13-year-old Chrissy Staten on the orders of her husband. The trial generated a barrage of international publicity for everyone involved, including Dax Hoffman, who is also living under a death sentence at the Norton Jones State Prison, about 100 miles away. . . .

Norma Sasser is determined that next Wednesday will be like any other day has been for the last 45 years. She'll walk into her first-grade classroom at Rockwood Elementary, give her students their final report cards and wish them a happy summer.

The problem is that however much "Miss Norma" follows her routine, it won't be the same. It will be her last day of teaching kids to read, write, count and be still.

She knows that, and even though she dreads the last day, she's looking forward to what comes after that: lots of travel, time to read and gardening, she says.

The day might be more normal if all she had to do was meet with this year's students. But soon after they've received their grades, a day-long celebration will begin at the school, all in her honor. More than 1,000 of her former students will be there, some of whom will travel from distant parts of the country.

"That's the part I dread, not leaving the classroom for the last time," she said. "I'm just afraid that a lot of people have gone to a lot of trouble to be here." . . .

some initial point that the story is to make, something that will hook the reader for the rest of the story.

The engine paragraph (also called the fat paragraph, the snapper, or the why paragraph) gives the reader this payoff and sets the stage for the rest of the story. It puts the story in some context for the reader and tells the reader why the rest of the story should be read.

The body of the feature story is the middle of the story that expands and details the subjects introduced in the lead. The body should answer every question raised in the lead, and it should fulfill every expectation raised within the reader. Like products bought in a store, features often promise more than they deliver. They tell the reader in the lead that the information they contain will be of interest or help to the reader, and they turn out to be neither interesting nor helpful. The body should contain the substance of the article, and it should be what the reader has been led to expect.

Newswriters using the inverted pyramid generally do not have to worry about the ending of their stories. Feature writers need to take care as to how a story ends. The ending of a story may be used to put the story in some perspective, to answer any lingering questions that a reader may have, or to make a final point about the story's subject. The major point about an ending is that a writer should not allow a story to go on too long. Like any other writer, the feature writer should stop writing when there is nothing of substance left to say.

Points for consideration and discussion

1. Why is the inverted pyramid structure such a common one for news stories? What are its advantages and disadvantages?

2. Some critics argue that the inverted pyramid news story structure should be abandoned by newspapers. They say that television and radio deliver news much faster than newspapers; therefore, newspapers should not be concerned so much with getting information to readers quickly as with getting more complete and accurate information. What do you think?

3. Chapter 3 discussed journalistic style and the conventions of journalism. How does what you learned in that chapter fit in with the principles presented in this chapter?

4. The author says you shouldn't go out of your way to find substitutes for the verb *said*. Do you think that is good advice?

5. The text says that a direct quote "should be the exact words of the speaker." Can you think of any circumstances where this would not be true?

6. Journalists often go to great lengths to keep their opinions out of the stories they write. Some people argue that this impossible to do, however. What do you think?

Further reading

Everette E. Dennis and Arnold H. Ismach, *Reporting Processes and Practices: Newswriting for Today's Readers,* Belmont, CA: Wadsworth, 1981.

Don Fry (editor), *Best Newspaper Writing 1987,* St. Petersburg, FL: The Poynter Institute, 1987.

Melvin Mencher, *Basic Newswriting,* Dubuque, IA: William C. Brown, 1983.

William Metz, *Newswriting from Lead to "30,"* Englewood Cliffs, NJ: Prentice-Hall, 1977.

M. L. Stein, *Getting and Writing the News,* New York: Longman, 1985.

Hiley Ward, *Professional Newswriting,* New York: Harcourt Brace Jovanovich, 1985.

EXERCISES

A NOTE TO THE STUDENTS: The following section contains a variety of exercises for news and feature writing. You should follow your instructor's directions in completing them. Some of the exercises are written in sentence fragments while others are written in complete sentences, often in narrative form. If you are assigned to write news stories from the exercises in this section, you should use the *information* but not the exact wording contained in the exercises (except for the direct quotes). Many of the exercises are badly written on purpose. It will be your job to rewrite the information you have so that it is better written than the exercise material.

Writing leads

Write a lead paragraph from each set of facts.

Wreck

Two trucks collided on I-59 last night

Caused a traffic jam because the road was blocked both ways for about 45 minutes

Fuel from both trucks spilled onto the highway and caused a big oil slick

One truck was refrigerated and most of the contents thawed, causing a loss of an estimated $10,000 worth of goods.

Accident happened on a part of I-59 undergoing repairs, so it was two lanes at that point; the trucks met head on.

Honor society

Alpha Alpha, university honor society, to hold inductions next Friday

5 sophomores, 20 juniors, 10 seniors will be named

names will be kept secret until ceremony

ceremony will be at 10 AM at Student Center

Faculty death

Education prof. Elizabeth Billson, dead at age 58

had taught here for 36 years

estimated to have taught 10,000 future teachers during her years

awarded University's "Outstanding Professor" award last year

had suffered from cancer for 10 years

Baseball star

Junior baseball star drafted by St. Louis Cardinals

Willie Ames says he won't turn pro this year but will stay in school

Ames says Mom advised him to stay in school: "She was never able to finish high school. It's important to her for me to get my education. I can play baseball later."

Ames was reportedly offered a signing bonus of $15,000 by the Cardinals

New course

Political science department announces new course, "Communism and Socialism," to begin next semester

Open to juniors and seniors who have had the freshman level beginning political science course

taught by Jerald Wiseman, associate professor

Wiseman: "These two political theories have been major forces in helping develop our 20th century political world."

Poll

Local polling firm, City Research Associates

poll of more than 500 city residents completed last week

showed 65 percent of citizens "satisfied" or "very satisfied" with the quality of life in the city; showed 75 percent of those with school-age children "satisfied" or "very satisfied" with city school system

poll sponsored by Chamber of Commerce

Computer donation

Mike McCracken, president of Computer Corporation of America, headquartered in the city, made this announcement this morning

his company donating 10 computers to local high school; donation worth more than $30,000

Schools Supt. Harvey Butterworth says computers will be used to teach word processing and business programs

computers should be in use by the fall term

Drinking bill

State legislature just finished marathon debate; 30 straight hours in the senate and then 30 hours in the house

bill would raise drinking age in state from 19 to 21

bill passed by house, 55-40, early today; passed by senate, 18-12, yesterday

bill sponsored by local legislator, Representative Tom Hartley

Water alert

Brownsville, twenty miles south of your city

last week placed on a "water alert" by state health commission because of "parasitic contamination"

alert lifted by commission

Jones Lamson, head of commission, says testing by commission shows the danger has passed. Residents had been boiling their water since the alert began

Theft investigation

Police chief Clayton Wheat, at press conference this morning

talks about department's continuing investigation into auto theft ring

says ring responsible for 200 to 300 auto thefts in city last year

says investigation has been expanded into surrounding counties

says most cars were disassembled and sold for parts

Industry returning

Local group of investors, lead by First Trust Bank president Joe E. Jamison

announcement made this morning

buying abandoned Lochs Papermill plant

investor to team up with Textron Corp. to start a machine tool plant refurbishing the plant will take about a year

when machine tool plant is opened it will employ about 200 people

Football game

School's football team defeats arch-rival, 2-0

final game of the season

only score, saftety, comes with 5 seconds left on the clock

breaks 3-game losing streak

arch-rival unbeaten this season until this game

Leads and follow-up paragraphs

Write a lead and second paragraph for each of the following sets of information.

Curriculum changes

University president announces changes in requirements for graduation

students entering next fall must take one math, computer science, and foreign language course

President: "We feel that these new course requirements will allow us to turn out better educated persons."

recent study showed only 15 percent of students took a foreign language course and only 20 percent took a math course while at the University

Arrest

Cathy Bensen, 22-year-old senior, arrested for driving under the influence of alcohol for third time in six months last night

daughter of locally prominent attorney Jim Bensen, 211 Green Grove Drive

mother, Sharon Bensen, lives in Canada

Cathy was this year's Homecoming Queen; has been cheerleader; straight-A student; going to Vanderbuilt University for graduate studies in biology

Protest

Group of citizens angry because University biology class is teaching evolution

Group led by Wilbur Straking, pastor of the Ever-Faithful Church of the Living Water

Straking: "I plan to lead a group of 25 dedicated Christians to the state capital next Monday to speak with legislators about this problem. We believe the teaching of evolution is against the principles of this Christian country, and we want to put a stop to it."

Class they're objecting to is taught by Laura Cliff, associate professor of biology; she wouldn't comment on the group's charges

Neither would University president

Law suit

Suit filed in Circuit Court today; for $100,000

Against Amburn's Produce Market

By Ellie Maston, 313 Journey Road

Charges market with negligence; suit says green beans left on floor of market; she walked through them and slipped and broke her hip

Suit says she "suffered permanent bodily and mental injuries, incurred medical expenses and lost income."

Accident happened April 1 this year

Agreement announced

Clyde Parris, president of Ambrose Steel Company, and Charles Pointer, president of United Steelworkers Local 923, make joint announcement

Company and union have reached collective bargaining agreement

Strike set for midnight tonight has been called off

Strike would have stopped production at Ambrose and put 457 steelworkers off the job

Terms of agreement will be read tonight to a meeting of the union, Pointer says

Parris says contract includes "substantial wage agreement" but won't say how much; that will be announced tonight

Union will vote on contract next week

Pointer says contract "the best we can get out of the company"

Malpractice suit

Two doctors being sued for malpractice; Barney Olive and Stephen Rogers, both of whom practice at Riverside Hospital

William Hamilton, lawyer for plaintiff, Bertie McNicholls, 623 Leanto Road

Hamilton, beginning final arguments in case, has heart attack

Quick work of Olive and Rogers save his life

Hamilton, 73, now recovering at Riverside Hospital

Trial to resume next week

Alumni festival

University Alumni Association planning spring festival for April

games, contests will be held on football field

barbeque lunch and exhibition baseball game

all proceeds to go to school library, plus alumni hoping to raise more money through pledges

date depends on whether or not baseball team makes it to playoffs this year

alumni president Bobby Don Willis: "This kind of activity is one of the positive things we can do to make this university a better educational institution."

Writing news stories

Write news stories from the following sets of information.

Vandalism

Two students at your school have been caught smashing windows in the new gymnasium

Identified as Bobby Ray Williams, 20, a sophomore, and George Hatfield, 22, a senior

Students are both from Snadeville; Williams majoring in Business; Hatfield majoring in Biology

Janitor, Eddie Vinson, caught them throwing bricks at the first floor windows at approximately 6:45 a.m. this morning

15 windows valued at $55 each were smashed

Two ran from Vinson after throwing bricks at him

He knew them both and reported incident to campus police

Police arrested them later in the morning

Said they did not deny their guilt

Punishment will be decided by Student Court in one week; Williams and Hatfield are suspended until the hearing

No charges will be filed with police, Chief of

Campus Security Harvey Oswald said

The new gym, a $1 million facility, was to have been dedicated today. Postponed until repaired

Williams is a stright-A student who plans to attend a summer honors program at a nearby university this summer. Hatfield has lettered in football and basketball for two years

Oswald: "I just can't understand how they could do such a thing. They weren't drunk or on drugs, they are good students who have contributed to the school, they've never been in trouble before. It's a real mystery to me. I have no idea what the Student Court will recommend in this case."

Vinson: "They were acting crazy, laughing and hollering. I heard one of them — I think it was George — say 'to hell with this school.'"

Hatfield refused to comment on incident; Williams said only, "We won't be fooled again."

Disruption

A fact-finding commission has been investigating a campus disturbance for three weeks since a campus incident. It issues a statement from which the following material has been excerpted by the college news office and distributed to the local press:

The disorders on May 7 in front of Laughton Library were the result of self-appointed guardians of student life deciding what their fellow students could hear and read. We have no sympathy with this act or its perpetrators regardless of their motives.

Nevertheless, we do recommend no action but the publicity that they have already received and that this report may achieve.

These six students who tore down banners, heckled speakers, and destroyed pamphlets of the Unifying Church on the afternoon of May 7 denied the young men and women of the Church their Ccnstitutional rights of expression and assembly.

We realize that the Church did not have college permission to use the campus, but students are not the enforcement arm of the administration.

Our commission of seven students, three administrators, and four faculty members voted as follows on the matter:

Condemnation without further sanctions: Students — 5–2 in favor; Faculty — 3–1 in favor; Administration — 3–0 in favor.

We thank President Ruth Pitts Renaldi for giving us full access to college files and records.

You check the clips at the newspaper and find out that the Unifying Church is a unit of a large proselytizing organization that has enlisted many young people in its Christian Crusade. There were four young men and three young women singing hymns and handing out pamphlets when the incident occurred. A group known as Youth Against Fascism and War had been picketing the Church members when suddenly several students casued a commotion. Campus guards took six students into custody and a study committee was appointed to examine the matter.

You call student members of the committee and learn Albert Towden and Steve Rabin cast the negative votes. They tell you:

Towden: "I wanted some kind of suspension. These students were rowdies. They are nothing more than fascists who would impose on us a way of life in which their ideas would be the only acceptable ones. I don't like people who in the guise of democracy would tear it down."

Rabin: "I was the student lawyer for the six students before the student judicial panel that recommended this study committee. Speaking on behalf of the six, I feel that they should not have been condemned.

"No democracy can thrive when it gives freedom to those who would brainwash innocents on behalf of a fascist ideology. We know the Unifying Church wants cadres of young people to propagandize the public to follow a charismatic leader. Foreign and U.S. business interests are financing this. We will continue to oppose the Church here and elsewhere."

Development

About six months ago the Roberts Development Company announced that it wanted to build an apartment complex on Park Lane, a residential area of the local community. The complex would be, a spokesman said at the time, about 120 units and would be built on a farm owned by P.T. Rodney, who had agreed to sell it for that purpose. The complex would cover about 15 acres. In order to get permission to build the complex, the company had to apply to the City Council for a rezoning of the area from "R–1," which allows only single-family residences, to "R–2," which would allow the apartment complex to be built.

Immediately after the announcement, the Park Lane Residents Association said it opposed the complex and would ask the City Council not to grant the rezoning request. The association's president is George Houghton. The association was joined in its opposition by the City Neighborhood Preservation Association. Both groups appeared before the council to fight the rezoning. The council voted 7-0 not to rezone the property, but Roberts Development said it would try to work out a compromise with both groups and resubmit the rezoning application.

Today, six months after this happened, you (a reporter for the local newspaper) receive a call from the president of the City Neighborhood Preservation Association, whose name is John Hedrick, saying his group is no longer opposed to the rezoning. Hedrick says, "We've had several meetings with Roberts Development people, and they have given us assurances about what will happen to the property. We're satisfied that the neighborhood will retain its character, so we will be backing them up when they go to the City Commission tomorrow to ask for another rezoning of the property." Hedrick said the reason for the turnaround by his group is that Roberts had redesigned much of their original plans so that the apartment complex would be more architecturally compatible with the neighborhood.

The city commission meeting is tomorrow morning, and you have to do a story on this situation for this afternoon's paper.

Olin Millsaps, president of Roberts Development Company, tells you, "We're very pleased with the preservation association's support. I think we have a shot at turning this thing around at the meeting tomorrow."

Gardner Houghton, who is president of the Park Lane Residents Association, says, however, that his group is still opposed to the petition. "I don't think the development people have changed their plans that much. What

they are trying to do would still disrupt the neighborhood. The way the streets are now, they just can't hold the traffic an apartment complex like that would generate. Frankly, and I don't have any evidence to back this up, I think the neighborhood preservation people sold out to the development company. I wouldn't be surprised if Roberts made a big contribution to their treasury."

The president of the city council, Harvey Latton, says he can't predict how the vote will go.

After numerous calls, you reach the other six council members, and none of them will tell you how he or she will vote on the issue. They all say they will wait until tomorrow before making up their minds.

Alcoholism

The Department of Health and Human Services (HHS) issued a 121-page report today. Congress recently passed a law which required the department to issue a report on alcoholism each year, and this was the first such report. The report was prepared by a committee of 11 within HHS.

The report said losses caused by alcoholism are high. It said alcohol causes 28,000 trafic deaths a year, and the deaths cost the nation a total of $15 billion. Nearly 9 million persons suffer from alcoholism or lesser drinking problems, and they constitute 10 percent of the work force within the United States.

The report also contained some statistics about the use of alcohol. It said that in the last year, the average American drinker drank the equivalent of 44 fifths of whiskey. The report concluded that alcohol is the "major drug problem in this country." It said HHS will spend $200,000 next year to pay for advertisements to warn the public about the dangers of excessive drinking. The liquor industry has endorsed the campaign. The advertisements will be used on radio and television and in newspapers and magazines. But an official added, "We will not tell people not to drink. That is a personal decision. What we are saying is that citizens have a responsibility not to destroy themselves or society."

The 121-page report suggests that the problem of alcoholism is not adequately understood by most Americans, who seem more concerned about other drugs, such as marijuana and heroin, even though those drugs do not cause as many problems as alcohol. To prove that point, the report pointed out that New York City has an estimated 600,000 alcoholics but only 125,000 heroin users. Yet the city spends 40 times more to fight narcotics addiction than it does to fight alcoholism. The report explained that most persons do not know much about alcoholism and do not consider alcohol a serious problem. People also are reluctant to admit that they have a drinking problem or that they are alcoholics.

Alcoholism is a particularly serious problem among certain groups. For example, the report said that on some Indian reservations alcoholism has reached epidemic proportions. On some reservations 10 percent of the residents are alcoholics, twice the national average, and the rate of alcoholism rises to as much as 25 percent on others.

Shooting

Write a 250-word story using the following information. The story is for the first edition of this afternoon's newspaper.

On your regular telephone rounds of the area police and sheriff departments, you talk with Sheriff Carmen Townsend of Sevier County. He says: "Yeah, we had a pretty bad incident here last night. A Mrs. Bertie Clancy was shot and killed by her husband. At least, I think she was killed. The hospital didn't expect her to live long. They lived on Caney Creek Road near Pigeon Forge. She was sixty-eight years old. The way I understand it, they had this kid — Randy — and he's the kind of kid who ain't all there, you know what I mean. Anyway, he and his old man, a fellow named Darris Clancy, got into an argument. Randy was all the time coming around, asking for money. He was drawing some disability money from the government, about $300 a month, but that was never enough. He was always hitting his folks up for some more, and as I understand it, they usually gave it to him. Well, they got into this argument, and the old man pointed a gun at Randy. The old lady tried to break it up and got in between them and the gun went off. She was hit in the head

and the shoulder. Well, you can imagine how the son felt and what it was like in the house then, so I guess what happened was that Randy grabbed the gun away from his daddy and shot him. It was a shotgun. Anyway, the old man dropped dead as a doornail. There wasn't even no use in taking him to the hospital. We just called the coroner and took him over to the funeral home."

A sheriff's deputy tells you that Randy Clancy is being held in the county jail without bond. His arraignment will be sometime this afternoon.

You call the hospital and a spokesman there says Mrs. Clancy has died. She died just a few minutes after she arrived at about 11 o'clock last night.

James Clancy, another son and an employee of the local Stokley canning company, tells you the following things about what happened: "No, Randy never was exactly right, but he was a good kid. I wasn't there. I just talked with him a little while after it happened. He says he don't remember much, but he said he couldn't live without mama. He was always her favorite, but he and daddy hadn't gotten along too well lately. I guess it happened about like the sheriff told you. I had talked with Randy earlier in the day, and he told me he was going up to see mama and daddy because he needed some money 'cause he was getting into some trouble with some people he had borrowed from. I think he was going to ask them for about $200. Daddy used to get really mad when he would ask for money. He got there about 9 o'clock. He told me that after the shooting he went upstairs to what used to be his bedroom and tore all the pictures off the wall. Then he went out into the yard and smashed the shotgun on a fence post. I found it later and showed it to the sheriff. As I understand it, after he had done that, he went to a neighbor's house and called the sheriff and told him to come get him.

The neighbor, Will O'Reilly, who lives next door to the Clancy couple on Caney Creek Road, tells you that's what happened: "I heard a lot of arguing coming from their house, I guess it was about 9 o'clock or maybe a little afterwards. Then I heard these shots, and I told my wife, 'There's trouble up there,' but she said I'd better not leave the house. Pretty soon, Randy come knocking on the door and asked to use the phone. I remember he was wearing a tee shirt with the words 'Gospel Baptist Church' on it. He was pretty calm, but I heard him tell the sheriff what happened and for them to come and get him."

Employee records at the Stokely plant show that Darris Clancy was 64 years old and had worked as a driver at the plant off and on for more than 20 years. He quit seven years ago because of arthritis and had been drawing disability payments ever since.

Bertie Clancy had lived all her life in the Pigeon Forge area but had never been employed anywhere for any length of time.

Caney Creek Road is a winding mountain road, and the dead couple had lived there for about 25 years.

Prosper

Prosper is a mining town of 909 people in the northeast corner of Crocker County. Since the deep-shaft coal mine was opened in 1901, it has provided a major source of employment for the town's people, and in the last 18 years has brought more than 800 people from other towns to work every day at the mine, United Coal Company's Mine No. 3, known locally as Hellpit. The company announced yesterday that the mine will close in two weeks for an indefinite period. Since 1980, when Propser was incorporated and became eligible for coal tax revenue, its budget has risen from $40,000 to $300,000 ($125,000 in coal severance tax monies, $125,000 in federal matching money for capital improvements). Mayor Lester Jenkins tells you that "With the mine closed, our revenue is just about gone." Some tax money will continue to dribble in as stockpiles of coal are depleted, but Wilma Foster, the city clerk, foresees a cutback for the fiscal year, which starts in 30 days, to $60,000. "That will cover essential services like police protection and utilities at city hall and at the new ball park," she adds. Councilman Ed Barnes tells you that most of the coal money went into building projects. "And we've got the city hall and the park paid for, so at least we're not in debt." The town council will talk about a new budget at its meeting tomorrow night. The mine employed 1,000 people. The shaft is a quarter mile deep, the deepest in the state. Company officials cannot be reached by phone, but a statement delivered to you gives the reason for the closing as a severe cutback in demand for coal because of a shutdown in manufacturing nationwide. It quotes Wilson Standridge, company president: "We hope to see an increase in demand, but until we do, the mine will remain sealed."

Murder

Francie Franklin, proprietor of a small bakery in Pleasant Grove, was killed during the night. Police Chief Wilburn Cole tells you over the phone that Miss Franklin did not deliver a wedding cake as expected this morning, and when the bride's mother went to the bake shop in Miss Franklin's home to check, she found the front door open and a display case smashed. "She didn't go no further," Cole says. "When we got there we found Miss Francie in the kitchen. She was shot dead." The little shop is in a shambles when you go by to check and you note the contrast to the neat tidy operation the woman kept. You can't find the chief, but the radio dispatcher reads this memo to you: "Francie's body was taken to Smith's Funeral Parlor where they'll do an autopsy. It must have happened before midnight because her television set was still on and she always turns it off after the late movie. She was shot once in the chest and her pistol is missing from the drawer under the cash register. Money was scattered around but they probably got away with some." Kenton County Homicide Investigator Kelton Kelly says she was shot with a .22 calibre bullet and that they didn't find any fingerprints. However, a strange, unidentified red wool ski cap was found under the body. Kenton County Coroner Ransom Cranwell tells you that death was from a single gunshot wound and that there were no other injuries. "It was crazy the way they messed up the place though," he adds. "She was always so proud of it. She was just an old maid who loved everyone and everyone loved her." Arrangements are pending. No known survivors. Age 68. Address, 504 Ash St. She started the business 20 years ago under the name Francie's Fancies. She recently expanded by building a small service area at the front of the house.

Sit-in

Students are angry because African-American candidate for Homecoming Queen did not make Homecoming Court in election held yesterday (Monday)

Homecoming Court of five girls is selected through a general election; girl with highest number of votes is Homecoming Queen

Protesting students have staged a sit-in in front of administration building

Began this morning; plan to continue throughout the week

About 10 students are participating

All have handmade signs - "Equality," "No Homecoming this Year," "We want fair treatment," and so on.

University President Jimmy Wilson has issued a statement warning other students to leave the protesting students alone. Here is an excerpt from the text:

"These students have chosen a non-violent form of protest against something they think is unfair. They are not excused from classes and will not be allowed to make up work they miss. However, they will not be punished in any other way unless violence erupts. Any students harrassing these protesters will be punished with immediate expulsion."

Wilson is a former president of the local NAACP

Yvonne Dees, the defeated candidate for Homecoming Queen: "I don't feel that the election was fair. We (African-American students) are 35 percent of the student body, and we should be represented on the Court."

Wendy Thomas, president of the Student Government and chairman of the Campus Election Committee: "It was absolutely fair. I don't think they have a cause at all. The African-American students just didn't get out the vote for their candidate, that's all, and they want to be represented without trying."

Bobby Dean Willis, a senior who organized the protest: "We are going to stay out here until something is done. We are tired of being treated like we don't exist in this school. We want representation on that court, and we will bring some real attention to this problem. I want all the media in here; I want the public to know what's going on."

Student government election

Student council elections were held yesterday

35 percent of student body voted

Votes were counted by a student-faculty committee last night

Four people ran for president:

Carol Lyndis, last year's Student Government Association secretary, won with 53 percent of the vote

Daughter of Mr. and Mrs. Ben Lyndis, 449 Holly Lane, Hollyville, Tx.

21-year-old junior, cheerleader for two years, on school soccer team, majoring in biology

Other candidates for president were Johnny Haynes, a junior who is president of the Lambda Delta Honor Society; Tania Wilson, last year's Student Government vice-president, a junior; and I.J. Weisburg, a sophomore who writes an advice column on love for the school paper

In the vice-presidential election, Gene Johnson was unopposed

His parents are Mr. Phil Johnson, 776 Union St., and Mrs. Sally Osborne, 2103 South Donley Rd., Johnsonville, Neb.

Johnson is a junior, 21 years old, Boys State Rep., president of Alpha Omega fraternity, majoring in political science

For secretary, there were two nominees: Freda Hance and Reba Wilkes

Hance won. She is the first freshman ever elected to a major Student Government office

Wilkes, a junior, was SGA treasurer last year

Hance is the daughter of Mr. and Mrs. Hanly Hance, 807 Queen St. (in the town where the college is located); She was president of the freshman class this year and was features editor of the student newspaper last year; majoring in journalism.

Keith Nelson was unopposed for treasurer. A sophomore, he was a Student Government senator for two years. He was Homecoming chairman this year and fund-raising chairman his freshman year

Lyndis: "I am really happy about the new officers we have. I think they will all do well in their jobs and all. I do want to thank all those who supported me in so many ways, especially my parents."

Here are the vote totals:

President:

Lyndis	1,126
Haynes	135
Wilson	612
Weisburg	232
Write-ins	125

Vice-president:

Johnson	1,854
Write-ins	39

Secretary:

Hance	1,169
Wilkes	954
Write-ins	2

Treasurer:

Nelson	1,966
Write-ins	20

Russel

Last New Year's Eve, John Page was found shot to death in his home. At first, the police and the coroner ruled the death a suicide, but that changed when they later found that Page had withdrawn a large amount of money from his bank account on the day that he died. Page is the owner of Page Auto Parts Store. He is also a real estate developer, a deacon in the First Baptist Church, a city councilman, and generally thought to be one of the wealthiest citizens in town. The amount of money Page withdrew from the bank that day was $10,000. Page's wife told the police that he had been depressed for some weeks before his death, but she didn't believe that he committed suicide.

Page's death and all of the subsequent events, including the police investigation and the trial, received a great amount of publicity from the city's newspapers and television stations.

A month after Page's death, the police arrested William Russel and charged him with first degree murder. William Russel is owner of Russel Realty, and even though they were competitors in business, Page and Russel were known to be good friends. They grew up together, and their families had been friends. Police said that several clues pointed to Russel as the murderer. Russel had been seen leaving the Page home late New Year's Eve by a neighbor who had been walking his dog. The bank provided the police with serial numbers of the money it had given to Page, and most of that money was found in Russel's house.

During the trial, which began a month ago, it came out that Russel had been having an affair with Page's wife, Geneveve. The district attorney, Hix Bradfield, tried to paint Russel as a desperate man whose business was failing and who was blackmailing Page. The key witness in his case was Page's wife, who said that Russel had threatened Page by saying he would "tell everybody in town about your slutty little wife" if he wouldn't pay. She said Page was worried that his reputation in the community would be damaged and it would mean the end to his political career. She said he had been planning to run for Congress next year.

Russel took the stand in his own defense and denied killing Page, and he denied having an affair with Page's wife. He said Page had asked him to keep the money because of a business deal he was about to make, but he didn't know any of the details. He said Page had been despondent because he had found out that his wife had been having affairs with other men. "I felt sorry for John," he said. "He married a little slut. I suspect that she was blackmailing him." Russel said he went to talk with Page on New Year's Eve but found him too depressed to talk. When he left, Russel said, Page was drinking heavily. Russel said he didn't tell the police about the visit or the money because "I got scared. It was a stupid thing to do."

Yesterday, after three days of deliberating, the jury found Russel guilty. Russel broke down and cried when he heard the verdict.

This morning, Judge Cecil Andrews sentenced Russel to death in the electric chair. In handing out the sentence, Andrews said, "This was a heinous crime — one that merits swift and severe retribution. The victim was a leading citizen in the community, a man who had made many contributions. In a cold-blooded way, the defendant ended his life while posing as his good friend. He has shown no remorse for his deed and has, in fact, lied about it. He showed no mercy to his victim, and I, in turn, can show no mercy to him." Russel, who looked pale and puffy-eyed when he came into the courtroom, had to be helped out.

Outside the court, Regina Wright, Russel's lawyer, said she would file an immediate appeal both of the verdict and the sentence. "Mr. Russel didn't get a fair trial. The massive amount of pretrial publicity surrounding this case prevented that. Early on, we asked for a change of venue, but that motion was denied. There was just no way that a person accused of killing a popular man like John Page was going to get a fair trial in this town." Asked about the sentence, Wright said, "I just can't believe he was given the death penalty. I believe Judge Andrews had it in for my client. He should have disqualified himself because he was a friend of John Page. He should have granted our change-of-venue motion. He did neither, and then he winds up sentencing my client to death."

After the sentencing, Bradfield said, "The sentence was a harsh one — not the one we would have recommended. We would have preferred a life-without-parole sentence, but I'll go along with what the judge said. It was an awful crime, and John Page was one of our leading citizens."

You try to get a comment from Mrs. Page, but her attorney, Frank Story, tells you she left immediately after the sentencing for New York to discuss writing a book about the trial and her experiences.

Write a story for tomorrow morning's newspaper.

Tornado

Yesterday afternoon was unseasonably warm for this time of year. Early in the afternoon, the temperature reached 70 degrees, and the people at the Weather Bureau became concerned. There was a lot of moisture in the air, and the conditions seemed just right for a tornado. At two o'clock they issued a tornado warning because of some buildup of moisture west of here.

At three p.m., after receiving several reports of funnel clouds, Lee Harper, chief meteorologist at the weather bureau, issued a tornado warning. Funnel clouds had been sighted just south of Midville, and there was one report that a barn had been damaged and some cows

had been killed. The tornado watch was to stay in effect for one hour.

At 3:33 a tornado touched down on Cleveland Street, a street with a lot of businesses and homes on it. The tornado damaged the following businesses: the Cleveland Street branch of the Trust National Bank; Red Cedar's used car lot; the Jiffy-Kwik 24-hour food store; and the Big Bank Sound Record Shop, which is located in the same building as the food store. Also, several homes were damaged, including that of Robert T. Mellon, the mayor. The bank was being housed in a mobile home while a permanent structure was built. There was no damage to the building site, which was located nearby. The mobile home was lifted completely off its foundation, however, and was totally destroyed. Clyde Plenty, vice president of the Trust National Bank said the following: "Thank goodness, the tornado hit when it did. We had closed up about three o'clock, and nobody was in the building." Some of the records housed in the building were destroyed, but Clyde said nothing of importance had been lost permanently, and all the records could be duplicated. There was also no money in the building to speak of.

The people at Jiffy-Kwik and the record shop weren't so lucky. At least four people had to go to the hospital to be treated for injuries due to flying debris and broken glass, according to hospital officials. Mr. and Mrs. George Jones -- his wife's name is Thelma -- were treated for minor cuts and lacerations and then released at Good Hope Hospital, and Irving Smalley was being kept overnight because of more serious cuts. He's listed in good condition. He lives at 123 Urban Street. The Joneses live at 1311 13th Avenue. Anna Patton had major injuries after being buried by an aisle of canned goods; she had just come out of surgery at 8 o'clock last night and was listed in critical condition. She lives at 12 Pinto Avenue. Killed was Evelyn Morrison as she was coming out of the record shop and getting into her car. She was a teller who worked at the Trust Bank, the same one that had been damaged by the tornado. She was on her way home. She lived at 67 Kent Street. She was dead on arrival at the hospital and her body was taken to Green Acres Chapel. None of the funeral arrangements have been set.

Holbert Morrison, manager of the Jiffy-

Kwik, said his store was not a total loss, but the damage was several thousand dollar's worth. "The worst thing was the looters," he said. "I just couldn't believe that some people would steal from us after something like this had happened." Police Chief Robert Sykes said they had arrested several youths for looting after the tornado hit, but they weren't going to release their names yet. Bill Belson, the manager of the record store and a noted area record collector, also said the damage to his shop would go into thousands of dollars. "Fortunately, none of my most valuable records were damaged."

Red Cedar said that one of his cars was damaged when some limbs fell on it, but otherwise nothing was hurt. Three homes in the next block of Cleveland Street were damaged, including that of Mayor Mellon. The roof was torn off of his home. "We were lucky because no one was home. I just feel awful about Miss Morrison, though. She was an old friend and a life-long resident of the town. Lots of people knew her, and I think it's tragic. You know, she used to be a teacher -- was a teacher at Elmwood Elementary School about ten years ago. She taught there for about 20 years before retiring and going to work for the bank. She didn't have much family, but everybody in town knew her." The roofs of the other homes on Cleveland Street were damaged by flying limbs, but none of the owners reported serious damage.

The police chief said the total amount of damage done by the tornado would come to about $150,000. "That part of Cleveland Street looks like a bomb has been dropped on it. It's going to take us several days to get it all cleared. It's amazing that all this damage was done in less than two minutes. I feel awfully bad about Miss Morrison, but we were lucky that more people weren't hurt. There were quite a few people in the area at the time." One of the people who was in the record store at the time said the noise right before the tornado hit was the "scariest thing." He was Josh Gibson. "It was like the loudest drum roll I ever heard. Then there was sounds of glass breaking and things crashing around you."

That night Dan Rather devotes about 30 seconds to the tornado. Your editor tells you that it is the first time the town has ever been mentioned on a network newscast.

Harper said this tornado was the only one that did any damage. At least three others were sighted during the afternoon.

City council

Here's what happened at the city council meeting last night.

The meeting started about five minutes late because city council member Harvey Haddix couldn't find a place to park. He came rushing in and made a comment about how the city police were going to have to crack down on illegal parkers. That brought a laugh from the overflow crowd of over two hundred people there. Mayor Ray Sadecki called the meeting to order, and Wilber Mizell, the minister of the Vinegar Bend Baptist Church, started the meeting with prayer. The minutes of the last meeting of the council were read, and no one had any additions or corrections to them.

The first item of business was a report from the Metropolitan Zoning Commission. Bobby Thompson, who is the chairman of the Zoning Commission, said the commission had met two days ago to consider a request by a local developer to move a cemetery so that he can build a supermarket. The developer's name is Carl Erskine. The cemetery is located in the 2800 block of Forbes Street, much of which is zoned for commercial purposes now. Erskine told the council that he will pay all the costs of having the graves relocated in Peaceful Rest Cemetery, which is located about a mile away from the present site. "I think rezoning will be good for the neighborhood and good for the city," Erskine said. "There's not another supermarket for at least a mile and a half in any direction." Thompson said: "We've studied the traffic patterns along Forbes Street, and we don't believe the supermarket will cause any problems." After several more questions by various council members, the mayor asked for any questions or comments from those in the audience. About twenty people spoke, and all but two of them were against the rezoning. It took about an hour. Here are some of the comments:

Early Wynn, 122 Forbes Street: "This thing is going to destroy our neighborhood. It's pretty quiet there now, but if you get this thing in there, it's going to turn noisy."

Dick Groat, 1811 Polo Grounds Road: "Nobody on my street wants the supermarket. We have plenty of places to go to shop. We don't need this. Besides, some of those graves are pretty old, and I don't think it would be the same if you moved them."

Sarah Yawkey, 555 Bosox Drive: "I just can't believe you'd do this. Anybody who'd do this would steal the dimes off a dead man's eyes."

Walt Dropo, 611 Forbes Street and president of the Forbes Street Residents Association: "We've been fighting this thing for two years now. All the zoning commission did was study the traffic patterns. They didn't consider what it would do to the neighborhood. Besides, that cemetery has some of the oldest graves in the city in it -- some of those people helped found this city. I'm sure that if you tried to move some of those stones, they would crumble in your hands. I can promise you that we will mount a campaign to recall any councilmember who votes for this thing." (That comment drew lots of applause from the people who were there.)

Harry Walker, 610 Forbes Street: "I'm afraid Walt's gone overboard on this one, like he usually does. I think our neighborhood needs a supermarket. We've got lots of people who have trouble getting around. Walt's one of these people who's against anything that is progress. He just wants to get some publicity for himself."

When the speakers were done, the council voted 5-2 against the rezoning petition. At that the crowd cheered, and most of them filed out, leaving a small audience of only about 35 or 40 people.

The next item of business was a one-cent sales tax proposed by councilwoman Wilma Rudolph. "The city desperately needs this money," said Rudolph, "or there is a chance that we'll have to start laying off workers next year." Mr. Joe Black, the city treasurer, agreed, saying the city's financial condition was pretty bad. A one-cent sales tax would raise about $400,000 for the city next year, and not only would that mean there would be no layoffs, but it's possible that the city could expand some services, such as having garbage pick-ups twice a week instead of just once a week, he said. "Besides, we figure that such a tax will only cost the average family in the city about $75 a year," Black pointed out. Mayor Sadecki is against the tax. He said, "I believe the people are taxed too heavily now. I don't believe they want this. I think they want to look at our budget and see where we can cut back." But the majority of the council didn't agree with the mayor, and they voted for the tax 5-2. Those voting for the tax were Rudolph, Haddix, Sam Jones, Eddie Matthews, and Lew Burdette; those against were Sadecki and Bill Mazeroski.

The last item of business was a proposal from councilman Mazeroski to license morticians in the city. "The state gives us the power to do this, and I think we should take advantage of it," he said. He said his proposal would assess an annual license fee that morticians would have to pay every year. Mazeroski said, "We've got more than 30 mortuaries in the city now, and assessing a fee from them would bring in a considerable amount of revenue." His bill calls for a $150 fee per mortuary per year. Several morticians were in the audience and spoke against Mazeroski's proposals. Don Blasingame, who owns Blasingame Mortuary and who is president of the city's Mortician Society, said: "We don't believe Mr. Mazeroski is correct when he says the state gives the city the power to do this. The state licenses morticians and gives the city the power to enforce this licensing procedure if it chooses to do so. Otherwise, the state enforces the licensing. I believe that if the city did this, it would just have to turn the money over to the state." Harold Reece, the city attorney, said there is some question about this in the law, and he has asked the state attorney general to give an opinion on it. Mazeroski said, "I don't believe we should wait for the opinion. I think we should go ahead and do it." Burdette made a motion to table the proposal, and that passed by a vote of six to one.

With that, Mayor Sadecki adjourned the meeting.

You find out later that when councilman Haddix got to his car after the meeting, there was a parking ticket on it.

Features

Write a short feature story on each of the following sets of information.

Bank robbery

Man named Jesse James tried to rob First Fidelity bank this morning

caught by passing policeman as he backed out the door

had $20,000

same bank had been robbed nearly 100 years ago by real Jesse James and his brother Frank; they too had been caught. Suspect says: "Jesse James was my great-great uncle. I was just trying to finish the job he started."

Police Chief Weldon Freeman: "This man has no sense of history."

Noise abatement

City Civil Court this morning

Judge Jan Sommerfelt

suit involved Lakeshore subdivision residents suing Weatherford Construction Co.

Company was building a road near subdivision

residents complained that noise the construction company was making violated city ordinances against loud noises

Judge ruled in favor of the residents but refused to stop the construction; said construction company would have to give earplugs to anyone who complained about the noise

Student sit-up

Local high school student Bobby Lott, junior at City Central, now sitting in tree in front of school

Will sit there until Friday's football game with County Central, City's arch-rival; winner of the game goes to state championship

climbed into tree at 9 a.m.

Principal Dick Barrett says Lott is a good student, "has his parents permission to do this," and "I won't make him come down. I don't think he'll get behind in his school work." Friends taking class notes for him, handing him food

Lott says this is his way of showing support for the team; he won't come down except to go to the bathroom; says he won't stay in the tree if there's a lightning storm. "I may be crazy, but I'm not stupid."

Features II

Write feature stories based on the following sets of information.

Tennis player

Bucky Haskiell is a tennis pro who graduated from your college two years ago. While in college, he led the team to the conference championship during his senior year and was named the conference's best player. When he graduated, he turned pro.

During this year's Wimbledon tennis tournament in London, England, Haskiell held the limelight briefly when he had to play John McElroy, the eventual champion, during the first round. Haskiell lost to McElroy, but only after he and the champion had played five full sets. The match was also highlighted by one of the fiercest temper tantrums McElroy had ever thrown. At one point during the match, McElroy stormed around the court cursing the officials and nearly got himself eliminated.

Haskiell has returned to the college for an exhibition tournament to raise money for the college tennis team's travel expenses. You are sent to interview him and here's how the interview goes.

What was it like playing John McElroy during the first round at Wimbledon?

Very hard (he says, laughing). In some ways McElroy is much like any other tennis player — only he's very, very good. When he concentrates on tennis alone, there aren't many people who can beat him. When he gets distracted, he tends to let down. But even then, he's hard to beat. I guess I found that out.

Was it the first time you had played him?

No, I had played him once before in a tournament in South Carolina. I beat him the first two sets, but he came back and won the last three to take the match.

Did he throw any tantrums that day?

No, he was pretty calm.

Do you think that the fit he threw at Wimbledon hurt your game that day?

I'm not sure. I've thought about that a lot. I don't think I played as well after he had finished his argument with the line judge as I had been playing. But I don't know if I was tired or what. I didn't really think about it at the time. I was trying to concentrate on my game.

Do you know McElroy personally?

Yes, I've been with him on several occasions. He's really a nice guy off the court and doesn't deserve his 'bad boy' image. Once he even gave me some pointers about how I was serving that really helped my game.

What was Wimbledon like? Everybody says it's a great place to be.

Well (laughing), I really wasn't there that long. As a player, it's not a great tournament because of the grass courts, which most of us aren't use to, and the accommodations aren't as good as some we've had at other tournaments. But the atmosphere at Wimbledon is hard to beat. There's so much tradition there — it makes you feel good just having a chance to play. Of course, next year I would like to win a match or two.

Do you expect to be invited back to Wimbledon next year?

I hope so. I'm having a pretty good year. I've won one tournament and have finished in the semi-finals in at least four others. My ranking with the tennis association is better than last year, so maybe I'll get back there.

What's it like having been a tennis pro for two years?

I really enjoy it, but it's not what people think. Tennis pros aren't pampered people. All of us have to work very hard just to maintain our forms. And we're required to travel a lot — it's not like being a tourist either. It's just one hotel or motel after another. The time you might spend seeing the sights is time you should spend practicing — and you do if you want to be any good. For instance, I saw relatively little of London when I was there for Wimbledon. I'd like to go back sometime when there's not a tournament.

Oldest tree

A plaque marking the oldest tree on campus will be dedicated today. Ceremonies for the dedication will take place under the tree at 10 a.m., and the event will also be used to announce a fund-raising drive by the alumni association for the school. A news story has already been written about this event. Your job is to write a feature story about the tree which will be used as a sidebar (a journalistic term for a secondary story) with the news story. You gather the following information about the tree:

The tree is a water oak and is thought to be about 100 years old. University records show that the tree was probably planted by students who had been hired to do some work on the campus. One record says that during the same spring 50 trees were planted in that area of the campus.

Marcus Maxwell, professor of history and University historian: "The University used to hire students to do odd jobs around the campus, so we think students planted this tree. There is no exact record of what was planted and by whom, so we're not sure about it.

"A number of buildings have been built in the area of the tree, but none has come so close to it that the tree had to be destroyed. The tree has some significance in university history. The first troop of soldiers that gathered at the University to fight in World War I assembled under that tree right before they left by train to report to their army base. A crowd of people gathered, a band played, and some politicians made speeches. It was a pretty festive occasion.

"Likewise, when the first of the University's reserve units was activated right after the beginning of World War II, they also gathered under the tree for a send off. I understand that it wasn't such a festive occasion then."

Elmer Hinton, a retired bicycle repairman in the town, was among the soldiers who started for World War I at the tree. He tells you: "It was hot as blazes that day, even though it was April. Fortunately, we got to stand in the shade, and I remember being thankful of that. I enjoyed the music the band played, but I coulda done without the speeches. Lots of people thought this war was going to be a lark — that all we had to do was show up and the Germans would fade away. It turned out not to be like that at all. The part of World War II I saw was pretty rough."

A number of legends exist about the tree. One is that a man was lynched on the tree around the turn of the century. He had killed the family of the mayor of the town, and one night an angry crowd broke into the jail, took him out and hung him. Newspaper accounts say that a man named Josiah Lindy was hung by an angry crowd in 1901; he was accused of killing the family of Mayor Tyree Jones — Jones's wife and two daughters – after the wife had let him in the house and given him something to eat. The news account doesn't say exactly where the lynching took place. Nor does it say that Mayor Jones was part of the crowd.

Another legend that was once popular with students is that the girl who walked under the lowest branch of the tree on the night of the full moon before the homecoming queen election would win that election. That legend became so popular in the 1920s and 1930s that students had a ritual of requiring all homecoming queen candidates to walk under the tree on the night before the election. That ritual died out during World War II.

Flora Handle, a professor in the biology department, says: "The tree is a good example of one of the major types of trees of this area. It is in remarkably good shape for a tree of its age. Usually a tree that old will have too many limbs and not enough foliage to support the whole system. That's not the case with this one. If something doesn't happen — if the tree isn't struck by a disease or by lightning — it should live another 50 or 75 years. It must be trimmed properly."

Your story should include a description of the tree and its location. (For that, you may pick any large tree on your campus.)

Hiker

A local high school teacher, Will Henderson, was lost for four days last week while hiking in the Great Smoky Mountains National Park. Henderson had been hiking along the Appalachian Trail and had gotten off the trail near a place known as Gregory Bald. After a couple of hours of walking off the trail, Henderson tried to cross a stream when he slipped and broke his leg.

Henderson is an experienced hiker. He is a member of the National Hiking Association. He had plenty of food with him at the time. He had been hiking for about 10 days before the accident. He had started in Georgia and was in Tennessee at the time of the accident.

After his fall, Henderson used some sticks and string to make a splint for his leg. He then began four days of crawling, pushing his 40-pound hiking pack in front of him. He crawled through a lot of thick underbrush. Finally, he made it back to the main part of the Appalachian Trail and was soon found by two other hikers.

The Appalachian Trail is nearly 3,000 miles long, stretching from Georgia to Maine. It is one of the most popular hiking trails in the country.

Henderson teaches biology at Jefferson High School. He is 39 and has been hiking since he was a boy of 10.

Henderson was hospitalized for several days in Knoxville during which time a number of stories were written about his ordeal. Now he is back home, recuperating in a local hospital, and your newspaper sends you to interview him. Here's some of what he tells you:

"I never doubted that I would be found. I got discouraged sometimes, but I figured that I had plenty of food and thought that if I could get back to a trail – particularly the main Appalachian Trail because it's so busy – somebody would come along before long.

"I'll tell you though, I sure was happy when I heard those first footsteps coming up behind me. Those guys thought I was some kind of animal at first. I guess I looked pretty rough. They kind of hesitated in approaching me, but when I said, 'Help' a couple of times, they came running.

"One of the guys stayed with me while the other went for help. They kept telling me not to go to sleep, and I didn't. I was so happy then that I probably couldn't have, even if I had wanted to. I'll never forget the feeling I had when they found me, not if I live to be a hundred. Those guys are going to get mentioned in my will.

"The hardest thing about being lost was thinking that other people might be worrying about me. I was supposed to meet some friends in Gatlinburg a couple of days after I got lost. As it turned out, they weren't worried but said if I had been gone another day, they would have contacted the park rangers and started a search.

"After a day or so of crawling, I had to discard most of my clothes and most of the other things in my pack. They had gotten too wet and heavy for me to push. Of course, I kept all of the food I had. It was mostly dry stuff — crackers, fruit, peanut butter, things like that.

"The mountain foliage was like a jungle. There had been a lot of rain up there this year, and it was really thick. If I had stayed where I was when I fell, I probably would still be there. At least, that's what one of the park rangers said. I think I knew that instinctively when I fell, so I never thought about staying put. I knew that I had better get somewhere where people could find me.

"Besides food, I did manage to keep a few small things with me. I had several pictures of my wife and two little girls. I looked at them a lot, especially when I got discouraged. I would spend a little time looking at those pictures, and then I would crawl a little bit more.

"I broke the first rule of hiking, of course. I hiked alone. If you're on the Appalachian Trail, it doesn't matter because you're not really alone. There are so many people on that trail. But when you get off the beaten track — that's when you need to be with somebody. I learned my lesson about that. My goal is still to hike the entire trail, but I guess I'll have to wait until I get my leg in shape."

Magazine writing

Travel article

A travel magazine is running a series of short pieces on several cities in your area. The series is geared toward college students and is trying to tell them things they would want to know if they visited them. Write about 300 words about the city where your college or university is located. Include some basic information about the city and the colleges and universities located there; also tell about places which are popular with students; finally, include something about places in the city which any tourist would want to visit.

Student budget

Write a short article (about 300 words) on how to live on a limited budget during your first year in college. This article is for a magazine which goes to high school students. You should talk about some of the unexpected expenses a new college student encounters as well as give some advice on how to save money on books, food, or other expenses.

A story with a moral

Write a short story, possibly based on some incident in your life, that has a moral to it. The story, which should be about 300 words long, is for a religious publication which is geared to teenagers. The story should not be heavily theological, but it should contain some moral message. The story can be completely fictional or based totally on a real incident.

Professor

The alumni magazine of your college or university wants stories on file about the professors who have been selected as the school's outstanding teachers: you have been asked to write one of them. (You will have to select the professor on whom you do the story.) There are four professors who have been awarded the Outstanding Teacher Award, and the editor wants a 400-word article on each of them. Be sure to include information about the teacher's background, research, personal activities and interests, and what makes this teacher outstanding.

"My Most Unforgettable Character"

Reader's Digest runs a regular feature article called "My Most Unforgettable Character." It is a character sketch about the author's encounter with an unusual and interesting character. Write a 400-word article on your most unforgettable character. What was your relationship with the person? What makes the person unforgettable?

6
Writing for Broadcast

Broadcasting is the world's most pervasive medium of mass communication. It is not unusual for the American home to receive 30 or more television channels from its cable system. A wide variety of radio stations has been available to anyone with a receiver since the early days of the medium. Underdeveloped areas that cannot get access to even a small newspaper will usually have a transistor radio which serves as a link with the rest of the world. Satellite broadcasting has drawn the world closer together (although not always with positive results) by insuring that we have instant, live coverage of major news events from almost anywhere in the world. In late 1992, when U.S. marines invaded Somalia, their landing was met not by hostile forces but by American, European and Asian television crews who broadcast live pictures of the event all around the world. (The marines, in fact, complained that the television lights made them more vulnerable to hostile fire.)

In America, broadcasting is arguably the most widely used and influential mass medium for receiving information. Americans get their news and information from a variety of sources, and it would be a mistake to believe that broadcasting is always the dominant medium in this regard. Newspapers and newsmagazines deliver a large amount of information to the American public and will continue to do so, but broadcasting is perceived to be the dominant medium. There are more than 6,000 local radio and television stations in America (and thousands more shortwave radio operators), as opposed to 1,700 daily newspapers.

A person who wants to succeed in the field of broadcasting needs to have intelligence, diligence, dependability — and the ability to write. Even though broadcasting is an audio-visual medium, almost everything you hear or see in the way of news or entertainment has been written down. The occasions for ad libbing before the cameras are relatively rare. Broadcasters consider air time too valuable to leave to chance. Even reporters who do live news spots often work from notes and have a good understanding of the forms of writing for the medium.

Broadcasters look for the same qualities in writers that have been discussed already in this book. They want people who know the language and its rules well, who are willing to research their subjects thoroughly and understand them well enough to report on them with clarity, who do not mind working hard and who are willing to rewrite their work and have it rewritten by others. In addition, they are particularly interested in people who can write under pressure and can meet deadlines.

Writing for broadcasting is similar in many ways to writing for the print media, but there are some important differences. Those differences concern the way news is selected for broadcast, the characteristics of writing and story structure and the style with which the information is presented.

Selection of news

Most of the same news values discussed in Chapter 4 apply to news selection for broadcasting. Broadcast journalists are interested in events that have an impact on many people, people in the news, current issues, events that happen close to home and conflicts or unusual happenings. Because of the opportunities and limitations of their medium, however, broadcasters are likely to view such events in somewhat different ways than thier counterparts in print journalism. The following are some of the factors that broadcasters use to select news.

Timeliness. Because of the nature of their medium, broadcasters often consider timeliness the most important news value. Broadcasters work on hourly, or less than hourly, cycles. A news broadcaster may go on the air several times a day. The news must be up-to-the-minute. News that is more than an hour or two old may be too stale for the broadcaster. When you listen to a news report on a breaking news story, you expect to hear the very latest news—what happened just a few minutes before.

Information, not explanation. Broadcasters look for stories that do not need a lot of explanation in order for listeners or viewers to understand them. They prefer stories that are simple and can be told in a straightforward manner. The maximum length for almost any story on a television newscast is two minutes; the more normal length is twenty to thirty seconds. In some larger markets, radio reporters are being told to reduce their story lengths to ten seconds and acutalities to five seconds. That amount of time is not enough to explain a complex story in detail. It is only enough time to give the listener or viewer a few pertinent facts. Of course, some stories are complex and important and explanation cannot be avoided. These are the ones the broadcaster must wrestle with, and it takes practice and talent to condense these stories to their essence.

Audio or visual impact. Broadcasters want stories that their audience can hear or see. Playing a part of the president's state of the union address (called an "actuality") is much more dramatic than a news reporter talking about it; pictures of a flood are more likely to be watched than an anchorman's description of it. Broadcasters often choose stories for their newscasts *because* they have sound or pictures, even though the stories themselves might not merit such attention otherwise. This is one of the major criticisms of broadcast news, but it remains one of the chief factors in broadcast news selection.

Characteristics of writing

The UPI *Broadcast Stylebook* says that while print journalism has the five Ws, broadcast journalism has the Four Cs — correctness, clarity, conciseness and color. These four Cs serve as the basis for broadcast writing and form a good framework for talking about broadcast writing styles.

The first commitment of a the broadcast journalist is to correctness, or accuracy. Everything a broadcast journalist does must contribute to the telling of an accurate story. Even though the broadcast journalist must observe some strict rules about how stories are written, these rules should contribute to, not prevent, an accurate account of an event.

One of the most admirable characteristics of good broadcast writing is its clarity, using clear, precise language that contains no ambiguity. Clarity is an absolute requirement for broadcast writing. Listeners and viewers cannot go back and re-hear a news broadcast as they might be able to read a newspaper account more than once. They must understand what is said the first time. Broadcast writers achieve this kind of clarity by using simple sentences and familiar words, by avoiding the use of pronouns and repeating proper nouns if necessary and by keeping the subject close to the verb in their sentences. Most of all, however, they achieve clarity by thoroughly knowing and understanding their subject.

Another important characteristic of writing for broadcast is its conversational style. Even the clearest, simplest newspaper style tends to sound stilted when it is read aloud. Broadcast writing must sound more casual because people will be reading it aloud. Broadcast news should be written for the ear, not the eye. The writer should keep in mind that someone is going to *say* the words and others will *listen* to them.

This casual or conversational style, however, does not give the writer freedom to break the rules of grammar, to use slang or off-color phrasing or to use language that might be offensive to listeners. As with all writing, the broadcast writer should try to focus attention on the content of the writing and not the writing itself.

Another characteristic of writing for broadcast is the emphasis on the immediate. While past tense verbs are preferred in the print media, broadcasters use the present tense as much as possible. A newspaper story might begin something like this:

```
      The president said Tuesday that he will
   support some limited tax increase proposals
   when Congress reconvenes this week. . . .
```

A broadcast news story might begin with this:

```
   The president says he's for higher taxes. . .
```

Another way of emphasizing the immediate is to omit the time element in the news story and assume that everything has happened close to the time of the broadcast. In the example above, the broadcast version has no time element since it would probably be heard on the day the president made that statement. The elimination of the time element cannot occur in every story. Sometimes the time element is important and must be mentioned.

The tight phrasing that is characteristic of broadcast writing is one of its chief assets and one of the most difficult things for a beginning writer to achieve. Because time is so short, the broadcaster cannnot waste words. The broadcaster must work to constantly simplify and condense. There are a number of techniques for achieving this conciseness. One technique is the elimination of all but the most necessary adjectives and adverbs. Broadcasters know that their stories are built on nouns and verbs, the strongest words in the language. They avoid using the passive voice. Instead they rely on strong, active verbs that will allow the listener to form a picture of the story.

Another technique is the use of short, simple sentences. Broadcasters do not need the variety of length and type of sentences that print journalists need to make their copy interesting. Broadcasters can more readily fire information at their readers like bullets in short, simple sentences.

The fourth C of the *UPI Stylebook*—color—refers to writing that allows the listerner to paint a picture of the story or event being reported. This picture can be achieved in a variety of ways, such as the inclusion of pertinent and telling details in the story or allowing the personality of the writer or news reader to come through in a story. The nature of the broadcast medium allows for humor and human interest to inject itself into many stories.

A final characteristic of broadcast writing is its almost complete subjugation to deadlines. Broadcast copy is often written in an atmosphere in which a deadline is imminent. Unless broadcast writers are able to meet deadline, their compact, understandable prose will never be heard.

Figure 6-1 Broadcast copy

This is the script sheet for the beginning of a local news broadcast that leads off with a national story. The directions on the left indicate that videotape or film is being shown while the announcer is speaking. (Thanks to Janet Hall, WBRC-News, Birmingham)

Slug SHUTTLE LANDS		Page 1
Directions	Script	
TWO SHOT	(2 shot) (s) GOOD EVENING, I'M RICHARD SCOTT. (J) AND I'M HALLIE JONES.	1
ON JONES/ FF SHUTTLE LANDING	***** MERCURY WELCOME BACK. THOSE WERE THE SWEET WORDS FROM MISSION CONTROL TODAY	
ROLLCSS--VO--- ---FT. EDWARDS AIR FORCE BASE	AS THE SPACE SHUTTLE MERCURY MADE A PICTURE PERFECT LANDING IN THE CALIFORNIA DESERT. THIS WAS THE MOMENT NASA HAD WORKED SO HARD FOR IN THE FACE OF MOUNTING OPPOSITION TO THE SHUTTLE PROGRAM. THE SHUTTLE CREW STEPPED OUT OF THE SPACE SHIP WAVING A LARGE AMERICAN FLAG AS SOME 340 THOUSAND SPECTATORS CHEERED. VICE PRESIDENT AL GORE AND SEVERAL NASA OFFICIALS WERE THE FIRST TO GREET THE	
ON JONES/CU	ASTRONAUTS. NASA ADMINISTRATOR JAMES JONATHAN SAID QUOTE, "THIS IS A BANNER DAY FOR ALL OF US AT NASA AND WE'RE VERY HAPPY THIS ONE WORKED SO WELL." (2 SHOT) (S)	

Story structure

The most common structure for broadcast news is called dramatic unity. This structure has three parts: climax, cause and effect. The climax of the story gives the listener the point of the story in about the same way the lead of a print news story does; it tells the listener what happened. The cause portion of the story tells why it happened — the circumstances surrounding the event. The effect portion of the story gives the listener the context of the story and possbily some insight about what the story means. The following example will show how dramatic unity works:

Climax

    Taxpayers in the state will be paying an
    average of 15 dollars more in income taxes
    next year.

Cause

    The state senate defeated several delaying
    amendments this afternoon and passed the gov-
    ernor's controversial revenue-raising bill by
    a 15 to 14 vote. The bill had been the sub-
    ject of intense debate for more than a week.

Effect

    The bill now goes to the governor for his
    signature. Estimates are that the measure
    will raise about 40 million dollars in new
    revenue for the state next year. Elementary
    and secondary education will get most of that
    money. Passage of the bill is a major victory
    for the governor and her education program.

Broadcast journalists should think of their stories as completed circles rather than inverted pyramids. While the pyramid may be cut without losing the essential facts, the broadcast story, if written in this unified fashion, cannot be cut from the bottom or anywhere else. It stands as a unit. Broadcast journalists and their editors are not concerned with cutting stories after they have been written to make them fit into a news broadcast. The reason for this is that the stories should be written to fit into an amount of time designated by the editor or news director. For instance, an editor may allot twenty-five seconds for a story. The writer will know this and will write a story that can be read in twenty-five seconds. If the story is longer than it should be, the editor will ask that it be rewritten.

Because they are so brief, broadcast news stories must gain the attention of the listener from the beginning. The first words in the story are extremely important. Getting the attention of the listener is sometimes more important than summarizing the story or giving the most important facts of the story. The broadcast news lead may be short on facts, but if it captures the attention of the reader, it has served its purpose. Here is an example:

```
     The lame duck keeps limping along.
     Congress met for the third day of its lame-
duck session today, and again failed to act
on the president's gas tax proposals.
```

The first sentence has very little in the way of facts, but it gets the listener into the story. This sort of story structure is only appropriate for certain stories, however. If the facts of the story are strong enough to gain the listener's attention, they should be used to open the story. For example:

```
     The five-cents-a-gallon gas tax is law.
     The president signed the bill authorizing
the tax today while vacationing in Florida.
```

In both of these examples, the writer has not attempted to tell the whole story in the first sentence. Rather, the stories have attention-getting leads and are then supported by facts and details in subsequent sentences. This structure for broadcast news writing is a common one that should be mastered by the beginning student.

Here are some more examples of newspaper stories and the attention-getting leads that could be written for broadcast:

Newspaper story

```
     Americans overwhelmingly oppose the taxa-
tion of employee benefits, and congressmen
who tamper with such tax-free worker benefits
may face trouble at the polls, two Roper Or-
ganization surveys say.
```

Broadcast lead

```
     Keep your hands off employee benefits.
     That's what Americans are willing to tell
congressmen who want to tax things like re-
tirement payments and educational allowances.
```

Newspaper story

```
     The United States is turning out inferior
products that are too costly for foreign cus-
tomers and the problems go beyond a strong
dollar, high wages and high taxes, a presi-
dential commission reports.
```

Broadcast lead

```
     Many American products aren't worth what
we are asking for them.
```

Newspaper story

```
     A lone juror, a city sanitation department
supervisor, forced a hung jury and a mistrial
```

of Midville Mayor Reggie Holder's trial on
perjury and conspiracy charges involving alleged illegal campaign contributions.

Broadcast lead

One man has made the difference in the
perjury and conspiracy trial of Midville May-
or Reggie Holder.

The broadcast writer should remember that stories are measured in *time*—minutes and seconds. While a newspaper can devote 300 words to a story, a broadcaster may have only twenty to thirty seconds for it. The broadcast writer should keep this time element in mind during every stage of the writing and editing process. Broadcast news stories cannot go into the detail and explanation that print stories can. The broadcast writer must remember that certain facts and explanations must be omitted from the copy if the story is to fit into the time allowed for it.

Broadcast writing style

The style and customs of broadcast writing differ somewhat from the style you have learned for print journalism. While the *AP Stylebook* is still consulted for many usage questions, broadcast writing has some rules and conventions. The following is a list of some of those conventions.

Figure 6-2 Local news copy
This is the script sheet for the beginning of a local news broadcast that leads off with a local story. What you see here is a lead-in for one of the station's news reporters to present her story.

Slug SOCIAL SECURITY		Page 1
Directions	**Script**	
TWO SHOT	2-SHOT (J) GOOD EVENING. I'M HALLIE JONES	1

ON RICHARD FF/
SOCIAL
SECURITY
	(S)
	AND I'M RICHARD SCOTT.
	***
	   IF YOU HAVE A PROBLEM WITH
	YOUR SOCIAL SECURITY
	BENEFITS, YOUR PROBLEM <u>COULD</u>
	BE SOLVED BY JUST PICKING UP
	THE TELEPHONE.
	   MIDDLETOWN IS THE NEW
	CENTER FOR A SOCIAL SECURITY
	TOLL-FREE PHONE SERVICE.
	   NOT ONLY IS THE CENTER
	CREATING A MUCH-NEEDED
	SERVICE FOR PEOPLE ALL OVER
	THE COUNTRY, IT'S ALSO
	CREATING 350-JOBS FOR
	MIDDLETOWN.	

TAKE CSS PKG--------	KARI LONEHART HAS MORE. CSS PKG	

Titles usually come before names. Just as in print stories, most people mentioned in broadcast stories need to be identified. In broadcast news writing, however, titles almost always precede a name. Consequently, while a print story might have "James Baker, former secretary of state," the broadcast journalist would say, "former Secretary of State James Baker."

Avoid abbreviations, even on second reference. Only the most commonly known abbreviations should be used in broadcast writing. The FBI and UN are two examples. FTC, however, should be spelled out as the Federal Trade Commission.

Avoid direct quotations if possible. Broadcast writers prefer paraphrasing rather than using direct quotations. Direct quotations are hard to handle in broadcast copy because signaling the listener that what the broadcaster is saying is a direct quotation is difficult.

Sometimes a direct quotation is essential and should be used. When that is the case, the writer needs to tip the listener off to the fact that a direct quotation is being used. The use of the phrase "quote . . . unquote" is awkward and should be avoided. Instead, phrases like "in the words of the speaker," "in his own words," "used these words," and "as she put it."

Attribution should some before a quotation, not after it. The sequence of direct quote-speaker-verb that is common in print journalism is not useful for the broadcast writer. Tagging an attribution onto the end of a direct or paraphrased quote is confusing to the listener. The listener should know where the quotation is coming from before hearing the quote.

Use as little punctuation as possible but enough to help the newscaster through the copy. Remember that broadcast news copy will be read by only one person, the news reader. That person should be able to read through the copy as easily as possible. The excessive use of commas, dashes and semicolons will not help the newscaster.

Numbers and statistics should be rounded off. While a print journalist will want to use an exact figure, a broadcast journalist will be satisfied with a more general figure. Consequently, $4,101,696 in print becomes "more than four million dollars" in broadcast copy.

Numbers themselves are handled somewhat differently than the *AP Stylebook* dictates for print journalists. Here are a few rules about handling numbers in broadcast copy: numbers one through nine should be spelled out; numbers 10 through 999 should be written as numerals; write out hundred, thousand, million, billion, and use a combination of numerals with these numbers where appropriate (for example, 15-hundred, 10-billion); don't write "a million" or "a billion," but rather use the word "one" ("a" sounds like "eight").

Personalize the news when possible and appropriate. In the example on page 148 the lead sentence could read, "Gas is going to cost you five cents more a gallon . . . ." Where possible and appropriate, broadcast stories should draw the listeners into the story by telling how the story might affect them.

International Widgets John Smith said today . . ." would become "International Widgets President John Smith says . . ."

Avoid using symbols when you write. The dollar sign should never be used. Nor should the percent sign be used. Spell these words out so there will be no mistake on the part of the news reader.

Use phonetic spelling for unfamiliar and hard to pronounce names and words. Again, you are trying to be helpful to the newscaster. Writing "California governor George Duekmejian (Duke-MAY-gen) said today he will propose . . ." helps the newscaster get over a difficult name. Notice that the syllable which is emphasized in pronunciation is written in captial letters. Difficult place names also need phonetic spellings. "A car bomb exploded in downtown Caracas (ka-RAH-kus) today . . ." Writers should also be knowledgeable about local pronunications of place names. For instance, most people know that Louisville, Kentucky is pronounced (LU-ee-vil); but most people do not know that residents of Louisville, Tennessee pronounce the name of their community as (LU-iss-vil). Pronunciation to the broadcast writer is like spelling to the print journalist. It should always be checked if there is any doubt.

Avoid pronouns, and when you have to use them, make sure the referents are clear to the listener. Putting too many pronouns in a story can be an obstacle to the kind of clarity a broadcaster must have. For instance, in the following sentences, it is unclear to whom the pronoun is referring: The president and the chief foreign affairs advisor met yesterday. They discussed his recent trip to the Mideast.

Avoid apposition. An apposition is a word or set of words that renames a noun. In "Tom Smith, mayor of Midville, said today . . ." the phrase "mayor of Midville" is an appositional phrase. These phrases are deadly in broadcast writing. They slow the newscaster down and confuse to the listener. Appositions, when they are found in the middle of sentences, are surrounded by commas. Listeners to broadcast stories do not have the advantage of those commas, however. Consequently, they may hear the example above as ". . . Midville said today . . ." Broadcast writers should keep subjects and verbs as close together as possible.

Use the present tense when it is appropriate. Using the present tense ("the president says" rather than "the president said") is one way broadcast writers have of bringing immediacy to their writing. Care should be taken, however, that using the present tense does not make the broadcaster sound foolish. For instance, if the president made a statement yesterday, a broadcast news story probably should not have the attribution in the present tense. The past tense would be more appropriate. The present tense should be used for action that is very recent or that is continuing.

Avoid dependent clauses at the beginning of sentences. Dependent clauses are troublesome to the broadcast writer because they are confusing and tend to hide the subject of the sentence. For instance, "Stopping on the first leg of his European tour today, the president said he . . ." gives the listener too much to digest before getting to the main point of the story. The broadcast writer should always remember that the simple sentence—subject, verb, object—is the best format to use.

Broadcast copy preparation

Copy is prepared for one person, the announcer. The copy should be presented in a way to make the announcer's job as easy as possible. The examples in this chapter should give you an idea of how you should prepare broadcast copy. Here are a few tips:

• Type only one story on a page. A story should have some ending mark, such as "—30—", at the end.

• Use caps and lower case. An old style of broadcast writing was to capitalize everything. That is changing. The all caps style is hard to read.

• Don't carry over a paragraph to another page. If a story is more than a page long, end the page at the end of a paragraph; begin the next page with a new paragraph.

• Don't hyphenate at the end of a line.

• Broadcast copy should contain no editing marks. X-ing through a mistake is acceptable, but if any other editing is necessary, the story should

Figure 6-3 Live reports
This script sheet shows a lead-in for a live report. The reporter will appear live on camera via satellite and give his report.

Slug	GADSDEN POLICE CHIEF		Page	1
Directions		**Script**		
ON HALL/ FF SKYLINK 6		(J) THE CITY OF GADSDEN HAS A NEW POLICE CHIEF TONIGHT DESPITE THE CONTROVERSY THAT SURROUNDED HIS HIRING. FORMER BIRMINGHAM POLICE INSPECTOR JOHNNY MORRIS WAS SWORN IN AS POLICY CHIEF THIS AFTERNOON.		1
ON HALL/LIVE RON		WE SENT OUR NEW SKYLINK 6 SATELLITE TRUCK TO GADSDEN TODAY . . . RON FUDGE JOINS US NOW VIA SATELLITE. RON, WHAT'S THE REACTION THERE TO THE NEW CHIEF TONIGHT?		
TAKE LIVE FULL SPR: SKYLINK 6 / GADSDEN SPR: SKYLINK 6 / RON FUDGE		(LIVE FULL)		

mistake is acceptable, but if any other editing is necessary, the story should be retyped. Remember, the announcer (and it could be you) needs to be able to read through the copy easily.

Broadcasters often want to work tapes (either audio or video) of interviews into their stories. The following example shows you how to indicate this on your copy.

```
        People who want to buy a Chevrolet next
    year are going to have to pay more. That's
    what company spokesman John Smith said today
    in Detroit. The new cars will cost about sev-
    en percent more than last year's cars. Smith
    blamed the increase on the new contract re-
    cently negotiated with the United Auto Work-
    ers.

        ROLL TAPE: The workers are getting more.
    . . .
        END TAPE: . . . really no way of avoiding
    this.
     [ :15]
        Labor leaders disputed this reasoning,
    however. Local auto workers president Stanley
    Porter said Chevrolet was raising its prices
    just to make the union look bad. At a separ-
    ate news conference in Detroit, he called on
    Chevrolet to roll back its prices.
        ROLL TAPE: The union gave up a lot. . . .
        END TAPE: . . .without good reason.[ :18]
```

The number in each of the sets of parentheses indicates the number of seconds of each tape.

Putting together a newscast

Broadcast journalists work with and against time. They use time to measure their stories, but they are also always working against the clock. Their stories must be completed for the next newscast. People working in radio feel this pressure keenly because of the hourly news shows that many radio stations produce. Many local television stations are also producing such hourly newscasts. For the broadcast journalist, the clock is always ticking toward a deadline, and the deadline cannot be delayed.

Many broadcast journalists—even those who are fairly new in the business—must worry not only about writing their stories but also about putting together a newscast. Producing such a newscast, whether it is a forty-five-second news brief or a half-hour telecast, involves many of the skills learned as a news writer.

The first such skill is that of exercising news judgment about what to include in the newscast. Writers must use traditional news values in deciding what events constitute news. Editors and producers use those same values in deciding what goes into a newscast. The key element in putting together newscasts is the timeliness of the stories. A newscast producer looks at the stories available and often decides which ones to run based on how recent the stories are. Because broadcasting is a medium that can emphasize the immediate, news producers often take advantage of this quality by telling listeners and viewers what happened only minutes before a newscast.

Timeliness is not the only news value used in these decisions. A story that is the most recent one available will not necessarily be the first one used in a newscast. Stories that have more impact or involve more prominent people may take precedence. All of the other news values come into play in putting together a newscast.

Another element that news producers use in deciding what to put into a newscast is the availablity of audio tapes, slides, film and videotapes. One of the criticisms of broadcast journalism is that decisions about what to run and what not to run are based on the availability of such aids. It is true that often such decisions are made, but broadcast journalists—especially television journalists—feel that they must take advantage of their medium to show a story rather than just tell it. Pictures compel viewers to watch, and the feeling of many in television is that the "talking head," the news announcer with no visual aid, is not as compelling to the viewer as the "talking head" with a picture or slide.

Time is the pervasive fact in putting together a newscast. Not only must stories be timely in themselves, but they must be written to fill a certain amount of air time. The producer or news director is generally the one who assigns the amount of time for a story to fill up. The writer must then write a story which can be read in that time. The producer, of course, must have enough copy to fill up the time allotted for the newscast. Sometimes, however, even with the most careful planning, a newscast producer will come up a few seconds short. The producer should always give the announcer one or two more stories than he or she will need in order to fill this time.

A news director for radio or television has a variety of formats from which to choose in putting together a newscast. The following is a brief description of some of those formats for radio. Generally, each of these formats, except the mini-documentary, runs for less than a minute.

Written copy/voicers. This format is a story without acutalities or sound-bites.

Sound bite or actuality. When possible and appropriate, a radio news writer will want to include some sort of sound effects from the event that is covered. This actuality may be someone speaking or it may be some other identifiable sound, such as gunshots or crowd noise, that will give the listeners an added dimension to the story. News anchors introduce the soundbite with the copy they read.

Wrap-around. A news anchor briefly introduces a story and the reporter. The reporter then gives the story and includes a sound-bite. The sound-bite is followed by the reporter giving a conclusion or "tag line."

Mini-documentary. This format allows a story to run for more than a minute, and some run for as much as fifteen minutes. They may include several sound-bites with a variety of sources or sounds, such as interviews, noise from events or even music. A reporter will weave in and out of the mini-documentary, guiding it along for the listener. A news anchor usually introduces a mini-documentary with a short lead-in that sets up what the listener is about to hear. This format is most commonly used on public radio news broadcasts.

Television newscasts can use any of the following formats:

Reader copy. This format is a story read by an anchor or reporter without visual or audio aid. It may have a slide or graphic in the background.

Voice-overs. A videotape of an event is shown with the sound of the event turned down. An anchor or reporter speaks over the tape to talk about about what the viewer is seeing.

Voice-over to sound-bite. An anchor or reporter speaks over a videotape that includes someone talking. The news copy is timed so that when the reporter stops, the sound on the tape is turned up and the person on the tape is heard speaking.

Package stories. An anchor, using what is called a "lead-in," introduces a story and the reporter. The pre-recorded piece then includes a mix of video, sound-bites, voice-overs, and a "stand-up" from the reporter who explains some element or the story or summarizes the entire story. These packages may run for as long as two and a half minutes.

Live shots. An anchor will introduce a reporter who is shown live at the scene of some news event. The reporter can then do one of several things: present a simple stand-up, interview someone, introduce and voice-over a videotape, or answer questions from the anchor. Satellite technology now allows even local news departments to use such live shots frequently.

Conclusion

The nature of broadcast news is changing dramatically, and the technology that is developing for broadcasters is placing new demands on broadcast journalists. Computer editing stations—allowing the reporter to do all of the editing of both videotape and copy on a single workstation—will give reporters more direct control in producing their stories. These systems will also allow reporters to call up file footage, videotapes that may have run in previous stories, for use or reference. Those entering the field of broadcast news must be increasingly computer-oriented.

Another development is the increased use of satellite technology to produce live shots from the scene of news events. This means that reporters will be called upon to do more stand-ups and that they must develop the ability to think on their feet, outline stories quickly, and read unobtrusively from their notes. Reporters must understand the forms and formats of broadcast news to be able to put these shots together. Even though it may occur in a different form, the ability to write clearly and concisely will continue to be a must of the broadcast news reporter.

All of these characteristics of broadcast writing place a heavy burden on the writer of broadcast copy. Producing such copy is no easy task. The person who can do it consistently and well, however, is likely to have a large audience for his or her work.

Points for consideration and discussion

1. The author begins the chapter by saying that many people believe that the broadcast medium is the most important medium of mass communication. Do you agree or disagree?

2. List the major differences between writing news for broadcast and writing news for print. Which of these differences makes writing for broadcast more difficult than writing for print? Which makes it easier?

3. Take a story from the front page of your local newspaper. Read it through completely. Now list, as briefly as possible, the three major facts of that story. That's the kind of thing a broadcast journalist must do. Try to write a thirty-second story using the three facts that you have listed.

4. Look at the lead paragraph of each of the stories in the figures in this chapter (pages 146, 149, and 152). What devices did the reporters use in writing these leads? Do you consider these leads good one?

5. Make a list of names of local personalities that might be hard to pronounce for broadcasts. Then write their phonetic spellings.

Further reading

Edward Bliss and John Patterson, *Writing News for Broadcast,* New York: Columbia University Press, 1971.

Irving Fang, *Television News,* New York: Hastings House, 1971.

Carl Hausman, *Crafting News for Electronic Media,* Belmont, CA: Wadsworth Publishing Co., 1992

Robert L. Hilliard, *Writing for Television and Radio,* 4th Ed., Belmont, CA: Wadsworth, 1984.

Peter E. Mayeux, *Writing for the Broadcast Media,* Boston: Allyn and Bacon, Inc., 1985.

Marcus D. Rosenbaum and John Dinges (eds.), *Sound Reporting: The National Public Radio Guide to Radio Journalism and Production.* Dubuque, IA: Kendall-Hunt Publishing Co.

Frederick Shook and Dan Lattimore, *The Broadcast News Process,* 4th ed., Englewood, CO: Morton Publishing Co., 1992.

Mitchell Stephens, *Broadcast News,* New York: Holt, Rinehart and Winston, 1980.

EXERCISES

The following section contains a variety of broadcast writing exercises. You should follow your instructor's directions in completing them.

Broadcast leads

Write a broadcast lead—the first one or two sentences of a story—based on the following information.

FCC official

James Graybeard, congressional liaison for Federal Communication Commission

Speaking to meeting of State Broadcasters, meeting in town today

"We are on a brink of new era in communication...new technology are not all that new—what's different is that costs are lower. Many more people can now use technology because the prices are going down and because equipment is easier to operate. Every day, engineers are making technology more accessible. Direct broadcast satellites (DBS) will be available to everyone in the U.S. for the price of a television set by 1995."

Car telephones

Survey by local telephone company

Number car telephones in area doubled last year

948 last year; 2110 this year

Survey shows mostly used by businesses for business purposes; personal use of car telephone limited but growing

Homecoming

Pep rally on Friday right before Saturday's homecoming football game

Begins at 7:30 p.m.

Featuring bonfire and music by pep band

For the first time this year a fireworks show, produced by fireworks artist Larry Lain, who designs fireworks for world's fairs

Fireworks to begin about 9 p.m.

Country music songwriter

Bill Gillespie, country music song writer; resident of Nashville; spoke to university music appreciation class today

Told students to "write if you feel like it; don't write if you don't"

Gillespie has written hit songs for Dolly Parton, Buck Owens, Charlie Pride

Most recent hit: "Sell Your Soul to the Devil"

House fire

House valued at $150,783 burned completely this morning

Address : 716 Ruppert Street, in Woodland Lake subdivision

Owner: George Mason, vice president of the First Trust Bank

No one at home at the time of the fire

Three engines fought the fire for more than an hour

Don Kerlinger, photograher for local paper, hurt by falling timbers as he tried to take pictures of the blaze; in satisfactory condition at local hospital with minor burns and bruises

Historic document

Letter signed by Robert E. Lee found by local woman this morning

Mattie Harrington, 718 Donald Avenue

She was going through some papers in a trunk in her attic

Says letter was written to her great-grandfather after the battle of Gettysburg

Says Lee talked about the battle, saying he had made some mistakes during the battle but still expressed optimism about the outcome of the war

Letter dated August 17, 1863

Letter now in the custody of the university history department;

Dr. Robert Weir checking its authenticity

Absence policy

New absence policy being considered by university

More than four absences from class during the semester will result in automatic failing grade

Neil Hendron, president of the Student Government Association, said today the policy is "unreasonable" and "outrageous." "I don't think it can or will be enforced."

Faculty senate last week passed a resolution endorsing the policy.

Newscast I

Construct a two-minute newscast based on the following items.

Capsize

A fifteen-foot boat capsized in rough waters off Point Lookout yesterday evening. Two men—Terry Reston, twenty-three, and Will Bendix, twenty-five—were in the boat. The men said offshore winds increased wave heights and capsized their boat. The men were picked up by a Coast Guard boat after an hour in the water. Both were hospitalized for observation, but the hospital lists their condition today as good. The men say they were hunting sharks about 200 yards offshore.

Basketball death

A fifteen-year-old freshman basketball player died this morning during practice at Central High School. The freshman, Todd White, collapsed while running during a practice game. White had not had any known illness, according to trainer Mike Way. White was pronounced dead at Central Valley Memorial Hospital after all efforts to revive him failed. An autopsy will be performed by the county coroner today.

Energy plan

The secretary of the interior announced a new $800 million energy plan while traveling through the western United States on a busy three-day tour. The secretary of the interior announced his plan at a Western Governor's Conference meeting in Salt Lake City. The plan calls for a five-year program to ease

strains brought on by strip mining and other energy ventures.

Abuse acquittal

A fourth-grade school teacher in Midville has been acquitted of child abuse for spanking a ten-year-old girl with a wooden paddle after the girl lied about having gum in her mouth. The District Court jury returned a verdict of not guilty after deliberating three hours. Lynda Kristle had been charged with child abuse after parents noted bruises on the child's buttocks.

Hotel opening

The world's largest casino-hotel opened yesterday in Reno, Nev. The MGM Grand is on a 145-acre site and will accommodate more than 1,500 persons. It has nineteen bars. Prices for rooms range from fifty dollars to $250 per day.

Newscast II

Construct a two-minute newscast based on the following items.

Retirement

The speaker of the state House of Representatives, Milton Bradford, has announced that he will not seek re-election. He has served in the state house for twenty-seven years and has been speaker for the past ten years. He is a Democrat from Logansville. He has always been closely aligned with the state's education lobby and has recently worked for substantial pay raises for the state's elementary and secondary school teachers.

New runway

The Airport Authority has announced that a new runway will be built some time next year. The airport now has three runways, and this fourth one will increase the airport's capacity. The new runway is being built to meet increased demands from airlines that want to schedule more flights into the city. The costs of construction for the new runway will be about $3 million, but Sam Peck, chairman of the Airport Authority, says the airport should recover the costs within about three and a half years.

Strike

Machinists Union Local 333 has called for an indefinite walkout of all local members against the city's General Motors plant. The walkout was called because the contract that GM has with the machinists expired last Friday. Since then, workers have been working without a contract, and Barney Olive, president of the union, said this situation cannot continue. "We have bargained in good faith, but we can see no evidence that General Motors is doing the same thing." General Motors spokesmen refused to comment about the walkout but said the plant will maintain its operation. The plant manufactures hubcaps for GM tires.

Concert

The City Community Orchestra and the City Chorus will combine forces this Sunday and present a joint concert which will feature the last movement of Beethoven's Ninth Symphoy. Lister Banks and Quenton Hill are leaders of the orchestra and chorus, respectively. Banks said this is the first time the two organizations have performed jointly. In addition to the Beethoven symphony, the chorus will perform works by Bach and the symphony will play works by Brahms. The concert will be at the City Auditorium at 3 p.m. Sunday. Admission is two dollars for adults and a dollar for students.

Custody battle

Bobby Ray Hacks, a native of the city and now a famous songwriter in Nashville, has said he will try to disprove a child-molesting charge and regain custody of his twelve-year-old son. In a Nashville courtroom, Hacks vowed to fight the charges brought against him by his former wife. They were divorced last year. He was convicted of child molesting last week, and his sentence hearing was today. He received a six-month suspended sentence but was also told that he had to give up custody of his son.

Newscast III

Write a two-minute newscast using the following information.

Bank robbery

The city hasn't had a bank robbery for six months. That changed this morning when two men, both wearing ski masks, entered the Fidelity Federal Bank, the downtown branch, just after it opened this morning. Police Chief Arthur Shultz said the men must have been waiting for the bank to open. They took $22,000 in cash and an undetermined amount in checks and securities, according to the bank's manager Jack Sherry. The men came into the bank brandishing shotguns, and one of them fired a couple of shots into the air. They made all the people in the bank lie down on the floor except for Sherry. "Fortunately, we hadn't taken all of the money we would have out of the vault, and they seemed interested only in the money they could see." Both men were tall and wearing leather jackets. They ran out of the bank and jumped into a red, four-door Chevrolet with a New York license plate. The county sheriff, Pat Gibson, said that roadblocks have been set up on all main roads leading out of the west of the county. That's all you have right now. A reporter from your station is working on the story.

Donations

The county's United Way drive has been going on for three months. Today it was brought to a close officially by this year's chairman, Sara Morris, a local attorney. She said that a record had been set. The county United Way raised $455,789.03. More than a hundred thousand people contributed. That's a record, too, according to Morris. "We couldn't be happier with the progress that we have made in this year's fund drive. The people of this city and county have responded far beyond our expectations." Last year's drive netted just over $400,000, and the goal this year was $400,000 again. United Way helps various community charitable and service organizations. Morris said the United Way board will meet soon to decide on how the money will be allocated.

Reactions

Don Seigel, the press secretary to the mayor, says that the mayor's office has received "literally hundreds" of phone calls this morning. Most of the people calling are mad because of the increase in property tax the city council voted last night. The council voted to increase property tax 10 percent across the board. That means everyone who owns property in the city will have to pay 10 percent more in taxes. "Actually, a 10 percent increase isn't that much because our property tax base is so low now," Seigel said. Mayor Lyle Fester proposed the tax, and after a heated debate, it passed 5-2. A number of people have called the radio station this morning complaining about the tax. It will go into effect next July 1. One citizen's group, the Taxpayer's Union, has announced that it is planning a recall movement against the mayor because of the part he played in proposing the tax. Seigel says, "We knew people would be upset. It was a tough decision, but it was the right thing to do. Most of this new money will go the the city school system, and they need it bad."

Books gift

Stanely Minion taught journalism at the local university for more than 30 years. He retired last year. Yesterday, the university announced that he had donated his entire collection of books and newspapers to the library. Minion was a noted collector of newspaper front pages, and his collection includes many pre-Revolutionary War newspapers. Quincy Mundt, the university librarian, said he is "thrilled" about the gift. "Dr. Minion has some newspapers that aren't available anywhere else that I know of. His collection is one of the best. We are looking into plans to remodel one floor of the library to house the collection. We would like to make the newspapers available to the public for viewing as well as to researchers." Minion's donation includes more than 7,000 books and 10,301 newspapers. Mundt said the collection is worth at least $133,000.

Traffic lights

A violent rainstorm passed over the city early this morning. It didn't last long, only a few minutes. But lightning struck one of the power company's substations and knocked out the traffic lights on one of the city's busy streets, McTerril Boulevard. Traffic was backed up for several blocks during rush hour, and several accidents were reported. At least three of them were caused by the lights being out, according to the police chief. Your reporter on the scene says traffic delays of up to forty-five minutes were reported in some areas. "The wet streets from the rainstorm didn't help us any," the police chief said. The power was restored by 8:30.

History of the county

The county historical society has been working on a comprehensive history of the county for several years. This morning, Lila Bancroft, president of the society, announced that the project has been completed and that a history of the county will be published some time early next year. She said many of the members of the society contributed to the work, but the main author was John Widner, a retired history professor at the university and a native of the county. The book will cover county history from the earliest settlers in the 1700s to the present day. "It's going to be a beautiful book—very well written and with lots of illustrations," according to Bancroft. The pre-publication price will be $17.50; after publication, the price will be $25. It will be available in all the local bookstores.

Newscast IV

Write a two-minute newscast using the following information.

Canine pacemaker

Last week, Marie Bruton's dog was sick. This week it's better. In fact, it's up and running around—"chasing the cat," she says. The reason is because the dog has had a pacemaker inserted to keep its heart going. Dr. Charles Eulau, a local vet, did the surgery, and he says it's the first time anything like this has been done in this area. Mrs. Bruton: "Wrangler had been pretty listless. Then last week he just collapsed. I didn't know he had a heart problem until I took him to the vet. Now he's doing fine. I think he knows that something has happened to him—that he's been given a new lease on life." Eulau says he used an old pacemaker provided to him by the local hospital. It cost about $100, and he charged $50 for the operation. Mrs. Bruton is a legal secretary for a local law firm.

Sentencing

A local man has been on trial for several months, accused of poisoning some Halloween candy. His name is Sam Gather. Two days ago a jury convicted him after a week-long trial. His attorney argued that he was insane, but the jury did not accept that defense. Less than an hour ago, Judge Harvey Eagle sentenced him to five years in prison. This was the maximum sentence the judge could give him since he wasn't trying to kill the children, just make them sick. At least ten children got sick from eating the candy given to them by Gather. He had put some cleaning fluid onto some hard candy, which he then gave to the kids.

Beerless St. Patrick's Day

M.A.D.D. stands for Mothers Against Drunk Driving. This organization is working to get drunken drivers off the road and to strengthen laws against them. It also helps victims and families of victims of drunken-driving accidents. Denise Clearly, president of the local chapter, has announced a "beerless St. Patrick's Day party." The party will be on March 17 at Palisades Park. It will feature a cookout and entertainment by a local bluegrass group, Ham'n Eggs. It will start at 5 p.m., and according to Clearly, "Everybody is invited. We want to show people that they can have fun without having to drink." She said that information about M.A.D.D. will be available at the party, and interested people may join. The annual dues are ten dollars a year.

Stabbing deaths

Frederic Church, a local contractor, and his wife, Sarah, were found in their $300,000 home Sunday, beaten and stabbed to death.

Their home is on Lake Smith. Police say they think the couple surprised a burglar because some jewelry and other valuable items were stolen. This morning the police announced that they had arrested and charged a 15-year-old boy with the crimes. They said he is a local youth, but his name is being withheld at this time. His name should be available from the district attorney's office later in the day. The police said he was seen by neighbors leaving the house on Sunday, and they said footprints in the mud outside the house matched a shoe belonging to the boy.

Depositers

Two months ago the Trust National Bank was declared bankrupt by the U.S. government. The bank was a state bank and not federally insured, so a lot of people lost their money. A number of people had their life savings invested in the bank, and they have been wondering about it ever since. Today the state claims board, which handles these kinds of things, announced that the state would provide about $60 million to pay back the investors. This amount of money would mean that investors would get about forty cents back for every dollar they had in the bank. The money would be paid out over a period of three years. The state legislature must still approve the plan.

Resignation

The state treasurer is a man named Manness Manford. He has been state treasurer for twenty years, which means that he has been elected to the post four straight times. Today, at the state capital, Mr. Manford announced that he is leaving office at the end of this month. He had just been re-elected to the position last November. He is leaving to become president of Fidelity National Bank in the capital city. Mr. Manford is from your town and a lot of people there know him. He is credited with revising the accounting procedures for the state, making it easier for the state legislature to predict the amounts of funding that will be available for the upcoming fiscal years. There have been rumors that he has been ill and not able to do his job. The governor made the following statement: "We believe that Manness Manford has served the state well. He has approached his job with imagination and foresight, and he has made the job of everyone in state government easier. He's my good friend, and I hate to have the state lose his services, but I can understand his desire to go into private business. We all wish him well."

More broadcast writing

Rewrite into radio and television style these stories from the UPI newspaper wire. Make a special effort to boil them down into capsule form. Watch for errors in style.

Hurricane

MIAMI, Fla.—Hurricane Nancy lurched toward the United States today after a brief pause last night during which she whipped up 160-mile-an-hour winds and developed into the most intense storm since 1935.

As the huge storm swung into motion, hurricane watchers warned persons in the target area of the possibility of monster tides being pushed ahead of Nancy.

Officials at the National Hurricane Center here said the storm was about 325 miles south of Pensacola, headed for the Florida Panhandle at a speed of twelve mph. At that speed she would strike the mainland tonight.

She was expected to hit the Panhandle with wind speeds of up to 156 mph.

Residents and travelers were told to move from low and exposed places which the up-to-15-foot tides could cut off from escape routes.

"Nancy is now very similar to the 1935 storm," said Dr. Robert H. Simpson, head of the National Hurricane Center. "She has a very large fury concentrated in an exceedingly small area."

Seismography report

WASHINGTON, D.C.—One hundred seismograph stations could keep Russia from violating an atomic test ban and at the same time provide new knowledge of how the earth is put together. This view was expressed by seismologist Frank Press of the California Institute of Technology at the annual meeting of the National Academy of Sciences.

Earth waves generated by quakes or large explosions provide science with a tool for studying the planet's structure from crust to core. Such waves are recorded by seismographs. Dr. Press said a network of 100 special seismograph stations could be established in a country the size of the USSR for less than $10 million and "operated at an annual cost of several million dollars." Such a system would spot any sneak atomic tests and at the same time, by recording earthquakes, provide a scientific bonus which "would justify much of the cost."

Authorities agree that no nation could start undetected tests of large nuclear weapons. But in the absence of a monitoring system small underground shots "present the possibility of evasion," Press said.

Collision prevention

SACRAMENTO—A device that has the capability of preventing in-flight airplane collisions through use of infrared rays has been described to a radio engineers conference here. The gadget, designed and developed by the Aerojet-General Corp. of Sacramento, uses invisible heat rays received from the oncoming aircraft to trigger an alarm.

Robert G. Richards, operations analyst for Aerojet's Avionics Division, told the Seventh Regional Conference and Trade Show of the Institute of Radio Engineers yesterday that the invisible heat rays are sent out by all engines, motors, electrical apparatus, or anything having a source of heat as part of its makeup.

It took about fourteen years of research to develop the device which, Richards explained, would have provided a warning in the case of the Grand Canyon disaster more than three minutes before the collision.

Interviewing for broadcast

Highway deaths

The State Department of Transportation today said that the total number of trafic deaths on the state's highways was 120. This is the lowest total in ten years. Your station sends you to do an interview with the State

Transportation Commissioner Dick Blocker about why this occurred.

Having the lowest highway death total in ten years is quite an accomplishment.

That's right, it is. I think the people of the state are to be commended for it. I think we must be doing something right.

What do you think we are doing right?

Several things. For one thing, I think people are just being more careful, observing the speed limit, having their cars checked, watching out for hazardous conditions – things like that.

The fifty-five-mile-an-hour speed limit – do you think that's had an effect?

Well, the fifty-five-mile-an-hour speed limit has been in place for more than a decade, so last year's low figure wouldn't necessarily be due to that. You know, it's interesting about the fifty-five limit. It was originally established to conserve fuel, but it's real effect has been to save lives. It's not that everyone is observing the fifty-five limit per se. But I think the fifty-five limit has made people drive more slowly than they would otherwise. So now, instead of the average speed being seventy-five, it might only be sixty-five—and that's an improvement.

Do you know of any specific reason that the death total should have been so low last year?

We're looking into that. One reason has to be the good weather we had generally last year. Hazardous weather conditions create a lot of accidents, and we didn't have much of that last year. Another reason has to be the tough new car safety inspection law the governor proposed and the legislature passed three years ago. I think that's gotten a lot of cars off the road that might have caused accidents.

Is drinking and driving a problem in the state?

Yes, definitely. Eighty out of the 120 people who were killed in automobile accidents in the state last year were killed in accidents where alcohol was involved. Alcohol is still the major safety problem in this state.

What's being done about that?

As you probably know, the governor has sponsored legislation to increase the penalties for those convicted of drunk driving. We were joined in this by M.A.D.D., Mothers Against Drunk Driving. We have also sponsored legislation that would raise the legal drinking age from nineteen to twenty-one. Unfortunately, neither measure was passed by the legislature this session, but we'll be trying against next session.

Hall of Fame

A local resident, George M. "Bucky" Barnett, has just been elected to Baseball's Hall of Fame. Barnett spent most of his career as a shortstop for the St. Louis Cardinals, from 1933 to 1946. He also played with the Boston Red Sox before he retired in 1949. He then spent twenty years as a coach and minor-league manager and has been living in your city since leaving baseball. Barnett was best known as a fielder. Grantland Rice, the famed sportswriter, once described Barnett as "personified lightning" on the field. In fact, he had the highest fielding percentage of any shortstop, .993 (fielding percentage is the number of chances handled without making an error). He had a lifetime batting average of .310. Your station sends you to interview him.

How did you get interested in baseball?

When I was growing up, you didn't get interested in baseball. Baseball was just there-kind of like milk. I don't guess it ever occurred to most of us not to be interested in baseball.

What's different about kids growing up today? Why aren't they as interested in baseball as your generation seems to have been?

There are a lot of distractions, I think. When I was growing up, baseball was about all you had, and you simply tried to survive the winter waiting for spring training to begin. Now kids have basketball and football and television to look at if they want to.

I take it you don't think much of football?

I don't have anything against football.

It's just that I love baseball so much. Nothing comes as close to being a perfect game as baseball. A good baseball game has lots of little dramas going on on the field at the same time, and it takes a keen, intelligent eye to see just a few of them. I'm sorry that many kids today seem to have adopted another sport. I think they're settling for second best.

What was the greatest thrill of your baseball career?

I think it was when the Cardinals won the World Series from the Boston Red Sox in 1946. The Red Sox had a great team with Ted Williams as their leading hitter. I don't think anything in my playing career gave me so much joy as beating the Red Sox that year.

People have said that you were the greatest fielding shortstop in the history of baseball.

That's flattering, but I'm not sure it's true. The game has produced several great men at short. It's funny because I always thought fielding was the easiest part of the game. It was just a matter of staying alert, knowing the hitters, and moving with the pitch. Usually, I just wound up where the ball was. Hitting was always the hardest part of the game for me — something I really had to work at. I think I was lucky to have such a high hitting percentage.

7
Writing Advertising Copy

Advertising pervades every part of our society. The products we use in our homes, the clothes we wear, the programs we watch on television, the books we read, the places where we shop and go for recreation—all of these things are affected by advertising.

Advertising is one of the country's major industries. One estimate put the money spent on advertising in 1984 at $85.4 billion. One company alone, Procter and Gamble, the nation's largest advertiser in 1982, spent $726 million in 1982. By 1992 that figure had gone up to more than $3.4 billion worldwide. Philip Morris Companies spends $2.7 billion worldwide. Major companies routinely spend thousands of dollars on the production of advertisements, and the costs of buying time in the mass media can be astronomical. In just one product category, soft drinks, Coca-Cola spent $141 million in 1987 to promote its chief product; Pepsi spent $135 million; and 7-Up spent $62.8 million. The entire retail soft drink market that year generated revenues of $40 billion.

Charges for network television advertising time during the National Football League Super Bowl are among the highest prices any advertiser can pay. In 1983, thirty seconds of air time during the Super Bowl cost $330,000. For the 1993 Super Bowl, those charges had risen to nearly $900,000. One of the most watched programs in television history, the final episode of "MASH" in the spring of 1983, cost advertisers about $450,000 for thirty seconds of air time. An average thirty-second prime-time television announcement costs more than $100,000 and about $200,000 to produce.

People who spend that much money obviously expect a return, and they often get it. Most companies recognize the need to advertise and the benefits of doing so, and they are willing to pay a price for it. Because advertising is so costly, however, there is little room for error or waste. This chapter discusses the writing of advertising copy, but the writing of the ad is only a part of the marketing strategy of a company. Writers of advertising copy must have more on their minds than how the ad will look and what the ad will say.

A love-hate relationship

Americans have a love-hate relationship with advertising. Many people claim that they never pay attention to advertising. They say they leave the room when a commercial comes on television, and they never read the ads in newspapers or magazines. Many will tell you they never make consumer decisions based on the ads—as if admitting to that would mean something is wrong with them.

More sophisticated critics of advertisements put them down as insulting and degrading. They criticize ads for creating desires and needs that are wasteful and unhealthy. Advertisers, they believe, use false, misleading, or deceptive measures to foist products on an unsuspecting public. They pollute the public's mind and its environment with their messages.

Despite these criticisms, advertising is one of the vital links in the modern economic chain. It is a major way of getting information to a consumer—information that a consumer often wants and needs. For example, a billboard near an interstate highway telling the location of a gas station may be an eyesore to some, but to the driver who is low on gas, it provides a vital piece of information.

Those who say that they never pay attention to advertising are not being honest. To live in today's society means receiving the messages of advertisers. There are few places people can go where advertising will not reach them. Even the "non-commercial" public broadcasting system contains advertisements in the form of credits to those who contribute to its programming and promotional spots for upcoming shows. One estimate has the individual consumer confronted with 1,600 advertising messages every day.

Not only do people pay attention to advertising messages, but they often act according to those messages. Advertising works. Check around any room in your house, and you will find plenty of items purchased, in part at least, because of the advertising you have encountered.

The field of advertising

The person who wants to enter the field of advertising has chosen an exciting and challenging profession. Advertising copywriters must be willing to work long and difficult hours researching their products and audiences and straining their creative forces to be successful. Like other writers for the mass media, they must understand the language and be willing caretakers of it. They must be willing to change their creativity into forms that others are willing to pay for and support. The rewards to the few who are able to do well in this profession are great.

Two concepts should form the base of a student's thinking about writing advertising copy.

Advertising copy is a different form of writing than the ones that we have studied in other parts of this book. Its purpose is to persuade and motivate. The basic precepts of good writing—simplicity, brevity, accuracy, word precision—remain in force with writing advertising copy as they do with all other forms of writing.

Advertising is based on the assumption that words have the power to produce a change—a change in thinking, attitudes, beliefs, and ultimately, behavior. Advertising that does not accomplish this, or aid in accomplishing it, is worthless. Copywriters must select the words and ideas that will help produce this change.

The process of advertising copywriting is in many ways the same as the process of news writing. The copywriter must process information and put it into an acceptable form for its medium. Like the newswriter, the advertising copywriter must conduct research before the writing begins. He or she must decide what is important enough to use and what should be left out.   The copywriter must choose the words and the structure for the copy that will best fit the product, media, and purpose for the advertising. The copywriter, like the newswriter, is subject to many editors—not the least of whom is the client who is paying for the advertising and whose ideas about advertising copy may differ radically from those of the copywriter.

But what about the "creative process"? Doesn't advertising copy require more creativity on the part of the writer than newswriting? In some respects, it does. Ad copywriters have a greater variety of forms for their work than do newswriters, and they have more tools with which to work.

Figure 7-1
Development of an advertisement
The process of writing an advertisement takes into account many factors, as pictured in this figure. We will discuss each of these factors in this chapter.

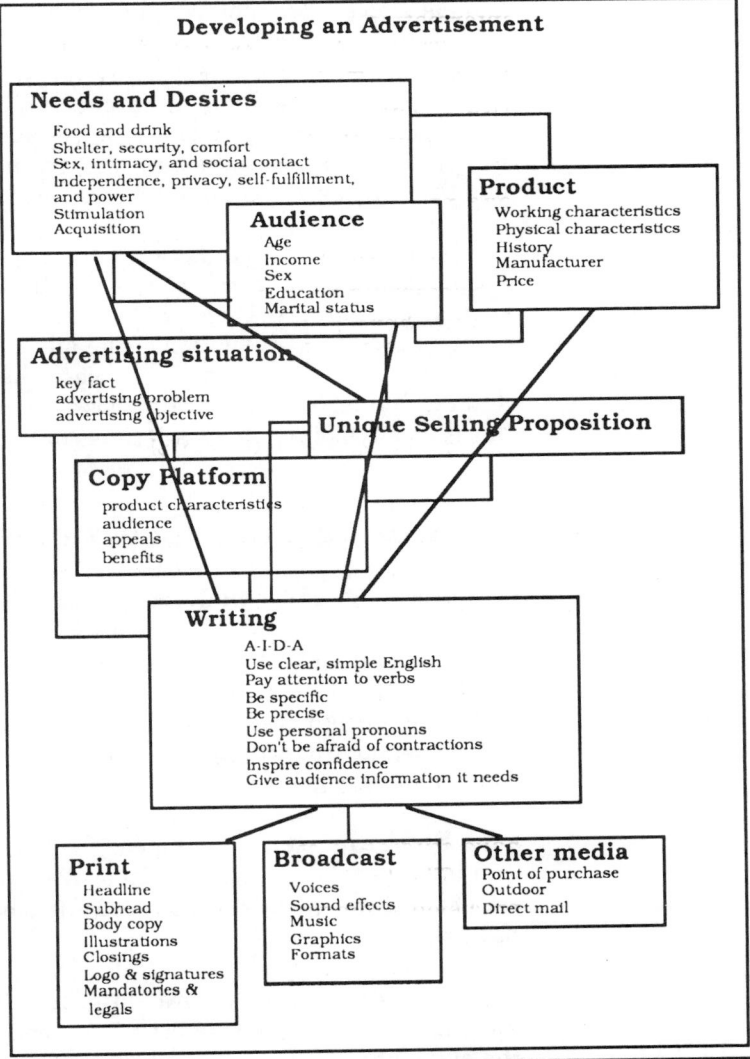

Those entering the field of advertising make a serious mistake, however, if they believe that because advertising requires creativity, they have complete license to write what they want when they want. A prime example of what many would consider a lack of creativity is found in the advertising for many Procter and Gamble products—household items such as Tide and toothpaste such as Crest. Advertisements for these products rarely win awards given to the more "creative" or attention-getting ads for the competition. Yet many of these products—backed by a large advertising budget—take a lion's share of their market, and Procter and Gamble remains one of the biggest spenders in the advertising industry. The evidence at the cash register is that the ads for these products work, despite their lack of creativity, and that is the kind of evidence that a client wants.

On the other hand, highly innovative approaches for ads are often effective, especially when products have established and well-rooted competition and when the purpose of the ad is to gain the consumer's attention. Possibly the leading proponent of the off-the-wall approach is Joe Sedelmaier of Sedelmaier Productions in Chicago. In 1984, Sedelmaier created an ad for Wendy's fast food chain that had an elderly lady in front of a fast food counter (at the competition's store, not Wendy's) shouting, "Where's the beef?!" That cry was taken up by a presidential candidate that year and became part of the national lexicon. More importantly for Wendy's and Sedelmaier, revenues for the fast food chain jumped 31 percent, net income went up 24 percent, and average sales per restaurant rose 13 percent from the previous year. Much of the credit for these increases was given to Sedelmaier's off-beat approach— one that he has repeated for clients such as Federal Express and General Motors Acceptance Corp.

Sedelmaier demands total creative control as a condition for taking on a client. His agency is one of the few that can do that. Most clients, whether they are spending a large or small amount of money on the advertising, want a say in the final production of the ad. A copywriter must take copy through a variety of approval stages, a process that demands a great deal of research and discipline. The creative process is a part of the process of producing copy, but it is only a part, and sometimes only a small part, of it.

Beginning the process: needs and appeals

The process of writing advertising copy begins with a recognition on the part of the copywriter that all humans have certains needs and desires. Effective advertising appeals to these needs and desires in a way that will make people act positively toward a product or an idea. We live in a consumer-oriented society where the list of needs and desires is a fairly long one. The first step in producing advertising copy is to examine some of the needs and desires of humans in a very general way.

Food and drink. The need for food and drink is among the most basic and universal needs that we have. We must have food and water daily to sustain ourselves. Beyond that, we want food and drink that is nourishing and palatable.

Shelter, security and comfort. Next to food and drink, one of our most basic needs is for shelter. We need a way of protecting ourselves from the elements.

Following closely on to the need for shelter is the need for security, the need to feel that we are protected from various dangers. Rational people understand that they cannot insulate themselves from every danger, but they can take some steps to ensure that they are not victims of certain calamities.

Once shelter and security are established, people want to feel comfortable. Physically, they want to be without pain, they want to be warm when it is cold and cool when it is hot. They want to live, work, and play in a comfortable and pleasing environment.

Sex, intimacy and social contact. Most people need to have contact with other people. That contact can take various forms in various stages of our lives. Our social relationships are important to us, no matter what form they take. They can be based on sexual intimacy, friendship, or casual contact. Whatever they are, we remain social beings, and lack of such contact can have physical as well as emotional consequences.

Independence, privacy, self-fulfillment and power. While we need social contact, we also have a countervailing need for independence and privacy. We need privacy even from those to whom we feel the closest. We have the urge to "get away from it all," and occasionally we do that, even if that means we simply draw inward rather than removing ourselves physically.

Related to this need is that for independence. Although we are social beings, we are also individuals, and we need to feel that we can develop our own personalities. This need for individual development continues through adulthood and governs many of our actions. We are all different from one another, and we need to confirm that to ourselves.

Independence is part of a greater need for self-fulfillment, much of which is met for many by their work. We need to be engaged in constructive activity that will give us satisfaction and confirm our worth as individuals. For many, the highest fulfillment of this need lies in the work we choose as adults.

At its best, the need for power means that we are able to make our own decisions and in some way control our own environments. Child psychologists argued that this need is one of the most important that children have. At a very early age, children need to be able to make choices—even if they are very small ones—so that they can develop their individuality. Adults also need to feel that they are in control of their lives and their surroundings. This need, of course, can develop into a need to control the lives of others. Many of us have this tendency to some degree, and our places in society may dictate that we exercise this power. Parents, particularly, feel the need to control the environment and actions of their children.

Stimulation. The need to be stimulated—to find life interesting—is one of the most important that we have. Despite the habits and routines that people have for themselves, they need to feel that life holds a variety of experiences. They read books, watch television, go to parties, shop, and engage in a variety of other activities in part to entertain themselves. Occasionally, they need to be excited, to have the feeling that something is going to offer them special enjoyment or a unique feeling.

Acquisition. The number and variety of goods and services that are available to those in Western industrial societies in particular would boggle the minds of people in other cultures and from other centuries. The availability of those goods and services has stimulated within many a need to acquire things. Part of our development as individuals is the acquisition of goods that go beyond those that meet our basic needs of food, clothing, and shelter.

On occasion the need overcomes common sense and the bounds of rationality. For instance, news reports coming from the Philippines in 1985 said that Imelda Marcos, wife of the deposed dictator of that country, had a closet full of shoes—more than 3,000 pairs. Her shoe collection became one of the standing jokes of the year, and she became a symbol of a consumer who was beyond conspicuous. What possible use, many wondered, could she have had for so many shoes?

Yet there is some of Imelda Marcos in many of us. Many people acquire

**Figure 7-2
Differing appeals**
The two ads below try to accomplish the same thing with the same audience. They make very different appeals, however.

What does this man know that you don't?

If you're not a regular reader of a newspaper, probably a lot.

Reading a newspaper every day tells you a lot about yourself, your community and your world – much more than television ever could or ever will. If you really want to know about what's going on, read a newspaper.

Don't say 'no' to knowing – read a newspaper.

Sponsored by the National Council on Newspaper Readership.

things for the sake of acquiring them—not because they are useful or because we need them for basic purposes. Children "collect" things like dolls, baseball cards, rocks, etc., and that collecting syndrome carries over into adulthood.

The foregoing list contains just a few of the needs that we all have. There are many others. The consideration of needs is one of the most important parts of the process of developing effective advertising copy. To understand that people need, or feel they need, certain things is vital to formulating the appeals that advertising can use.

Appeals are the words, phrases, and ideas used by advertising copywriters to tap into the needs of the audience. It is in formulating these appeals

Boring?
Hardly.

Newspaper readers don't often complain about being bored.

Television tells you what to watch. Newspapers let you choose. That's why you don't hear newspaper readers complaining about newspapers being boring. There's always something there to entertain them.

Treat yourself – read a newspaper.

Sponsored by the National Council on Newspaper Readership.

that copywriters must choose their langue carefully. They must understand that certain words, even those that may have similar meanings, can evoke strikingly different images. The copywriter must have a highly developed ear for the language to couple with an understanding of the needs of the audience.

Just what needs are most salient to an audience? The next section discusses how marketers find this out.

The audience

Most manufacturers and advertisers want to sell as many units of their product as possible. They recognize, however, that most products are not universal; that is, not everyone will want what they sell. In addition, distributing a product to a massive audience can be costly. Consequently, it is not efficient to try to sell most products to everyone. Marketing a product or service begins with deciding what part of the population is most likely to buy it.

In considering the audience for a product, advertisers need to think about two groups. One is the people who are already using the product. They cannot be taken for granted. Many advertisements are directed at reinforcing the behavior of people who have already bought a product. (For instance, readers of car advertisements in magazines are often those who have already bought the car; they are simply trying to reinforce their belief that they made the correct decision.) Advertisers need to have some idea of how strong a user's loyalty is to a product.

The second group is people who do not use the product but are most likely to. These potential users provide the greatest opportunity for product sales to grow. Finding out who they are and what kind of advertising message is most likely to motivate them is the job of market research, and the answers have a direct effect on the advertising copywriter.

How does an advertiser get this information? Researchers can employ a variety of methods for this purpose. They may include personal interview surveys, telephone surveys, mail surveys, focus-group interviews, consumer product testing, intercept interviewing (the kind of interviewing conducted by people in shopping malls), and many other methods. The data produced by this research are vital to the advertising copywriter.

The major concept that the beginning advertising copywriter must understand is that of **demographics.** Demographics is a way of dividing the population into groups. People who share many of the same demographic characteristics are likely to share many consumer behaviors. In the 1980s, the term "yuppie" was coined to describe an important segment of the population. A yuppie is a young, upwardly mobile professional. All of these categories are demographic characteristics, and they provide researchers with a way of looking at different segments of the population.

There are many demographic categories. The following section discusses some of the most basic demographic characteristics.

Age. How old people are is one of the most common determinants of how likely they are to use many products and services. Our needs and desires change as we get older, and often they change in the same way for most of us. Most children want toys, but as they get older, the desire for toys decreases and the desire for other products increases. The changes that accompany age are not only physical but also psychological and emotional.

Gender. Boys and girls are different; men and women are different. These differences are of primary importance to the advertiser. These groups have different needs and desires, due not only to different physical characteristics but also to differing roles they are likely to play in society. For instance, within a household, a man is more likely to earn more money, but a woman is more likely to make most of the household buying decisions.

Income. How much money people have to spend is important in determining how likely they are to buy a product. Some products and services are marketed to people who do not have as much income as others, and the appeal the advertisers use is often based on price. This kind of appeal is likely to motivate potential customers. On the other hand, many producers want to direct their advertising toward an "upscale" audience, those who have high incomes or whose incomes are likely to increase.

Education. Education is an important demographic variable for two reasons. One is based on the assumption that education changes people; it changes their attitudes and values. For instance, the more education people have, the more likely they are to place a value on getting an education. The second is that education is often related to the demographic characteristic of income. The more education a person has, the more likely that person is to have a higher income.

Marital status. If a person is married, that means he or she is in a household. That inevitably leads to different consumer behavior than if that person were single. Knowing whether or not a person is married is important for the advertiser because of the different appeals that may be used to sell a product.

There are many other demographic characteristics that advertisers may need to consider in finding the consumers for their products. For instance, race, home ownership, number of adults and children in a household, occupation, place of residence, and type of housing are just a few of the many variables that can be examined by researchers.

As a step in developing an advertisement, an advertiser might want to draw a "demographic profile" of those who use the product already or those who are potential users. For instance, a manufacturer might find that those who have found the product are women between the ages of eighteen and thirty, single, with at least a high school education. Chances are that not all consumers who fit this profile are buying the product, so advertising directed at this group might not only persuade others to buy it but also reinforce those who already do. On the other hand, an advertiser may decide that the product could be marketed to older women as well as to those already likely to buy it. In that case, the advertiser might use a different appeal—one that would work for women thirty-one to forty years old.

In addition to these demographic factors, advertisers must also take into account psychographic variables. In general, psychographic variables refer to the values and attitudes of people and how they feel toward various things in their environment. Market researchers want to know what people feel is important and valuable. If people use a product, they want to know how they feel about that product and if they are likely to use it again.

As you can tell, making decisions based on just this small amount of in-

Figure 7-3
The product factor in advertising
The design of the Macintosh, unusual
for a computer, helped establish its
place in the market.

formation is not a simple task. An advertiser may take a variety of routes in marketing a product. Good research is essential to making the correct decisions about marketing and advertising. But the audience is only one factor to be considered in trying to sell a product; of equal importance is the product itself.

The product

Along with knowing who the audience is for a product, the advertising copywriter must know the product itself. To say this is to state the obvious, but knowledge of the product—particularly from the standpoint of developing advertising for it—is not as simple as it might first seem. (Note here that when we talk about a product, we are speaking of anything the advertising is designed to promote. It could be a product, such as a vacuum cleaner, a business, such as an auto body repair shop, or an idea, such as quitting smoking.)

The advertising copywriter must ask, "What is it about this product that I am trying to sell?" The answer may come from a close examination of the product, and it may be surprising.

First, the copywriter should know **what the product does.** A vacuum cleaner may clean a floor, but how it cleans the floor may be important to the advertising of the product. Does it introduce some new cleaning method—something that no other vacuum cleaner on the market does? A line of sofas may come in fifteen different patterns; it may also be comfortable to sit on. Which one does the copywriter emphasize? A copywriter may find that there are a number of advertiseable facts about any product, and someone—the copywriter, the advertiser or a combination of them—will have to decide what it is about the product that will be advertised.

The **physical characteristics of the product** also provide the copywriter with some useful considerations in developing the advertising. Sometimes a product will be designed to do a job more efficiently than competing products. Sometimes it will be designed to do a part of a job. Small, hand-held vacuum cleaners are vacuum cleaners, but they're not meant to vacuum an entire house, or even an entire room. They're for small jobs that need to be done quickly. The physical characteristics of the product help promote the feeling that the product can do the job.

Sometimes the physical characteristics of a product can have little to do with how the product works, but they can still be useful in helping to sell the product. When the Macintosh computer was introduced by the Apple Computer Company in 1984 (with an engrossing surreal commercial aired only once, during the Super Bowl that year), one of the characteristics that helped set the Macintosh apart from other computers was its unique, small, box-like design. That design helped establish the Macintosh as "the computer for the rest of us," as its advertising slogan said. One of the most legendary campaigns in the history of advertising, the 1960s promotion of the Volkswagen Beetle, also used the car's unique shape to distinguish it from other cars. Some of the ads even poked some good-natured fun at the car in order to establish this difference in the minds of the consumers.

The **history and reputation of a product** are characteristics that also need consideration when formulating advertising. A product may have a long history, and that may be something that a copywriter will want to emphasize. Many businesses use the phrase, "Established in —— (year)" to let people know that they have been around for a long time and thus can be considered reliable and stable. If a product has existed only a short time but has gained a good reputation, the advertisement may reflect that reputation.

Sometimes an advertising campaign will be designed to overcome the history or reputation of a product. It could be that the product has not worked particularly well, and a manufacturer has taken steps to correct that. Or, it may be that manufacturers want to sell the product to a different audience. One classic case of this redefinition of a product was done by Miller Brewing Company. For many years, its main product had been known as the "Champagne of Bottled Beers." The slogan had little appeal for the Sunday afternoon, football-watching crowd, who were mostly men. When Miller began making a lite beer, Miller Lite, the company sponsored a series of commercials that had ex-jocks arguing as to whether the product "tastes great" or was "less filling." The commercials were good entertainment in themselves, but they also established Miller Lite as a beer that could be enjoyed while watching a football game.

Another classic advertising campaign that reestablished a product was the one the Chicago-based advertising agency Leo Burnett developed for Marlboro cigarettes. Marlboro had been a red-filtered cigarette when filtered cigarettes were thought to be products for women. Marlboro also had the slogan "mild as the month of May." Burnett developed a series of ads that put the cigarette in the hands of men and put those men outdoors. Eventually, the Marlboro Man, a rugged outdoorsman (usually a cowboy with a horse), became a staple of the advertising industry. The campaign was so successful that the Marlboro Man is still with us today, more than thirty years after he was created.

The **manufacturer of a product** is another characteristic about a product that an advertising copywriter may want to give attention to. Many products are indistinguishable from their competition, but if the manufacturer is well-known and has a reputation for reliability and stability, that can help set the product apart. International Business Machines (IBM) has a reputation for servicing its products, and that has established for IBM a broader reputation for reliability. IBM often uses this reputation in advertising its individual products. More recently IBM advertising has tried to build on this reputation by emphasizing its ability to find innovative solutions to computing problems.

Many advertising and marketing campaigns emphasize the brand name of a product. This emphasis occurs for a number of reasons. Consumers often exercise what is called "brand loyalty." Having made a decision to buy a product at some point, many people are reluctant to change. A brand may also be positively associated with other products that carry the name. Nabisco, for example, appears on a number of crackers and cookies because of the strong brand identification that name has. Such identification makes a product, especially a new one, easier to sell.

One of the most important product characteristics is **price**. People want to know how much something costs. They also want to believe that they are getting the best product for the money they spend. Sometimes, price is the most notable factor about a product, and it will be the characteristic the copywriter will want to feature.

Another factor copywriters will want to consider is the **competition** that a product has. Much of what we have said already has made reference to a product's competition and the means by which advertising can distinguish it from others like it. Rarely is a product the only one of its kind. It may have some individual characteristics, but there are usually other items that will accomplish the same task. One of the copywriter's main jobs is to set a product apart from its competition.

The list of product characteristics just discussed is only an indication of the many variables that may be considered in developing advertising for a product. The key here is that the copywriter should know as much about the product as possible so that the best characteristics may be selected for the advertising.

In advertising terms, this process is called finding the Unique Selling Proposition (USP). A product's USP will give potential consumers their first clue as to why they should want to buy that product. Once a USP has been identified, the selling process has begun.

Finally, advertisers must recognize the **social aspects of their advertising**, that is how their products and advertising fit into society and whether or not the approaches they use are appropriate. For example, many women feel that much of the advertising for and about them is degrading. One watchdog group, Women Against Pornography, annually gives awards to advertisers who use non-sexist approaches in their advertising, and at the same time the group criticizes advertisers who, according to the group, degrade women. In 1983, the group criticized the Hanes company for the way it implied in its hosiery ads that men preferred women with "shapely, sexy, silky legs."

More recently, the British auto maker Austin Rover received many compaints about an ad that focused on the walnut interior of one of its models and quotes an old English saying, "A woman, a dog, a walnut tree, the more you beat them, the better they'll be." The makers of Opium and Obsession perfumes have also been criticized by those who believe that the names of these products and their advertising glamorizes degrading conditions within society.

The Center for Science in the Public Interest has criticized the alcoholic beverage industry for ads which it said were aimed at starting young people to drink and at inducing alcoholics to return to the bottle. Ethnic minorities are often sensitive to the way in which they are portrayed, and advertisers are wise to be aware of their concerns.

This is not to say that advertising should always avoid controversy and that advertisers should construct ads so bland that absolutely no one will be offended. Controversy might well be an advisable marketing strategy, as when Burger King directly criticized McDonald's in a recent advertising campaign. The point here is that advertisers should never be surprised at the effects of their ads. They should know what society, or groups in society, expect of them, and they should have thought through their advertising campaigns well enough so that the ads produce the intended results.

The advertising situation

The marketing environment is an important consideration in the development of an ad. This environment is created by the audience and product—factors which have already been discussed, but also by the more immediate situation surrounding the advertisement. We are at the point where the copywriter is beginning to make decisions that will determine the content of the ad.

First, ad writers must know and be able to state the **key fact** about an advertising situation. This key fact sets the stage for the thinking about an ad, and writers who do not have a key fact clearly in mind will be confused and prone to wander in several directions. The key fact may involve the competition: A new product may have entered the market two years ago and now accounts for more than fifty percent of the sales in the market. The key fact may involve the audience: Few people know about the product. The key fact could involve the product itself: Some improvements have been made in the product. Discovering this key fact is sometimes difficult and time consuming. It often takes extensive research and discussion with the manufacturers. But being able to write down the key fact of the situation orders the thinking of the advertiser and helps to produce effective ads more efficiently.

Distilling the key fact of the advertising situation leads directly to the next step in the process of ad development: **stating the problem that the ad should solve.** The problem statement should be a specific one and should evolve from the key fact. For example, the key fact may be: A product's percentage of the market is down. The problem then would be: The product's share of the market needs to be raised. Problems may also involve the product itself: The product has a bad reputation; or the product costs more than its competitors.

If the key fact and the problem of the advertising situation are clear in an advertising copywriter's mind, the third step in the process should follow: **the objective of the advertisement.** The objective needs to be stated clearly and precisely. Just what is the advertisement supposed to do? The following are some statements of advertising objectives: the ad should make people aware of the product; the ad should change people's attitudes toward the product; the ad should tell consumers of the product's improvements; the ad should encourage people to shift from buying another product to buying this product.

Once an advertiser has thought through to this point—and assuming that the proper amount of research has been done—the next step is to develop a copy platform.

Copy platforms

A copy platform is a way of getting the ideas and information of an advertising situation down on paper and of organizing those ideas in such a way that effective advertising copy can be produced from them. A copy platform is not an ad itself, but it will contain many of the ideas that will later appear in the ad, and it will provide valuable information for the ad copywriter. One version of a copy platform is on page 179 in this book, but it is not the only type of copy platform there is. Copy platforms vary according to the advertising agency and the advertiser, but most contain this basic information.

The copy platform is where many of the factors in developing an ad begin to come together. The copywriter must finally commit what he or she has learned about a product and about an audience to paper and develop ideas from the information that is there. The example of the copy platform in this chapter shows some of the elements that make up the platform. Note that the advertising problem is the first piece of information that is called for in the copy platform. Stating this problem directly and simply sets the stage for many of the other ideas that will appear on the copy platform. A problem may be encountering a number of different advertising situations, but generally the copywriter will zero in on just one—the one that the advertiser considers the most important. The product characteristics are those that might be helpful in formulating the ad. This list cannot be all-inclusive; the copywriter will have to limit the list to those items that relate directly to the advertising problem and items that might otherwise make the product distinctive and beneficial to the consumer.

The advertising objective is then drawn directly from the advertising problem. The objective should be a way of solving the problem.

The target market is the audience to whom the advertising will be directed. A description of this audience should be stated as simply and specifically as possible. Knowing exactly who the audience is will help the copywriter in coming up with the next, and most important, part of the copy platform—the statement of benefit and appeal.

Advertising should tell its audience the benefit of a product—the "what's in it for me." The advertising should state, implicitly or explicitly, why the product or service is good for the consumer, why the consumer should buy it, or what the consumer can expect from it. This statement of benefit and appeal is the most persuasive part of an advertisement, and its importance cannot be overestimated. Here are a few examples:

> You'll save money if you buy our product.
> You'll be safer if you use our product.
> You'll live in more comfort if you have our product.

These benefits relate directly to the discussion of needs and wants at the beginning of this chapter. Such appeals are highly potent ones for advertising, and they have been highly effective in many advertising campaigns.

The creative theme in a copy platform allows the copywriter to use some imagination in formulating the appeals of the advertising. The creative theme might be a slogan, or it might be a description of the way in which the advertising will be presented.

Supportive selling points is a list of product characteristics or factors about the advertising situation that will help sell a product. They may vary somewhat from the main statement of benefit, but they can be used to reinforce a tendency to use the product.

Writing the ad

With the copy platform in place, the copywriter is almost ready to write an ad. Among the decisions that still need to be made are which medium the advertisements will appear in, how many ads there will be for a product, when they will be placed, how large or long the ads will be, etc. All of these are marketing decisions that go beyond the scope of this book. Our focus here is the writing of the advertisement.

This section looks at some of the common ad writing practices and guidelines. There are few "rules" in the writing of an advertisement, and there are no dominant structures for ads as there are for news stories and for broadcast news. Instead, each ad is a combination of the factors already discussed in this chapter, plus the limits and opportunities provided by the medium in which the ad is placed.

Still, there are some things that we can say generally about the writing of advertisements. One of the oldest advertising copywriting formulas is A-I-D-A: attention, interest, desire, action. According to this formula, an ad should do four things, in this order. It should gain the attention of the viewer or listener. An ad that doesn't do at least this is not going to be able to do anything else.

Figure 7-4 Copy platforms
The copy platform to the right (for a fictitious product) shows how a copy platform can be put together.

Copy Platform

Ad Subject: General Motors Spinout
Ad Problem: This new model needs to gain some identity and find its place in the market.

Product Characteristics:
reasonably priced against competing models
dependably built (experts say it should have an excellent maintenance record)

Advertising Objective: Help model establish itself by building on brand loyalty to GM.

Target Market: Young, single people who are just graduating from college, ages 21-24. These folks have just taken their first job and need transportation.

Competition: Toyota Tercel, Honda Civic, Ford Escort.

Statement of Benefit or Appeal:
1) Spinout is reasonably priced.
2) Spinout is a member of the GM family.
3) Spinout is dependable.

Creative Theme:
Take the spin -- Spinout.

Supportive Selling Points:
1) Depreciation in 3 years expected to be only about 30 percent.
2) Part of GM, so it's built in America.
3) Priced so that someone starting out can afford it.

After getting the consumer's attention, the ad must hold his or her interest. The ad should use words and pictures that will draw the reader or listener into the ideas that the ad is trying to present. An ad may be about an interesting or important subject, but it can be so dull that the consumer is lost before the message gets across.

The ad should create a desire for the product, service, or idea presented in the ad. It is important for the copywriter to choose the appeal, the benefits, and the proper words that will develop this desire.

Finally, the ad should stimulate the consumer to some action. In most cases, what you want the consumer to do is go out and buy the product.

With this formula in mind, we will look at some of the commonly accepted guidelines for writing effective advertisements.

Use clear, simple English. This rule reappears throughout this book. It is basic to communication in the mass media. Obscure words and complex sentences will not encourage people to read an advertisement. You cannot impress someone with your wide vocabulary in an advertisement.

Another reason for using simple language, particularly in advertising, is that it is more believable. People will tend to believe advertising messages that are presented to them in language they use or are used to hearing.

Figure 7-5
Advertising critique
The headline of the ad to the right offers a benefit to the reader; the headline of the ad on page 181 —combined with the illustration—is designed to get the attention of the reader.

Notice the liberal use of pronouns in both ads, particularly the one on the right.

Notice, too, the short, direct sentences. Each one builds on the previous one.

The ad to the right gives the location of the store and the hours of operation.

Now You Don't Have to Go Out of Your Way To Be Good

You know frozen yogurt is good for you. Better than ice cream. But until now, you had to travel more than a mile from campus to get it.
Now there's Milo's – just two blocks from the center of campus.
All the frozen yogurt you want, any time you want it.
New flavors every day, plus all your old favorites.

See how good being good can be.

Milo's Frozen Yogurt

323 Elm Street
Open 11 a.m. to Midnight every day.

Pay attention to the verbs. Verbs are the most important part of the language. If your ad has mostly "to be" verb forms (is, are, was, were, etc.), the ad will probably sound flat and lifeless. If it contains mostly action verbs, it will be alive and interesting.

Good copywriters use verbs, rather than adjectives, to describe their product. They associate verbs with how the product looks, what it does, and how it makes the user feel. A list of those verbs helps them develop good advertising copy.

Another rule about the verbs in advertising copy is to stick with the present tense (whenever appropriate) and the active voice (almost always). The present tense implies immediacy and puts the reader into an advertisement more quickly. The active voice allows the writer to make a stronger statement than the passive voice.

Be as specific as possible, but don't let too many details get in the way of the advertising message. An advertisement should be balanced. Facts—specifics—are more likely to sell a product than general ideas or concepts. Yet too many facts are likely to confuse the reader or listener. Consumers like to have reasons to buy a product, and an ad should give them enough of those reasons that they will be motivated to do so.

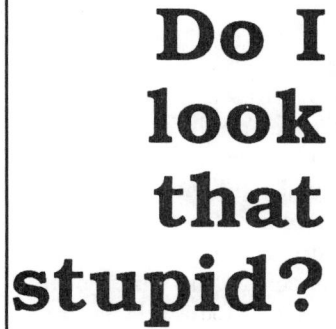

Do I look that stupid?

You think I don't know it when you buy me cheap dog food. You think I don't understand that you're trying to save a few pennies at my expense. I'm the guy who's here every day when you get home – giving you a lift, no matter how I feel. Think about that the next time you reach for that cheap dog food at the grocery store, and ask yourself, "Is this what he deserves?"

A message from the dog's point of view, brought to you by
Gino's Dog Chow
"The best there is for your dog."

Be precise in the use of the language. Here's where intelligence, art, and creativity mix together for the copywriter. The copywriter needs to know the language intimately. He or she should be sensitive to the subtle meanings of words—not just their dictionary meanings but the images they provoke.

For example, the words "laugh," "giggle," and "guffaw" have essentially the same meaning, but they provoke different images. Most of us laugh; little boys and girls giggle; old men don't usually giggle but guffaw; and so on. Writers need to understand the subtle differences between words and to take unusual care with them. They need to select the words for their copy that evoke exactly the images that they want to convey; that will describe the product in exactly the way they mean for it to be described. You should select the words that relate directly to the benefit you are presenting with the product.

Use personal pronouns when appropriate. Let the reader, listener, or viewer of an advertisement know that you are talking directly to him or her. Using personal pronouns, especially "you," is an effective way to do that, but like any good idea, it can be overdone. Occasionally, you should ask a question (although only occasionally; we'll discuss this more in the next section).

Don't be afraid of contractions. Contractions are a good way of making sure that your tone is informal, and the informal tone is preferable in most advertisements. Like personal pronouns, they can be used too much, particularly if they sound forced. A copywriter should develop an "ear" for the language and recognize when a piece of copy "sounds" right or wrong. If a contraction sounds right, use it.

Inspire confidence in the product and the advertiser. Ads should contain messages that will help people believe and trust a product. They should not sacrifice a long-range trust for a short-term goal. They should, however, tell an audience that the product being advertised is one that will benefit them and will live up to expectations. Not only should the messages in an ad inspire such confidence, but the ad itself should contribute toward this goal. Ads that are in good taste, that use English properly, that are not cutesy or smart-alecky, and that do not insult the audience are the kinds of ads that build confidence. A manufacturer should be as proud of the ads commissioned for a product as of the product itself. Advertisement writers should feel that same pride in what they produce.

Give the audience all the information it needs. An ad does not have to tell everything about a product or a manufacturer, but it should not leave hanging any major questions about the product or service being advertised. For example, a power company recently advertised that energy audits were available to its customers. These audits involved representatives of the power company coming to the home, inspecting it, and recommending actions to increase the efficient use of energy. The service was free. What the ad did not say was how a customer could get this service: Whom should the customer call or write; what was the procedure? The ad left the clear impression that the power company was not very interested in having customers take advantage of this service.

Elements of a print ad

Unlike the newspaper reporter, who generally does not have anything to do with the physical appearance of a story in the newspaper, an advertising copywriter must always be aware of the design of an ad. Design is an integral part of the ad writing process, and it often is a determining factor in what the ad says. In this section we will discuss the different parts of a print ad, keeping in mind that, depending on the work situation, it may or may not be the copywriter's job to design the ad as well as write the copy.

Illustration. The illustration an ad uses is often the most important attention-getting item in that ad. It is the part of an ad most likely to achieve the attention-getting part of the A-I-D-A formula. While we are not concerned here with the design of the ad or the selection of the illustration, the copywriter will often write the copy based on the kind of illustration that is used. The illustration, the headline and the body copy—the three most important parts of the ad—must be closely tied to one another. If the relationship between these three elements is not readily apparent, the ad runs the risk of losing the reader who will not want to figure it out.

Headline. The headline is often the most important part of an ad because it gives the reader the first solid information about the advertisement. The headline will most often achieve the "interest" part of the A-I-D-A formula and will determine whether or not the reader's interest is aroused enough to read the rest of the ad.

The most effective headlines appeal to the self-interest of the reader—the "what's in it for me?" The copywriter must decide what appeal is being made and what benefit is being offered.

The headline should consist of just a few carefully chosen words (many ad writers say the limit is eight words) that will set the tone for the ad and implicitly promise some reward to the reader for reading through the ad. Many advertising copywriters believe that headlines in ads should be treated much like headlines for news stories in newspapers. That is, they should give the reader some information that the reader does not already have. Although this approach is not the only one to writing headlines in ads, it is a useful one for many ads.

A headline may deliver a promise about a product. It may challenge an assumption on the part of the reader. It may make a claim about a product. It may play on the reputation of the advertiser. It may simply try to provoke a mood for the reader.

Above all, headlines should involve the reader in the ad quickly. They may do this by asking a question ("When will you get an opportunity like this again?"), offering some information ("How to save money"), or making a provocative statement ("Not all men are created equal").

Finally, caution should be exercised when writing headlines. Some headlines are clearly misleading and inappropriate, and an advertiser will use these at his or her peril. Misleading or deceptive headlines can get an advertiser into legal trouble, and inappropriate headlines can destroy the advertiser's credibility with the reader.

Subheads. Subheads allow the copywriter an opportunity to expand on what has been said in the main headline. They also allow the writer to introduce new material that may draw the reader into an ad. Subheads are set in

Figure 7-6
Advertising headline
These headlines demonstrate the wide variety of techniques available to get the attention of the reader.

Invest your cash where you can get to it. But taxes can't.

Here's a better way to manage your money

Amazing!

Be all that you can be

There are a million reasons to celebrate the New Year. Here are three.

We've figured out a new way to look at the bottom line

While others talk about the future, we deliver it.

How fast can you make it through the grocery store these days?

Saturday and Sunday Specials

Entire Stock 50% Off

a smaller size of type than the main headline, and they are generally longer. Most often, the thoughts presented in a subhead are tied to those presented in the main headline. For instance, if the main headline poses a question, the subhead may answer it, as in the following example:

IS NOW THE TIME TO BUY A NEW CAR?
Most experts agree that it is.

Not every advertisement needs a subhead. They are not attention-getting devices; rather, they are informational devices, and they should be used only when necessary and appropriate.

Body copy. The body copy is the heart of the advertisement. If the art and headline get the attention of the reader, the body copy is where the reader should be rewarded for taking the time to read the ad. That reward should come in the form of information about the product being advertised and answers to questions raised explicitly and implicitly in the headline.

Writing body copy can take a number of approaches. The factual approach is a direct one. Essentially, it says: Here is some information about the product; here is why you should buy it. The narrative approach is a less direct one. It generally tells a story about the product, emphasizing the selling points of the product. The narrative approach is used when the ad needs to hold the attention of the reader. The stories or situations used in a narrative approach should be projective. That is, they should be situations that the readers can relate to or imagine themselves in.

The rules for writing body copy are the same as those for writing in any part of the mass media—simplicity, brevity, word precision, etc. Ad copywriters should take special care with the verbs they use and think of them as the chief descriptors of a product.

Avoid mistakes in grammar. Mistakes call attention to the writing and not to the message. Sentence fragments—one or two words or short phrases that do not make complete sentences—can be acceptable, but they must be de-

Figure 7-7
Copy sheets
This figure shows how copy is translated from a copy sheet to the completed ad.

Copy Sheet

Product: Sun Spa Systems membership
Medium: Newspaper
Client: Sun Spa Systems
Writer: Smith

Headline: Feeling like a beached whale?

Subhead:

Body copy:
It's been a long winter. Cold. Damp.
Exercise? You kidding?
But spring is coming, and those days at the beach lurk in the near future.
You need to get in shape - quick.
At Sun System Spa, we can help. We've got a full line of exercise equipment and a full schedule of exercise classes - led by trained instructors.

Subhead or slogan
Let us help you
get out of the sand
and onto the beach.

Signature: Sun Spa Systems, 3929 Muscle Beach Road
Call us today at 333-6666

liberate, and the writer should exercise complete control of the language.

Avoid exaggeration. Saying that something is the "greatest in the world" or even "the cheapest in town" is not likely to help sell a product. Readers are more likely to want facts and specifics.

The writer should have a simple message in mind, and everything in the body copy should relate to that message.

Tell the reader what you want him or her to do—"Call today," "Go out and buy it," or "Clip this coupon." Whatever the action is, do not assume that the reader will know it without being told.

Above all, the copy should be interesting if not compelling.

Closings. Closings may be thought of as subheads that come after body copy rather than before it. A closing will make a fairly strong point for the reader. Often it will summarize what the body copy has been implying. Sometimes, it will give a direct command to the reader; at other times, it will only suggest that the reader do something. Like the subhead, a closing may not be necessary for every advertisement.

Mandatories, including legals. Mandatories are items that must be included in the advertisement. For instance, an advertiser may want an ad to mention the name of the company president or that a product is manufactured in a certain area. The words, "an equal opportunity employer," are a mandatory for the employment ads of many organizations.

Legals are items that are required by law to be in an ad. For instance, all cigarette ads must give the Surgeon General's warning; all automobile ads must include the mileage ratings. The Federal Trade Commission and other federal agencies, such as the Food and Drug Administration, have issued many regulations about the content of advertisements. These regulations often require that certain things be in an advertisement. A professional copywriter must be familiar with these regulations if the ads he or she writes are to remain legal.

Slogans, logos, signatures. These items may be included in an ad, although they are necessary in every advertisement. Slogans are short phrases that become identified with products. A slogan should be short, easily understood, and appropriate to the product. Sometimes, whole advertising campaigns are built around slogans, such as Coca-Cola's slogan, "The Real Thing," or that of McDonald's, "What you want is what you get."

A logo is a design that represents a company. The Volkswagen logo, for instance, is a "*v*" sitting in the middle of a "*w*," all of which is in a circle. Volkswagen has been using this logo for years. It has become a symbol of the company. Advertisers will want to use well-designed logos in their ads because of the distinctiveness they add to the advertisement. Signatures generally refer to the name and address of the company, which are often necessary or useful in an ad.

Writing advertising for broadcast

Much of the advertising that we pay the most attention to comes from the broadcast media—television and radio. Broadcasting has advantages over print in being able to deliver a message with immediacy and impact. It can bring a product to life and show it in action. But broadcast advertising is expensive to produce and air, especially on television. And broadcast advertising gets only one chance at a time with the listener or viewer. If the message is not delivered immediately, the consumer cannot turn back the page and listen to it again.

Whereas print ads are space oriented, broadcast ads are time oriented. Broadcast ads should be simple. They should be designed to achieve maximum impact in a short amount of time. In addition, copywriters should write for the ear. The visual and oral messages should complement one another. They should key in on the sounds, words, and pictures that will help sell the product.

The copywriter for broadcast advertising has certain tools available, and it would be useful to take a brief look at what they are and how they can be used.

Voices. The most commonly used tool of the broadcast advertiser is the voice. Talking is the most direct and effective form of communication for broadcasting and the easiest to produce. Most of what the advertising copywriter will write for broadcast advertising is a script for what people will say. To write conversational language, however, is neither easy nor simple. It takes practice and much writing and rewriting. The script must be suitable for the voice that is using it as well as the other elements of the ad.

Sound effects. Like voices, sounds can be a very effective means of communication. Sound effects are often vital to radio ads. Car engines, crowds cheering, quiet walks in the woods, children laughing—all of these sounds can take listeners to the scene of an advertisement. They evoke pictures and images inside the heads of the listeners. They can "demonstrate" the way a product looks or works.

Music. Like sound effects, music can provide the proper background for a commercial, or it can be the main part of the commercial's message. Selecting the proper music for a commercial's background is an important consideration for the producers of an advertisement. The haunting music of Vangelis (part of which was used in the score for the movie *Chariots of Fire*) was one of the most memorable parts of the famous Ernest and Julio Gallo "Wedding" commercial. The commercial needed only the music, the superb photography, and the tagline, "All the best a wine can be" to gets its message across.

In the days when radio was the dominant broadcast medium, the jingle—the one-or two-line musical message about a product—was one of the most popular advertising technique. The jingle is still popular for radio but has also become a staple of the television commercial. In fact, the simple one-or two-line jingle has developed in a number of ways. Some advertisers have produced orchestra-score songs to promote their products, and Coca-Cola's "I'd Like to Teach the World to Sing" became a popular hit when it was recorded and sold to the public.

Pictures. Pictures are not available for radio, of course, but they constitute one of the major advantages of television. Not only can television show pictures, but a well-produced advertisement can direct the eye to exactly the images that it wants the audience to see.

Pictures bring a commercial to life. They can show real people talking to one another and doing real things. While most people realize that commercials are most often dramatic presentations (not pictures of real life), they still have a believability about them that makes people accept them and consider the messages they have to send.

Visual effects. Graphics and special effects have always been a part of television and have proven themselves to be a useful tool in the production of television advertising. Today their value has been enhanced because the computer hardware and software to create complex and eye-popping graphics are readily available and easy to use.

While broadcast commercials can vary widely in approach, there are two basic formats that can be used: dramatic formats and announcer formats. Dramatic formats emphasize the action on the screen or within the script. One of the best and oldest ways to make a point is to tell a story. Radio and television commercials are often small dramas packed into just a few seconds. They may also be just a set of scenes and sounds that lead to a point about a product. While they may use announcers, the announcer plays only a partial role in the ad. There are four types of dramatic formats:

Problem-resolution. Presenting a problem and then resolving it is one of the most common ways of selling a product. The outline for a problem-resolution commercial is a simple one. For instance, a person has a headache; he takes a brand of aspirin; he no longer has a headache. The problem-

Figure 7-8
Radio script sheet
This sheet demonstrates how radio script advertising is organized by the writer for production.

Radio Script Sheet	
Product: Shipler's Soup	
Client: Shipler's Soup Company	
Title: Home from the Hills	
Writer: Smith	
Length: 20 seconds	
Source	**Audio**
	SDX: Wind blowing, door slams
ANNCR #1	Hi, honey, I'm home.
ANNCR #2	Oh, Jack! You're home. It's been two years. Where have you been?
ANNCR #1	Crossing deserts, sailing oceans, climbing mountains — you know, that sort of thing. I'm hungry. Got any Shipler's soup?
ANNCR #2	No. We ate the last of it yesterday.
ANNCR #1	Well, see ya!
	SDX: Door opens, wind blowing, door slams.
ANNCR #3	Shipler's Soup. Good enough to make them stay home.

resolution technique is popular with advertisers because it can make a strong point in a short amount of time.

Whatever the problem is, the commercial is structured so that its solution is directly attributed to the product. You can think of the problem-resolution commercial as a "before" and "after" structure: "Before" using the product, we had this problem; "after" using it, we no longer have the problem.

One of the secrets of the problem-resolution commercial's success is the speed at which a problem can be established. A copywriter can waste no time in letting the audience know what the problem is. Usually, that is done with the very first words and pictures. The idea of the problem has to be clear and simple: The people in the commercial are hungry; or they're uncomfortable; or they're looking for something; and so on. The product then comes to their rescue just as quickly. All this is done usually within the space of thirty seconds, sometimes even fifteen seconds.

Slice of life. Normally, the slice-of-life-commercial shows people doing things in which the advertised product is involved. These may be mini-dramas with a problem and resolution that have little to do with the the product itself, but they show the product in a very good light. Or they may be sketches that revolve around the product. For example, a popular commercial

Figure 7-9

A television storyboard sheet
This sheet shows how a writer would organize a short television commercial. Simple drawings inside the rounded boxes would demonstrate the scenes that would occur at various parts of the script.

Television Storyboard

Product: Shipler's Soup
Client: Shipler's Soup Company
Title: Home from the Hills
Writer: Smith
Length: 30 seconds

Video	Audio
Frame time 3 seconds	SDX: MUSIC; winding blowing, door opens, closes MAN: Hi, honey, I'm home.
Frame time 5 seconds	WOMAN: Oh, Jack! You're home. It's been two years. Where have you been?
Frame time 10 secconds	MAN: Crossing deserts, sailing oceans, climbing mountains — you know, that sort of thing. I'm hungry. Got any Shipler's soup?
Frame time 2 seconds	WOMAN: No. We ate the last of it yesterday. MAN: Well, see ya!
Frame time 4 seconds	SDX: Door opens, wind blowing, door slams. ANNOUNCER: Shipler's Soup. Good enough to make them stay home.
Frame time 6 seconds	MUSIC UP

for Coca-Cola shows a baseball team on a bus after a game that the team won; the team is hot and thirsty, and the bus stops at a small diner; the team descends on the diner, and everyone who works at the diner must work harder; finally, the team quenches its thirst with Coca-Cola, and one of the team members gives his baseball cap to one of the waitresses right before the team leaves.

In a similar type of commercial, a father drives his pre-teen daughter and her friends to McDonald's, where they may run into some boys they have been discussing. When they get to McDonald's, the father gets out, and his daughter, horrified, says, "You're not going in, are you?" The father waits in the car, realizing that his daughter is growing up. He takes comfort in eating some McDonald's french fries.

Slice-of-life commercials must be entertaining, but more importantly, they need to identify the product with a situation or feeling that is familiar and comfortable. They try to demonstrate that the product is part of the life that the people on the screen are living, and it should also be part of the viewer's life.

Documentary/demonstration. These kinds of commercials use fewer dramatic techniques than others. They may simply show how a product works (for example, how a fabric cleaner "lifts out" the stain from a sweater). They may demonstrate how a product works in comparison to its competition. They put a product in an unusual situation to demonstrate something about the product (such as Timex watch's slogan, "It takes a licking and keeps on ticking," or Master Lock's demonstration of the durability of its lock by firing a rifle bullet into one of them). Occasionally, a commercial will present the way a product is made in order to demonstrate something about the product.

Fantasy. Putting people and products in unreal or abnormal situations is another way of making a point about a product. Fantasy also includes the use of animation, such as in commercials for Keebler cookies or Jolly Green Giant products, and special camera techniques, such as dancing cats and talking dogs.

Fantasy characters are not always without controversy. During a mid-1980s campaign, Duracell used a fuzzy, pink bunny beating a small drum to say that its batteries lasted longer than those of the competition. One member of the competition, the Eveready Battery Company, took exception to this

Figure 7-10

Through the grapevine

In the mid-1980s, a group of California raisin growers undertook an advertising campaign to increase the consumption of their product. The animated raisins that they used spurred a modest growth in the raisin market. The merchandising of the raisin characters, however, reached $500 million in 1988—twice the size of the raisin market itself.

message and brought out an ad feating a garish, hot-pink bunny with sunglasses pounding a bass drum. "For years, one of our competitors has been telling you they have the longest lasting battery. But they haven't invited us to the party," the voice-over announcer says. The Duracell Energizer bunny has proved to be remarkably long lasting. Several years after it originated, its new tact was to interrupt fake commercials with the tag line, "Just keeps on going."

Dramatic presentations have either no announcer at all or an announcer who plays only a minor part in the commercial. Announcer formats are those in which the announcer is the main character, or one of the main characters, in the commercial. There are two types of announcer formats: the spokesperson and the anonymous announcer.

The spokesperson. The spokesperson is another popular format for broadcast commercials. Spokespersons may range from celebrities to unknown but real people to actors. They may or may not be experts on the product they are advertising. The Federal Trade Commission has a wide variety of rules governing the use of spokespersons in advertisements. In general, celebrities who endorse products have some responsibility for the claims that are made about the products; people who are identified as "real people" or "typical users" in advertisements must be who the ads says they are; actors may play the part of "real people" or "typical users" as long as they are not identified otherwise. In other words, if a commercial identifies a speaker as "Joe Smith of Hoboken, New Jersey," that speaker must be Joe Smith of Hoboken, New Jersey.

Famous people (usually actors but not always) can become spokespersons and even symbols for the manufacturers that hire them for their products. Actors Cliff Robertson and James Garner have become identified with ATT and the beef industry, respectively, because of their appearance in commercials. Jesse White has for two decades been the Maytag repairman, "the loneliest guy in the world." The advertising industry took special note when Maytag announced in 1989 that Gordon Jump, a star of the "WKRP" comedy series, would replace White in this role.

Testimonial. Closely associated with the use of the spokesperson is the testimonial commercial. The testimonial differs from the spokesperson commercial because of the credibility of the person doing the testimonial. In the testimonial, the person in the commercial is saying, in effect, "I have some expertise about this product, and I think it's the best there is." Sports figures are often asked to endorse sporting goods products because it is believed that they have high credibility in this area. In some cases, their endorsements have gone as far as allowing their names to be placed on the product itself, such as with Michael Jordon's line of sports shoes.

Anonymous announcers. In the anonymous announcer format, the announcer does not appear and is not identified but is only heard. This format is popular with advertisers who want to direct all the attention of the audience to the product itself. The attributes of the product, not the spokesperson, are emphasized.

Sometimes "anonymous" announcers may not be so anonymous. A number of people have such distinctive and widely recognizable voices that viewers of a commercial will know who is speaking even when they are not identified. Burgess Meredith's voice has become closely identified with Honda cars, and Jimmy Stewart has done the voice-over parts for Campbell Soup commercials. This technique of having a recognizable voice in a commercial can heighten the interest in a product without distracting from the message of the commercial.

Students should recognize that many commercials do not fall strictly within the categories just outlined. They are often combinations of two or more of the types of commercials. They use techniques from a number of sources to help sell their products. On the other hand, you should remember that the most common characteristic of a television ad is its simplicity of structure. The time constraints of a television commercial demand that you get the message across to the viewer simply and quickly.

One of the most useful tools that writers of television commercials have is the television storyboard. The storyboard allows a writer to begin visualizing the commercial as it is being written. It uses a series of scenes from the commercial along with the words to give the writer an idea of how the commercial will look when it is produced. An example of a television storyboard can be found on page 189.

Storyboards are useful in other ways. Besides helping the writer visualize the commercial, a storyboard can give a client an idea of what a commercial will be like before any expensive production work has begun. It can also give the producer and director of the commercial insights into what the writer has in mind for the commercial.

No one has to be a good or clever artist to use a storyboard. The most basic drawings of commercial scenes, even using stick figures if necessary, will be sufficient for transmitting the visual ideas in a commercial.

Other media

Three other types of media should be mentioned briefly as part of our overall discussion of advertising. They are point-of-purchase advertising, outdoor advertising, and direct mail. These are important forms of advertising, particularly in supporting advertising campaigns that are carried on in other media. Because they involve many decisions beyond those of the copywriter, however, they are discussed only briefly here.

Point-of-purchase advertising refers to the packaging and display of a product. One study by the Point-of-Purchase Advertising Institute indicated that as many as two-thirds of buying decisions are made after the customer has entered the store. All other advertising is useless unless a product can be found. That means that it must be well packaged and well displayed. It must stand out from other products—particularly the competition, which is likely to be displayed beside it on the store shelves.

Point-of-purchase's effectiveness can be found in the history of one product—Hershey's candy bars. For decades, Hershey's declined to advertise in any media except its own packaging. Its market strategy was known as mass availability. That is, the company tried to place its product at as many locations as it could. That strategy worked, and Hershey's products became some of the most popular in its area. It has only been in recent years that the company has produced mass media advertising.

Outdoor advertising is a multimillion-dollar business. In 1991 advertisers spent about $684 million on this medium. In May 1992 McDonald's bought 20,000 outdoor boards all across the country. Because the messages on almost all types of outdoor advertising must be brief, this medium is also used to supplement advertising campaigns in other media. One of the chief assets of outdoor advertising is its repetitive nature. A person may pass by a poster or billboard many times, and yet the advertiser has made only one advertising purchase.

Finally, **direct mail** advertising offers an advertiser many possibilities and advantages. Direct mail includes a variety of marketing techniques, including sales letters, post cards, pamphlets, and brochures and catalogues. Direct mail allows advertisers to target a very specific audience and to get a message to that audience very quickly. It can carry a great deal of information. One of the problems with direct mail is that it can be very expensive. It can, however, give an advertiser some fairly precise information about how well an advertising campaign has worked.

Conclusion

Writing advertising copy calls for a high degree of intelligence, hard work, creativity, and competitiveness on the part of the writer. It is not a job that everyone can do, but it is one that has great rewards for those who are successful.

Points for consideration and discussion

1. The text lists some major demographic characteristics that advertisers want to know. Can you think of other demographic variables that would be important to advertisers? What would make these important in selling a product?

2. Think of a member of your family. What needs are most important to that person. What advertising appeals would work best to sell a person that product?

3. Take an ad from a magazine. To what audience, in terms of demographic variables, is that ad targeted? What appeals does the ad use?

4. The text says that ads should tell people what they should do (for example, "Go out and buy one today.") Find an ad that does *not* do this and then find one that does. Which do you think is more effective?

5. Select an ad that you think is a good one from a magazine. List the verbs that are used in the ad. Does this tell you anything about how the ad was written?

6. What characteristics does advertising copy writing have in common with news writing? How are they different?

Further reading

Advertising Age. For the person who wants to keep up with the world of advertising, this weekly publication is must reading.

John W. Crawford. *Advertising.* Boston: Allyn and Bacon, Inc. 1965.

Donald Jugenheimer and Gordon E. White. *Basic Advertising.* Columbus, OH: Grid Publishing, Inc, 1980.

S. Watson Dunn and Arnold M. Barban. *Advertising: Its Role in Modern Marketing.* New York: Dryden, 1978.

David L. Malickson and John W. Nason. *Advertising – How to Write the Kind that Works.* New York: Charles Scribner's Sons, 1977.

EXERCISES

The following section contains a variety of advertising situations for students to use to practice advertising copywriting. The advertising copy sheets contained in Appendix E may be used for these exercises.

Non-product advertising

College promotion

Pick a slogan or theme for an image advertising campaign for your college or university (example: It's a great place to learn.) and write 200 words of copy for three ads centered around that theme. You will also need to write a four- to ten-word headline for each of the ads.

Forestry company

Write an image ad for the Houseware Forestry Company, a national firm which owns two-thirds of the commercial forest land in Alabama. Houseware is seventy-five years old. It began as a small family business in 1907 near Oshkosh, Wisconsin. It did not stay confined to Wisconsin for long. Frank and Joe Ware were natural entrepreneurs who expanded into Michigan in 1915. By 1920, they had begun to buy up forest land all over the country, planting it with appropriate trees.

Houseware is currently embarking on an image campaign to emphasize the care it takes to replant the land from which it harvests trees, the family beginnings of the company, and the research the company conducts concerning the preservation of the ecosystem in the areas it harvests.

Houseware also takes great pride in its strict employee safety standards and generous employee benefits. Employees working with heavy, loud equipment must wear earmuffs, hard hats, and heavy gloves. No employee works unsupervised until he or she has completed a two-week training course.

Houseware has had only fifteen accidents during the time it has been in existence. None of the accidents was fatal.

Houseware replants the areas it harvests and also restocks some of the larger areas with wildlife. The company works closely with environmental protection groups, sharing the results of its research. The twenty-person Houseware research staff has found evidence that their company's forestry activities have improved the ecology of areas overcrowded with wildlife and trees.

The current chairman of the board of Houseware is Joseph P. Ware III.

Guns

Several politically oriented groups in your state have begun a lobbying effort with state legislators and city councils to outlaw the sale of handguns. These groups seems to be making some progess. In the last session of the state legislature, a bill to restrict the sale of handguns, was passed by the House of Representatives but barely defeated in the Senate.

The state chapter of the National Rifle Association (NRA) has decided to fight this movement through an intensive advertising campaign. The central thrust of this campaign is to oppose the handgun legislation which the state legislature is currently considering. The bill is known as Senate Bill No. 3, and it would outlaw the mail order sale of handguns. Persons buying handguns in stores would be required to fill out a long application stating why they want to buy the handgun and supply personal information about themselves and the people in their households. This application would then go to the State Gun Control Board for approval.

The state NRA retains your advertising firm for the campaign, and you are asked to design three ads opposing this legislation and urging people to write or call their local state legislators about it. When you talk with the head of the state NRA about the campaign, he tells you, "We think guns are good for people, not bad for them." The ads should have headline, subhead if necessary, and seventy-five to 150 words of copy

Retail advertising

Baseball team

A National League Baseball franchise has been granted to Washington, D.C. The last time the city had a team was 1971, when the Washington Senators moved to Texas to become the Texas Rangers. The owners of the new team have not selected a name for the team yet, and they want your ad agency to propose a name and design a set of advertisements to promote ticket sales during January and February. Ticket prices are $6.50 for box seats, $5.50 for reserved seats, $4.50 for general admission, and $2 for bleacher seats. Those wanting more information or wanting to buy tickets should write to the Washington National League Baseball Team, Box 3995, Washington, D.C. 20006 or call (202) 555-1212. The owners tell your agency that the ads for tickets should emphasize the advantages of buying early, the excitement of baseball, and the fact that the game is finally back in the nation's capital. Write a headline, subhead, and copy for three ads. The copy should be seventy-five to 100 words long.

Wedding dresses

A local wedding shop wants to run a series of ads in April and May with the idea that it has "the best prices in town" on wedding dresses and accessories. Wedding dress prices begin at $150, and bridesmaids dresses begin at $100. The shop has lots of sizes and colors, and it also carries many accessories for weddings such as veils, ring pillows, etc. The store, the Bride's Boutique, is going to remain open extra hours during these two months for its sale. It will be open until 9 every night and Sunday from 1–5 p.m. One of the owners says she especially wants the ads to mention that brides who have looked everywhere else in town and haven't found what they wanted should come to the Bride's Boutique. They'll probably find something they like. Write four ads which include a headline, subhead, and seventy-five words of copy.

Classical record sale

A local shop, Sound Advice, normally advertises and sells a lot of rock and country recordings. The owner wants to expand his business by offering "the best collection of classical records in the area." He wants you to write some ads promoting this part of his business. But you must be careful, he says, because he doesn't want to drive away his current customers. He is starting the new part of his business by offering all his single classical records and tapes for $1.99 for this weekend only. Come up with a slogan that the owner can use for this expansion in his business and write the ads, which will run in the local paper on Thursday, Friday, and Saturday. The owner says he has a full line of classical music, from Bach to Stravinsky.

Frozen dinners

Good Foods, Inc., is a manufacturer and processor of many foods commonly found in grocery stores. The company produces many canned goods, distributes fresh produce in many areas of the country, and has a large line of individually frozen fruits and vegetables. The company is now seeking to enter the frozen dinner market. The company has done extensive research in this area and has found two major negative characteristics of frozen dinners among consumers. One is that frozen dinners lack taste—the food found in most frozen dinners is simply not very good. The other negative characteristic is that, generally, frozen foods do not have a very good reputation. That is, "good" cooks don't serve frozen dinners to their friends; "good" wives and mothers don't serve frozen dinners to their families. People who serve or eat frozen dinners are thought to be lazy and not very good in the kitchen. Frozen dinners have these reputed characteristics despite the fact that research shows frozen dinners are eaten in the average American home at least once a week.

Good Foods doesn't know which negative characteristic to attack in its advertising and comes to your ad agency asking for prototype ads to help company officials decide which approach to take. Choose one of the negative characteristics above and write some advertising copy designed to counter it. It is up to you to come up with a name for Good Foods' frozen dinners, and the name should help in countering the negative characteristic you choose. Here are some more facts about the advertising situation which are included in a copy platform written by your agency.

Target market: Middle- and upper-middle class women who work but still have the responsibility of fixing meals for their families; age range twenty-five to forty-five.

Competition: Two major brands of frozen foods now dominate the market: Swan Foods has a wide variety of frozen dinners, which are generally advertised as the cheapest on the market; their average price is ninety-one cents per dinner. Wholesome Foods doesn't have as many varieties of dinners but research shows that people generally think they're a little tastier and more nutritious. They cost about $1.03 per dinner. These two companies sell 75 percent of the frozen dinners in America. The rest are sold by a variety of small companies, many of whom specialize in foreign dishes, such as Chinese foods.

Supportive selling points: Good Foods dinners will average about $1.25, making them almost the most expensive on the market. Good Foods will have fewer varieties than Swan but more than Wholesome, with more vitamins and minerals than any dinner on the market. One line of the Good Foods dinners will feature rib-eye steaks which have been pre-cooked "well done," "medium," and "rare." The dinners will also have more vegetables than the dinners now on the market, and Good Foods has come up with a process that will preserve more of the natural flavor of these vegetables.

Writing copy for advertising layouts

On the pages at the end of this exercise section are layouts for print ads for the next five exercises. All of them have illustrations. Spaces are indicated on the ads for the headline, subhead, body copy, slogan, and signature. You or your instructor may want to use these ads as they appear, or you may want to cut them out and change them around. You may

also want to photocopy them in case you need to write a series of ads. Below is the information for writing each ad:

Local flower shop

Pearsall Florist Shop, the manager says, "wants to put a flower in every business in town at least once a week." She wants to promote the idea that fresh flowers enliven a business and make both customers and employees feel better about that business. The advertising will be pitched to downtown area businesses where the flower shop is located. (It's at 222 Main Street, and the telephone number is 643-ROSE.) For businesses that order one bouquet of flowers each week for a month, there will be a 20 percent discount. Because the shop is located in the downtown area, it can offer quick delivery to businesses in the area. In fact, they guarantee delivery within two hours of getting a telephone order. The manager says the florists at the shop are experts in designing "specialty bouquets" for special occasions or locations and that they can design something that is appropriate for any business.

Suggested assignment: Design a series of four ads to run in the local newspaper in four succeeding weeks. Each ad should carry the same slogan but have a different headline and body copy. Each block of body copy should be about fifty words long. You may want to keep the same design and illustration for the ads, or you can change things around.

Car repair shop

Wright's Auto Repair, located at 126 Wesley, is the oldest car repair shop in town. It has operated continuously from the same location since 1923. In fact, that makes it one of the oldest businesses in town. The steam engine in the illustration is a nineteenth-century railroad engine, and it represents the kind of longevity that Wright's is known for.

At least, that's what it wants to be known for. Hank Wright, the current proprietor, has just taken over as manager of Wright's from his dad. It was Hank Wright's grandfather who began the business in 1923.

Hank wants a set of advertisements that emphasize the reliability of the work he does. He wants to appeal particularly to those people who have used other repair shops—especially those who use the shops at dealerships where they bought their cars and those who have been dissatisfied with them. Hank says his shop offers not only a guarantee on the work, but also a guarantee on when the work will be finished. If the shop cannot meet that deadline, it will provide a loaner car to the customer, if needed. The shop takes care of all types of car work, from car maintenance (changing oil and filters) to engine and brake repair. They also have a specialist trained to repair car radios and sound systems.

Suggested assignment: Write the copy for three ads. The body copy in each should be from fifty to seventy-five words long.

Local newspaper

For National Newspaper Week, the local newspaper wants to run a series of advertisements about how widespread newspaper reading is. The target audience for this ad campaign is potential advertisers, particularly those advertisers who use other media, such as radio and television.

Here are some supportive selling points: The newspaper is subscribed to by two out of every three households in the area. More than 80 percent of the adults in the area say they read the newspaper regularly. More than 90 percent say they have seen the newspaper in the last week. By contrast, only 30 percent of the adults in the area say they listen to the top-rated radio station. The top-rated television show in the area, "Fly by Night," a syndicated game show, is watched by only about 25 percent of the households each night. Consequently, the argument can be made that the newspaper is the only "mass" medium in the area. If advertisers want a "mass" audience, they should choose the newspaper rather than radio or television. This information comes from a marketing survey that was commissioned by the newspaper within the last three months.

The newspaper wants you to come up with a slogan that would convey this theme.

Suggested assignment: Write three advertisements using the layouts on pages 209, 211, and 213. Use the slogan you have created for the campaign in each of them. The body copy in each should be fifty to seventy-five words.

Daycare center

Daycare is one of the fastest growing parts of the service sector. As more and more women work outside the home, the demand for quality, affordable daycare has skyrocketed.

The Sunshine Daycare Center is open from 6:30 a.m. to 6:30 p.m. It is located at 1212 Wiltshire Blvd., one of the city's major thoroughfares, so it is convenient to many people, especially to those who work downtown. The center takes children up through kindergarten ages and has a fully accredited kindergarten class.

The center knows that one of the major concerns that parents have for their child's daycare is to make sure that the child is properly cared for and that the child gets a lot of individual attention. Responding to this concern, the center makes sure that there is at least one adult for every ten children at all times in the center. Most of these adults have some academic or professional training. The center has an open, bright environment inside, with a large, well-equipped playground in the back.

Current advertising should be pitched toward people who work downtown and who are concerned about the quality of care their children receive during the day. These people are not as concerned about price (the Sunshine Daycare Center is one of the most expensive in town) as they are convenience and quality.

Suggested assignment: Write three advertisements using the same theme or slogan. The ads should be at least seventy-five words each.

Computer store

Computerware, a store that has been in business for nearly ten years now, specializes in selling and servicing a wide variety of hardware and software for many types of computers, particularly Apple (the Apple II line and the Macintosh line) and IBM and IBM-compatible computers. For the next month, the store is offering special prices on upgrades for many of the models of computers it sells and services.

Computerware is located at 717 Coventry Street, telephone 516-5523.

The folks who run Computerware realize that many people who bought computers for their homes or businesses two or more years ago will have machines that are beginning to get out of date. Because computer manufacturers like Apple and IBM are constantly bringing out new lines of equipment, the people who have owned their computers for two or more years may find that they cannot use much of the newest software that is made for their machine. Or they may find that they need more "internal memory" for their computers. ("Internal memory" is the capacity of a computer to store data and run programs faster.) The upgrade prices vary according to the brand of computer.

Computerware says the price of an upgrade includes everything, even installation. There are no extra charges, and satisfaction is guaranteed. People who want an upgrade should call the store.

Suggested assignment: Write two ads for Computerware. Each should be fifty to 100 words long. Use the layouts on pages 217 and 219.

National advertising

Doughboy soft-serve dessert

The Doughboy Company, which produces a variety of frozen foods and mixes, is attempting to broaden its stake in both the dessert and frozen foods markets with a soft-serve dairy dessert. The company has been researching the potential for the product for about two years. It comes in vanilla, chocolate, and strawberry flavors and will be sold in rectangular half-gallon cartons.

Soft-serve frozen desserts typically contain between two and a half percent and less than 10 percent butterfat, qualifying as ice milk; ice cream must contain at least 10 percent butterfat. The primary ingredients in the new product are skim milk and mellorine (which substitutes vegetable fat for animal fat). The product has the nutritional value of ice cream. Doughboy says it "approximates the texture of soft-serve" desserts sold primarily through food service outlets like Dairy Queen. This product will be sold only in the dairy products section of grocery stores.

Give this product a name and write a headline, subhead, and the copy for three advertisements that will be placed in *Good Housekeeping, Time,* and *Newsweek* magazines. One of the ads should promote the product's nutritional value, another should promote its taste, and the third should emphasize its convenience. Each ad should be 100 to 150 words long.

Perfume

The Soft Lights Perfume Company has been marketing Wild Abandon perfume for a number of years, and recently it has found that its share of the perfume market has been decreasing. Essentially, the company wants to advertise a "new and improved" Wild Abandon perfume, but company officials are uncertain exactly how to do this. They tell you that this new perfume, which they want to market under the same name, has a slightly stronger scent and that it comes in a variety of colors, including purple, crimson, and gold. (It used to be transparent.) In a radical move, the company has decided to increase the price of the perfume by 50 percent, so that now it costs sixty-five dollars for a half ounce. Write five advertisements for this product which will run in successive issues of *Vogue.* Each ad should have a headline and about fifty words of copy. The ads will have a common illustration—a gorgeous woman, dressed in a leopard-skin dress and accompanied by a leopard.

College beer

A new brewing company, Real Beers, Inc., is about to enter the crowded beer market with a new product. Company officials have decided that the part of the market they have the best chance of capturing with their new beer is college students. They believe the new beer will appeal to college students for several reasons. In the first place, this new beer is much cheaper than most other beers, with a base price of about $1.50 per six pack. Second, it comes in extremely thin aluminum cans. Fi-

Be Smart, top your head w/ Smart Tops.

nally, this beer will not come in a light version. In fact, the name of the new beer is Not Light Beer. The company wants to base its advertising campaign on the appeal that this beer is "a lot of fun to drink." It wants to advertise in your college newspaper, and you have been asked to write two ads. Each should have a headline, subhead, and 150 words of copy. Write the ads and designate appropriate illustrations.

Smart Tops, Inc.

Most men don't wear hats. That's what the research shows. Smart Tops, Inc., is going to try to change that. Smart Tops is a small firm but owned by the clothes conglomerate Giant Size, a respected name in clothes. Giant Size isn't a charity, however, and Smart Tops has been losing money for years. The managers of Smart Tops fear that Giant Size will close the company down unless they can show a profit in the next two years. They have decided to embark on a major advertising campaign and have come to your agency for help.

The research that your agency has done into why men do not wear hats has come up with two major reasons: men don't wear hats because they don't consider them necessary; and they don't wear hats because they think hats are for "older" men. Smart Tops wants to market its hats to younger men, those in the twenty-five-to-forty range. The managers aren't sure which would be the most effective advertising campaign. Should they take on the "old" characteristic directly and try to convince men that wearing a hat is a "young" thing to do? Or, should they try to counter the negative characteristic that hats are unnecessary with some convincing arguments that hats really are necessary?

Your agency wants you to pick one of these advertising strategies and design some advertising for Smart Tops. The following is some information that the agency research office has provided you which may eventually go into a copy platform.

Competition. Smart Tops now has about a 7 percent share of the market, down from 10 percent two years ago. Almost every other manufacturer of men's hats has seen a drop in sales during the past two years also, so there is no evidence that hat wearers have anything against Smart Tops. The biggest advertiser in the market is Smith, Inc., which manufacturers a line of hats known as Good As Gold. These are some of the most expensive and well-made hats on the market. Other hat manufacturers do relatively little advertising.

Supportive selling points. Smart Tops says that its hats are as well made as the Good As Golds, but they sell for an average of twenty-five percent less. The hats range in price from $15 to $50. All the hats contain at least 50 percent natural fibers, especially cotton and wool. They are extremely well crafted and backed by years of tradition and experience. Smart Tops has been making hats since the 1880s. The hats are guaranteed against any defect in workmanship and against any damage for a year. If a customer is dissatisfied with anything about a Smart Tops hat, all he has to do is send the hat to the company office and he'll receive a full refund. Smart Tops can also be counted on to provide the latest in new styling in men's hats, as well as a wide variety of traditional styles.

Audience. The marketing research has turned up the fact that women make about forty percent of all hat purchases for men.

Your assignment is the following:

—Write a slogan for Smart Tops hats that can be used in all their advertising.

— Write two print ads, each with a headline and at least fifty words of copy. Be sure to use the slogan you have written.

— Write a thirty-second radio spot or a thirty-second TV storyboard, also using the slogan you have written.

Professional advertising

Hymnals

A publishing house has asked your advertising agency to market a new hymnal which it has just produced. This hymnal is designed for use in all Christian-denomination churches. It has all the classic hymns in it, such as "The Old Rugged Cross," "Onward Christian Soldiers," and "Amazing Grace." It also contains some new songs that have never before been published in a hymnal but that viewers of television religious programs are likely to recognize. The hymnal is organized alphabetically by song title; it has an index; and it has traditional rituals for baptism, dedication, and other services. You are to write two magazine ads attempting to sell this hymnal to ministers and song directors of smaller churches. The name of the hymnal is *Sing Unto the Lord*. If ordered in quantities of less than 100, it sells for $3; more than 100, $2.75. The publishing company is New Life Publishing House, 200 Sixth Street, Dallas, Texas. The two ads you write should have a headline, subhead, and body copy of at least seventy-five words.

Electronic editing equipment

Signalcorp, a corporation which manufactures computers, is trying to break into the market of selling electronic editing equipment to smaller newspapers—those with circulations between 25,000 and 100,000. A market study has indicated that this is an expanding area and one in which the company can make a lot of money fairly quickly. Signalcorp has manufactured a good line of electronic editing equipment, as good as that made by any competitor. The corporation's problem at this stage is to distinguish itself from the competition. The corporation's management has asked your ad agency to help solve this problem. The management wants you to develop three prospective ads for use in *Editor and Publisher* and other trade magazines. These ads should say little about the equipment and more about the company and the services it offers. Each ad should have a headline, subhead if necessary, and seventy-five to 100 words of copy. Develop a common slogan that you can use in these ads.

Magazines

The Scientific Media Corporation has recently begun to publish a new magazine called *Working Scientists*. The magazine attempts to interest children in scientific professions. Its publishers feel strongly about the neglect of scientific and technical education in the United States.

The magazine is written simply, perhaps on the traditional ninth-grade level. Its articles, submitted by professionals as well as by staff writers, deal with many subjects, including astronomy, biology, genetic engineering, energy, and geology. The articles discuss advances in each field. Recent topics covered included microsurgery, the Galileo Jupiter mission, and the future of solar energy. Each issue of the magazine includes two feature stories on two professions. The stories may be personality sketches of men and women working in the profession or may simply outline the job opportunities and responsibilities found in the chosen field. For example, one issue spotlighted career opportunities and pitfalls in astronomy. It described the career of a well-known astronomer who had been the first to research the atmosphere in detail. He had named the various layers of the atmosphere, determining their chemical composition and temperature. Later, he worked at the Jet Propulsion Laboratory in Pasadena, participating in the Apollo, Mariner, and Voyager missions. The magazine is careful to describe the problems as well as the benefits encountered in such professions, mentioning, for example, the astronomer's vulnerability to federal budget cuts. Also included in the career articles are approximate salaries and the type of education each requires.

Write an ad for *Working Scientists*. It will appear in such publications as *Time, Newsweek, Astronomy,* and *Business Week*. A year's subscription costs $15. Each issue is illustrated with color photos.

Selecting advertising problems

The following exercises present situations that have a variety of problems that might be solved by advertising. In reading and thinking about these situations, consider yourself an advertising consultant and not just a copywriter. Follow the directions of your instructor. You may be asked to select one of the problems and produce some advertising for it, or you may need to produce several ads that attack a variety of problems.

Hershal's Department Store

Hershal's Department Store is one of the largest department stores in town. It's located in the same shopping mall as a Sears and a J.C. Penney store, but Hershal's has a larger variety of clothes than either of these two chain stores. The store's line of women's clothes is especially large, and the store has a reputation for having the most up-to-date styles of women's clothing. It is locally owned and has been in operation for more than fifty years. The president of the board is John Hershal, Jr., the son of the founder. The store's general manager is John Hershal III, the president's son. Hershal's is considered to be the major store in the mall where it is located.

Hershal's recently conducted a marketing survey, as it has for several years, but this survey turned up some surprising results. The survey found that there is a reservoir of good will about the store, something Hershal's has cultivated for many years. For instance, people in the survey said they liked Hershal's refund policy, which has always been a very liberal one. However, the survey found that people did not like a number of things about Hershal's: The store hours were not long enough (Hershal's closes at 8 p.m., while the other stores in the mall stay open until 9 p.m.); it takes too long to check out; many of the departments don't have enough people to wait on the customers adequately; there is some feeling that Hershal's has raised prices more than other stores have; and many younger women try smaller shops, especially those close to the local college campus, before shopping at Hershal's.

In light of these findings, Hershal's has done several things: Store hours will be extended to 9 p.m. beginning next month; new people will be added to departments that have been understaffed; the store, which conducts three major sales each year, will conduct five during the coming year.

Hershal's also wants to increase its advertising and comes to your agency for help.

At this point, you should identify some of the possible advertising problems and follow the directions of your instructor on handling this advertising situation.

Wayfarer Restaurant

The Wayfarer Restaurant was established in 1865 and is the oldest restaurant in town. It has been in several locations but has been at its present location, 505 Sixth Street, for more than fifty years. The Wayfarer is famous for its breakfasts. It has a tradition of serving the finest country ham in the area, but each item on the menu is of exceptional quality. A food critic for the state's largest newspaper once reviewed the breakfast at the Wayfarer and called it the "best place to wake up in the state."

The Wayfarer Restaurant is small and usually crowded, especially in the morning. It seats only about thirty people, and that's one of the problems. The owners feel that they are losing customers who are put off by the thought that they will have to wait for a while. There is no thought being given to expanding the restaurant, however. There is no room to expand, and if there was, the owners probably wouldn't because they like the cozy, intimate atmosphere the small space affords.

The owners have also noticed that many of the people who eat at the Wayfarer are "regulars," people who come there often. They feel that they should be attracting some new customers, especially younger people, like students from the nearby college.

Finally, one of the "hidden secrets" of the restaurant, according to the owners, is its dinner menu. The owners say they offer the best steaks in town—they reject a lot of the meat the packers offer them because it isn't good enough. Their steaks cost seventy-five cents to one dollar less than comparable steaks in the best restaurants in town.

At this point, you should identify some of the possible advertising problems and follow the directions of your instructor on handling this advertising situation.

Apple Growers Association

Apples are one of the most popular fruits in America, but in the last few years, the Apple Growers Associaton has been disappointed with retail sales and has been somewhat disturbed that growers of other fruits have been advertising so heavily—especially the orange growers. Even raisin growers have gotten into the act lately with a television campaign that emphasizes the various uses raisins can have. Apple producers feel they need to increase the visibility of their fruit and reinforce its top spot in the market.

There are more than twenty major varieties of apples sold in this country, and most of these varieties are available in most parts of the nation. They range from the large yellow Golden Delicious, a very sweet variety, to the traditional tart green apple, used mostly for cooking. There are also varieties like Winesap and Red Delicious. Apples have a wide variety of uses, and the creative cook can do a lot with apples. The problem is that people don't think about apples very much and don't consider the uses they can make of them.

Another thing about the apple is that it is considered a "traditional" rather than an "exotic" fruit. It's old fashioned. It still bears the image of "an apple a day keeps the doctor away." (The apple is packed with a lot of vitamins and minerals and other things that are healthful.) The Apple Growers Association is divided on how to approach this image. Some want to emphasize the traditional image and uses of the apple, while others believe that image isn't attractive enough, especially to gain younger customers.

The Association comes to your advertising agency with these feelings and this information and wants your advice on possible advertising campaigns it can conduct.

At this point, you should identify some of the possible advertising problems and follow the directions of your instructor on handling this advertising situation.

Toyota Tercel

For several years, Toyota has been using the slogan, "Oh, What a Feeling–Toyota!" in most of its advertising. That slogan has been pitched at creating a good feeling, a feeling of excitement about Toyota cars. The slogan has also been a central theme for the advertising of all models of Toyotas, from the smallest Starlet to the most expensive Cressida.

Toyota has decided to change its marketing plan in a couple of important ways. For one thing, the company wants to begin to get away from the "Oh, What a Feeling!" theme for all of its models and wants to emphasize more substantive selling points for each of its cars. Second, it wants to begin to distinguish

more carefully one model from another in its advertising. The thinking with company officials is that the name "Toyota" is the only central theme it needs to use in its advertising since the company has built a reputation for producing quality cars.

Toyota wants to begin this new marketing plan with one of its models, the Tercel. It has chosen the Tercel for a number of reasons. The Tercel used to be part of the Corolla model, the smallest in that line. The company found that the car was so popular that it evolved into its own full line, so that the former Corolla-Tercel is now simply the Tercel. A second reason is that while the car is a popular one, it will be facing stiff competition from several American-made models of the same size during the next two years. Toyota wants to cement the Tercel's position in the market.

Your advertising agency has been asked to bid on the Tercel account. You are to come up with a central theme and a slogan for all of the advertising and then produce some sample ads. Toyota and your agency's research department have provided you with the following information you may use for constructing the ads.

Competition. The three major models that compete with the Tercel are the Honda Civic, the Chevrolet Chevette, and the Ford Escort. The Civic, like the Tercel, is a Japanese-made car, while the Chevette and the Escort are made in America. Tercel's base price is $8,995; Civic's is $8,495; Chevette's and Escort's are both $8,495. (All of these prices exclude taxes, options, transportation and dealer preparation charges—which must be mentioned in the ad if the price is mentioned.) The Honda is a very well-made car, but the Chevette and Escort have had some problems with recalls. Both have had problems with the transmission. Toyota has not had a major recall of any of its models in seven years.

Supportive selling points. Tercel has a higher-than-average price, but the resale value of the Tercel is also much higher. While most cars depreciate about half their value in three to five years, the Tercel depreciates only about 30 percent. The maintenance record for the Tercel is "outstanding," according to *Consumer Companion*, a highly respected consumer and product-testing publication. In a recent article on subcompact models, the magazine said, "Taking into consideration price, dependability, low running and maintenance costs, and resale value, the Tercel is the best subcompact on the market today. Owners will pay a little more at the beginning, but they will save money in the long run."

Audience. Toyota wants to pitch its advertising for the Tercel to young, single people who are just graduating from college. The age range for this group is twenty-one to twenty-four, and your marketing research shows that these people are likely to begin looking for a new car soon after they land their first jobs.

Your assignment is the following: Write a slogan that can be used in all the Tercel advertising. Write two ads for the major national newsmagazines. Each should have a headline and at least fifty words of copy. They should also use the slogan you have written. Write a thirty-second radio spot or a thirty-second TV storyboard, also using the slogan you have written.

**Layout for
Local flower shop
(see page 197 for information)**

**Layout for
Car repair shop
(see page 197 for information)**

**Layout for
Local newspaper
(see page 198 for information)**

Layout for
Daycare center
(see page 199 for information)

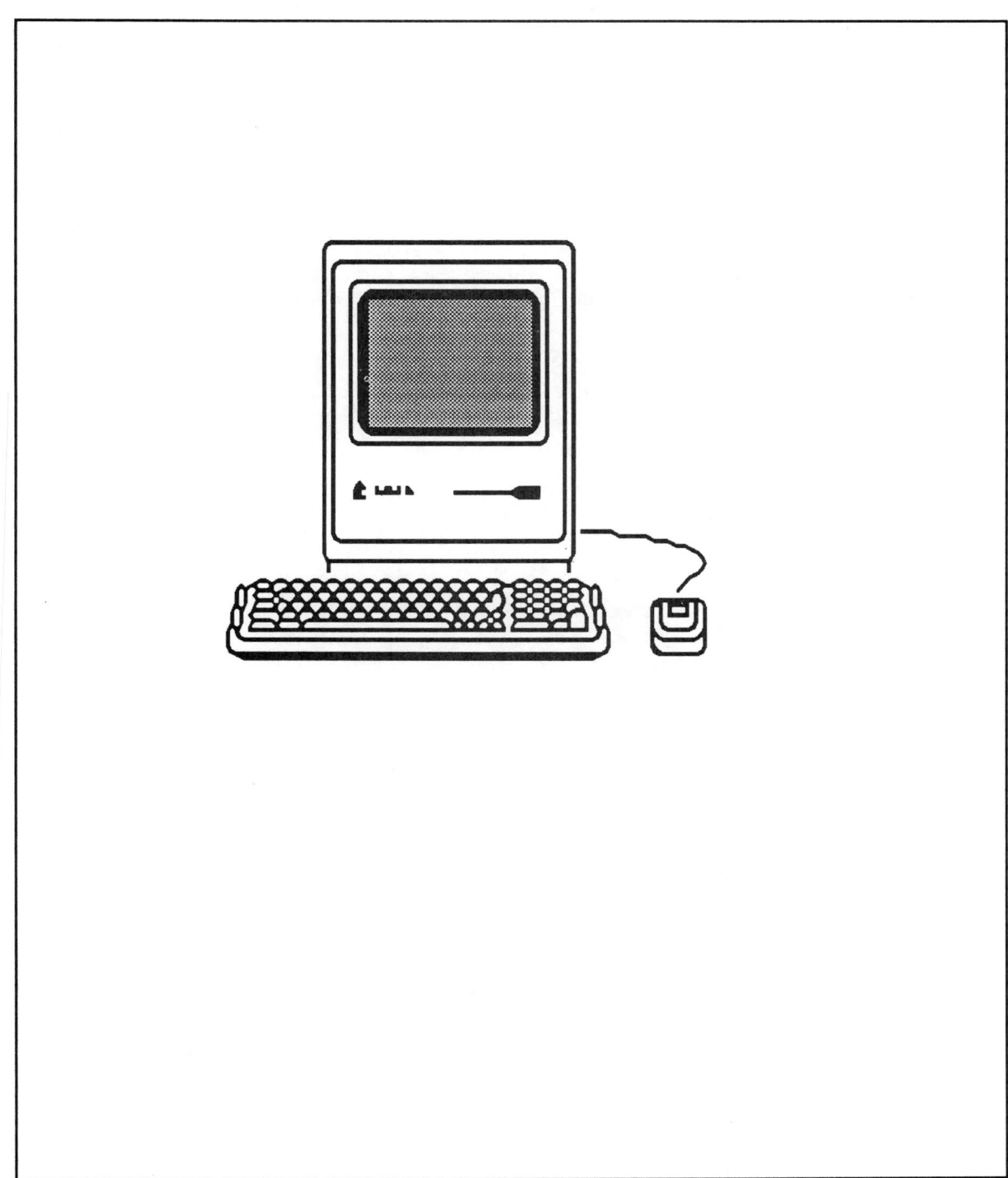

**Layout for
Computer store
(see page 198 for information)**

Writing for Public Relations

Public relations ranges across the organizational map. Public relations means communicating, and in today's business and social community, an organization must communicate at every level. Public relations practitioners are communication specialists, hired by organizations to perform and advise on a variety of communication tasks.

Only a few years ago, many organizations, particularly private businesses, saw no need to have such specialists. They sold their products or performed their services for a specialized public, and they were content to believe that they were doing all of the "communicating" that they needed to do. One example is a large corporation that specializes in operating sites around the country that handle toxic chemical waste material for other industries. The company performed this necessary but unpleasant task and did so within the legal regulations that governed such operations. The company felt that it had little need to communicate with the public. After all, it was not trying to sell a service to the general public. It dealt exclusively with other industries. In the last two decades, however, with more public attention focused on the environment—and on dangerous toxic waste sites, such as Love Canal in New York—the company found that it could no longer afford to take such a cavalier attitude about its communication needs. As the issue of hazardous waste disposal has become not only an industrial one but also a political one, this company and many others like it has found itself in the communication business.

This situation has occurred for many organizations. Corporate chiefs are discovering that they need professional communicators as well as budget managers, salespeople, scientists, engineers, and secretaries on their staffs. The field of public relations has expanded a great deal in the last few years, and more and more students are finding excellent employment opportunities in this field. In fact, the public relations major has become one of the most popular fields of study in mass communication.

Traditionally, the career path into public relations has been through journalism programs and working in the mass media. People who had either or both of these credentials were thought to make good public relations practitioners. While this is still the case, many colleges and universities have instituted public relations majors. These programs teach many of the specifics of working in the field of public relations. More and more students are obtaining internships in public relations agencies and PR departments within companies and organizations.

Despite these burgeoning opportunities, public relations remains a very competitive field. The person who would enter this line of work must be intelligent, disciplined, and willing to work difficult and long hours. Public relations jobs carry with them a great deal of responsibility, and the people who accept them must be willing to live up to that responsibility.

What do PR practitioners do?

People who work in public relations jobs do a great many things. In fact, that is one of the attractions of a career in PR. The variety of activities that a practitioner can engage in is enormous. On the other hand, that variety requires that practitioners be skilled in many areas and that they be able to deal with many differing and sometimes conflicting assignments. They should also be comfortable with many different people.

The following are some of the jobs of a public relations practitioner:

Handle communication with the external publics of an organization. The term **publics** is one that is used often in public relations. It refers to the various groups that an organization attempts to reach through its communication efforts. External publics are those groups outside of the organization that an organization wants to communicate with. They may include the public at large, buyers of a product, users of a service offered by the organization, potential contributors to the organization, members of the news media on whom the organization depends to distribute its information, or any number of other groups. A public relations practitioner must assist not only in getting information out but also in making sure that information is properly interpreted. Some of the means by which information from an organization is distributed are news releases, letters, brochures, and quarterly and annual reports.

Handle communication with the internal publics of an organization. Just as there are groups outside the organization that need to be reached, there are also groups within the organization that must receive information. These are the internal publics. They can include employees, independent contractors, stockholders, members, and the families of any of these groups. In companies that have a larger number of employees, this communication function is often critical to the organization. Keeping employees properly informed is often vital to the company's health. Associations—those that have memberships that are not part of the day-to-day operation of the organization—also depend on good communication with their members to keep their organizations healthy. Communication with these internal publics can take the form of newsletters, company magazines, letters, notices, memoranda, and periodic reports.

Work with the news media to get information about the organization. In most organizations, one of the chief responsibilities is that of media liaison. The PR person is called on to help find out information about the organization that would be useful to the news reporter in putting together a story. This kind of information goes beyond that produced in a press release. The PR person must find the person within the organization that has the information the reporter wants and must often make arrangements for those people to meet. The other side of this responsibility for the PR practitioner is that of advising the organization's officials on media relations. When and how to release information is often the responsibility of PR practitioners. They may also have to give advice on speeches, press conferences, and interviews that the organization's officials may give. In short, any time the news media deal with an organization, a PR person will be involved.

Help produce public functions and events. Public relations practitioners are often involved in the organization's public activities. A company may announce an advertising campaign; officials of a local charity may hold a news conference to kick off its annual fund drive; a local business may make a donation to a school with a ceremony marking that donation; a university may break ground for a new building. Any number of such events may occur, and PR practitioners are usually a part of the planning. They are most likely the ones who see that the public is properly informed about such events. Almost all organizations have the need to produce public events at some point, and the public relations practitioner will have a major responsibility for their success.

These are some of the day-to-day activities that PR practitioners might be involved in. On a more general level, they contribute to their organizations by helping formulate a continuing, long-range public relations plan. That plan may have many parts and may certainly be revised as new needs arise and old needs subside. At this level, most experts agree that public relations consists of four parts:

Planning. An organization should develop a plan for how it intends to deal with its publics. Some means of communication are not appropriate for certain publics, while others are. A well-conceived plan will allow the organization's officials to figure out what publics the organization needs to communicate with and how that communication should take place. An integral part of planning is setting goals for the various communications with the organization's publics. Planning is a constant process with many organizations.

Research. Hand-in-hand with planning is research. A public relations practitioner may have to find out exactly with whom the organization wishes to communicate. And that person may also have to discover the best means of communicating. These are complex questions for which there are no ready answers. A public relations person will need to have these answers if a plan is to be properly executed.

Another part of the research process is finding out what information the organization wants to communicate or should be communicating. Again, this is no easy or simple task. The process of research may involve talking with people in the organization in order to write a news release. It could mean poring over financial and technical papers and holding long discussions with many of the organization's top officials in order to put together an annual report.

Communication. This is the part of the process that we are concerned with most in this book. Putting information into the proper form—and often doing it very quickly—is one of the most important jobs that the PR person can perform. A PR practitioner's ability to do this, more than anything else, will determine that person's worth to the organization.

Evaluation. The evaluation phase of the practitioner's work is when he or she asks, "Did our plan work? Did we get the right information out to the right publics? Did our efforts have the effect we wanted?" Plans need evaluation to see if they are working, and it is often up to the public relations person to devise a means of evaluation for the plan.

Evaluation, of course, is related to the goals of the plan. If the goal of an organization was to gain new members, evaluation is fairly easy. Looking at the number of new members that joined while the plan was being executed is a straightforward means of evaluating the plan. Sometimes, however, goals are much more complex, and evaluation is more subjective.

What does it take to be in PR?

Whether you work for a major public relations firm, a particular company, a government agency, a hospital, a university, or another institution, if you work in public relations the chances are quite good that you will have to write. The overwhelming majority of jobs in the field of public relations are writing jobs. Public relations departments produce brochures, press releases, letters, speeches, scripts, and public service announcements for television and radio, posters, reports, books, formal documents, magazines, newsletters, newspapers, and information directories on a wide variety of topics. While photographers, artists, designers, production managers, and editors may also be required in producing such items, each begins with a writer. Even a flier announcing a company picnic has to be written by someone.

Gathering information and structuring it for specific formats is the basic process for all writing in the mass media. The best people in the public relations profession can take a scribbled set of ideas and produce a fifteen-minute speech for a vice-president to give at a company dinner in much the same way that a good reporter takes a tip from the telephone and eventually produces a polished story. The differences between public relations writing and news writing are primarily differences created by the intent inherent in public relations writing. A public relations writer must bear in mind a complex set of purposes and interests while producing any piece of copy for any particular publication.

If you wish to write in a public relations environment, you should be prepared to work very hard on a relatively small set of assignments directed at a limited audience. It is not unusual for a piece of writing to be scrutinized by several "editors" (that is to say, your bosses), who will criticize and often change your work. Public relations writing is usually done for an explicit purpose, and the expenditures involved in producing any item must be justified by the degree to which the writing fulfills that purpose. For example, if you are asked to write an article for a company publication outlining a new policy about how raises are awarded, you will be expected not only to write a factually correct story but also to express the attitudes and intentions of management in a manner acceptable to employees.

This idea of intent in public relations writing puts an extra burden on the writer. All of the rules of good grammar, spelling, usage, style, and structure apply to public relations writing. The requirements of brevity and clarity that help make for crisp news stories also hold for writing brochures. Above and beyond these considerations, public relations writers must constantly bear in mind the interests of the institutions for which they write and the purposes of their writing.

Public relations writers are not merely propagandists for the people who pay them. Rather, the good public relations writer is a professional, able to write honestly and clearly about complex and varied issues in a manner acceptable to people who may know little or nothing about writing but who know a great deal about what they want to see in print.

Public relations writers have a dual role, however. Their responsibilities extend not only upward to their employers but also outward to those who will read what they write. In a sense, public relations writers act as translators. They must completely understand the company or institution they write about. If it is a company that makes computer parts, they must know a great deal about computers. If it is a hospital, they must have a working knowledge of medical terms and procedures. Yet they must write about these things in ways their readers can understand. Their role becomes much like that of newspaper reporters covering particular beats they know intimately.

This intimate knowledge of the institution a writer "covers" engenders a particular problem with the use of language. Public relations writers should take care not to become so immersed in their topics that they take on the jargon of the company to an inordinate degree. Readers of newspapers that use press releases from a hospital may not know what a "cardiovascular microsurgery specialist" really does unless you explain cardiovascular microsurgery in simple terms. The same is true for any highly specialized topic. Central to this concept is the idea of audience. As a public relations writer, you will write for a variety of people—company employees, the general public, management, government officials—and the use of language will change depending on who the audience is. A piece intended for the board of trustees of a university will differ substantially in tone and content from something intended for release to state newspapers, even if the topic (the hiring of a new dean, for example) is the same.

A public relations writer must be something of a verbal acrobat, leaping from form to form with seemingly effortless ability. By the same token, the writer must be skilled at structuring information into a variety of widely differing formats. One person may be required to write speeches, letters, brochures, news releases, promotional copy, and formal reports—all on the same topic and all in the same week! This is particularly true of small firms or departments. Doing this kind of work requires an absolute command of the basic tools of writing, good reporting abilities, and a mental flexibility which allows the writer to think about the same or related topics in a multitude of ways.

A final point should be made about PR writing. Essential to all writing for public relations is understanding the purpose of the communication and knowing what the audience is for the communication. In other words, a writer needs to know why he or she is writing and what the audience is likely to do with that information. That knowledge comes not only from the research the writer does on what he or she is writing but also from a sensitivity and respect the writer has for the audience.

The ability to write—and to use the language effectively—is at the heart of almost all public relations activities, but it is not the only skill necessary for the successful public relations person. That person must also have the ability to deal effectively with many people in various situations. He or she must know how to use tact or persuasion in obtaining information from others within the organization. The PR professional must be able to satisfy the various publics that the organization communicates with. The professional must also be persuasive with the leaders of an organization in advising them on their public relations efforts. The PR practitioner is often one of the most visible persons within the organization and must keep the purposes and goals of the organization in mind during all of his or her contacts.

The successful PR practitioner must have the ability to organize effectively and work efficiently. That means meeting deadlines that are imposed quickly and arbitrarily. That person must be a quick study—one who is able to quickly grasp an idea or situation and give it form and substance. And that person must be able to make sound judgments about the effectiveness of public relations efforts.

The PR professional should combine a belief in the goals of an organization with a high standard of personal ethics and integrity. In the tenth century, so the story goes, Eric the Red sailed west from his native Iceland and discovered a large, desolate land. He wanted to colonize it, but the land was so forbidding that he felt that even his hearty Icelanders would be reluctant to do so. To make the land more appealing, he named it Greenland. With this name, Eric the Red was able to persuade a number of people to follow him to a place that is covered mostly with snow and ice. Eric the Red, many have said, was one of the world's first flacks.

Public relations has had a widespread reputation of being practiced by "flacks." These are people who stretch or ignore the truth to gain something for their organization. They spout the "company line," knowing but not caring that it is self-serving and inaccurate. They seek only publicity, even if it is bad publicity. These kinds of people, unfortunately, make it into almost every profession, and the public relations field has certainly not been immune from them. Yet, most public relations practitioners consider themselves professionals with high standards of ethics and a deep regard for accuracy. The people who believe in what their organization is doing and make genuine efforts to provide accurate and useful information to the organization's publics make the best PR professionals.

Writing news releases

One of the most common forms of public relations writing is the news release. The news release is information, usually written in the form of a news story, which an organization wishes to make public through the news media. A news release, like a news story, should follow a consistent style; it should be written as concisely and precisely as possible; it should answer all of the pertinent questions about the story; and it should emphasize what an editor will think is the most important part of a story. In short, a good news release differs very little from a good news story.

The last point about news releases—that they should emphasize what an editor will think is the most important part of a story—is one that sometimes gives public relations writers some problems. The first problem can be overcome by knowledge and application of the news values discussed in Chapter 4. The second problem is that corporate managers, who have very little knowledge of news values, will often want to emphasize what *they* think is important rather than what rates as important to an editor.

This attitude puts the writer in a difficult position. Most news releases are discarded by editors most of the time. One reason for this is that editors get many news releases every day, and they do not take the time to go through each of them carefully. If a news release does not give the editor some news immediately, the editor is not going to spend much time with it. Another reason that editors discard news releases is a prejudice on the part of many editors against running news releases. News releases are often seen by editors as propaganda or promotion—or even free advertising. The way a writer can overcome these problems is by writing a news release as close to the news story form as possible. Editors are much more likely to use news releases that have the most important information in a simply written lead paragraph and that follow a consistent style than those releases that do not.

Many corporate managers do not understand this, and they often want a non-newsworthy item emphasized in a release. For instance, a manager may want to announce a new plant opening in the following way:

```
    John Jones, president of the American South
Corporation, announced today that American
South Corporation will open a new copper-wire
manufacturing plant in Midville next year.
    Mr. Jones said the plant will employ about
75 people initially and about 250 when it is
fully operational....
```

The public relations writer will have to convince the manager that this style will not help the news release get used. A better way of writing this release would be the following:

```
    A copper-wire manufacturing plant, which
will employ about 250 when it is fully opera-
tional, will open in Midville next year, ac-
cording to officials of the American South
Corp.
    The opening was announced by John Jones,
president of the corporation....
```

While the content of a good news release is the same as that of a good news story, the form differs slightly. Generally, a news release should contain three things at the top of the first page. One is a headline or slug-line telling what the story is about. The styles of various public relations departments are different, and the writer must learn what style his or her department uses. In the example above, a headline might look like this:

```
NEW PLANT TO OPEN
IN MIDVILLE NEXT YEAR
```

A second item that should be at the top of a news release is the name and telephone number of a person in the organization who can be contacted for more information. Again, this will differ according to various public relations departments, but it should always be there. Editors who are interested in using a story may want to know more about it. They are more likely to pursue a story if a name and telephone number are easily available to them. The form this information takes could be as simple as the following:

```
For more information contact
James E. Smith
American South Corporation
555-1616
```

A third piece of information that should be at the top of a news release is a release time. This tells the editor when the information may be used. Often, the information may be used as soon as the editor gets it, and in this situation the words "FOR IMMEDIATE RELEASE" should be used. Sometimes, however, editors may be sent releases before they should be used. For instance, some sort of a ceremony in the mayor's office may be set up to announce the new plant mentioned in the example above. It may be that corporate officials do not want word of the plant getting out until the official announcement is made, but they still want to cooperate with editors who have deadlines to meet. In these cases, they will put an **embargo** on the release. An embargo is simply a time when a piece of information may be used, and it may look like this:

```
For release after 10 a.m.
Friday, October 13
```

Editors will generally abide by embargo times and not release information before they should. There is nothing an organization can do, however, if an editor chooses to run information before an embargo. Consequently, public relations practitioners should be careful in releasing information with an embargo and should do so only to those editors who can be trusted.

News stories are generally written in an inverted pyramid form. The most important information is presented first, and the information comes in a descending order of importance. For the writer of the news release, this means that the background information that often must be included about the organization should come at the end of the story rather than toward the beginning.

The writer of a news release—like the writer of a news story—should keep the commonly accepted news values that contribute to defining news in mind when writing the release. The writer should ask, "Is the story timely? What impact will it have? Is there conflict in this story? Are prominent people involved in the story? Is there something bizarre or unusual about this story?" Reviewing the news values of a news release will help the writer in producing a release that is more likely to be used.

The most important part of a news story—and also a news release—is the lead paragraph. Remember, the first reader of a news release is likely to be a busy editor who must decide whether or not to use it in his or her publication. You should let that editor know quickly what your story is about. Just as a news writer needs to "sell" a story with a lead that is interesting or informative (or even both), the writer of a news release needs to sell an editor on the story in the same way. If the editor thinks the news release is interesting or important, he or she is more likely to use the information.

Another point about news releases should be made here. A news release might have only one reader—the editor or reporter to whom it is sent. Yet, if that person uses the information it contains in a story or uses it as the basis for getting more information, the release has been a success. In most cases—particularly in larger cities—newspapers and trade publications rarely run press releases, so the writer of a news release rarely expects to see his or her

Figure 8-1 News release
This news release has a number of problems. As we noted in the text, the lead emphasizes the wrong details. In paragraph 1, instead of having John Jones' name at the beginning of the lead, the fact that a new plant employing as many as 200 people should begin the story.

In paragraph 3, the facts about the company are too high in the story; they should be moved to the end of the story.

In paragraph 5, some company jargon is beginning to sneak into this story. The writer should make sure that the readers can understand everything that is in the story.

The location of the plant is very important, especially to readers in Midville, where this story is likely to get the most attention (see paragraph 7). This fact should be placed higher in the story. Also, the projected beginning and ending dates of construction should be placed higher in the story.

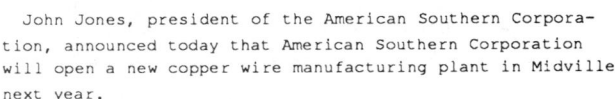

News from

For more information contact
James E. Smith
American Southern Corporation
(404) 555-1313

For release after 10 a.m.
Friday, October 13

NEW PLANT TO OPEN
IN MIDVILLE NEXT YEAR

American Southern
"Making America Grow"

John Jones, president of the American Southern Corporation, announced today that American Southern Corporation will open a new copper wire manufacturing plant in Midville next year.

Mr. Jones said the plant will employ about 75 people initially and about 200 people when it is fully operational.

American Southern Corporation has plants in more than 30 states and manufactures a variety of materials that are used for industrial and technological purposes. The company employs more than 15,000 people and is headquartered in Atlanta, Ga.

The copper wire plant planned for Midville will be part of the industrial parts division of the corporation.

"The computerized rotating process that will be installed at the Midville plant will be state-of-the-art for this industry," Mr. Jones said in making the announcement in Midville today.

"We plan to hire many people from the Midville area to work in this plant, but a number of them will have to be trained in this process. We will be giving those people that training as soon as possible.

The plant will be located on a 50-acre site on Sherrill Road, five miles south of downtown Midville. Construction of the plant will begin immediately, and company officials estimated that the plant should be fully operational within three months.

"We looked at a number of sites for this plant but chose Midville for a number of reasons," Mr. Jones said. "Among those were Midville's location near some major rail transport sites and the overall quality of life that Midville offers."

own words in print. The purpose of a news release is to get information to the people who work in the mass media. If the information in a news release results in the information being used by the media, the news release has done its job.

The rules about sentence and paragraph structure apply to news releases just as they do to news stories. Sentences should be short, and the paragraphs reasonably brief. Editors, just like newspaper readers, do not like to get involved with long paragraphs.

A news release writer has to pay particular attention to jargon and wordiness that might creep into a news release. Every organization or association develops its own language—abbreviations and acronyms that speed up communication among those with a knowledge or interest in the field. PR practitioners must also know this language in order to communicate within the organization, but they should be careful to use only language that is widely familiar in their news stories.

Wordiness is another danger to the well-written news release. Wordiness is particularly a problem if a news release must be approved by those who are not professional writers. People who do not understand how to use the language often believe that the more words you can use—not the fewer words—the more you will impress the reader and the more likely you are to get your point across. Professional writers know that just the opposite is the case. A news release should use only the number of words it takes to convey the information you want to convey. Anything more is wasted.

News release writers should pay particular attention to proper identification of all the people mentioned in a release. A news release is an official document coming from the organization. Journalists count on a news release to be correct when it mentions information about the organization. Journalists may also want to contact directly the people mentioned in the news release. They assume that those mentioned in a news release are correctly identified and that their names are spelled correctly. A PR practitioner who fails at either of these tasks can cause much embarrassment for everyone involved.

Finally, another form of the news release with which PR practitioners must deal is the video news release. The VNR can range from a short news story produced by the organization on videotape and distributed locally to longer feature items (or even half-hour shows) that large companies distribute nationally. VNRs for news items are written in much the same way as broadcast scripts for news stories are written. They are "reported" by someone within the organization or someone hired by the organization, put on videotapes, and distributed to TV news departments in the area. Larger companies produce longer and more expensive VNRs that are likely to emphasize the generic products they sell rather than the brand names. For instance, a soup manufacturer may produce a tape on the nutritional value of soup, or a brokerage firm might produce a piece on the advantages of buying stock.

From the PR practitioner's point of view, the two major problems with producing VNRs are the expense and the uncertainty of their use. VNRs can take a lot of time and money from an organization. The people and equipment involved in producing a high-quality VNR can involve thousands of dollars. For a company with many assets, the costs may not seem out of line, but for smaller organizations, spending several thousand dollars—or even several hundred—on a single item like a VNR is not worth it. The second problem is getting VNRs used by television stations. Many stations are unwilling to use material that is not produced by their own news departments. And even where stations are willing to use this material, they may not have the air time to do so.

Despite these problems, VNRs remain a valid tool for information distribution by an organization. With improvements in video technology, the costs of producing and distributing a VNR are coming down, and more and more companies are finding video a useful means of providing information to their publics.

Letters

Despite increased use of the telephone and advances in other forms of communication, letters are still one of the most important and effective means of communicating in the business world today. In fact, they have increased in importance with the installation and use of fax machines. The well-written letter is impressive and appreciated by the receiver. The poorly written letter can establish negative feelings on the part of the receiver that are extremely difficult to overcome. PR practitioners are often called on to write letters for their organizations. These letters may serve a variety of purposes, such as selling a product or idea, explaining company policy, answering complaints, and raising funds. Each of these letters must be carefully crafted to accomplish its purpose.

Letters are a good way to direct a message straight to the persons you want to receive that message. Most people read their mail; at least, they begin to read their mail. If a letter does not quickly give its information and make its point, it is likely to irritate or lose its reader—or both. Letters are expensive for organizations to produce and send. They take time and care to write. Like all other communication, they must accomplish their mission for the organization.

Like any other kind of writing, letter writing requires a precise and concise use of the language. Letters require that writers come directly to the point, that they do not waste the time of the receiver. Letter writing requires more, however. The letter is a very personal form of communication. Even if a letter is obviously written for a large number of people, it is still taken very personally by a receiver. Letters, then, should have some personal touch. The reader should get the feeling that the letter was written to and for him or her.

One technical requirement is that letters should *never* contain any spelling, grammar, or punctuation errors. They should also never show any editing.

The first rule of letter writing is to understand the purpose of the letter. The letter writer should ask, "Why am I writing this letter?" and if necessary should make a list of those reasons. There may be a number of reasons for a letter to be written, but there should be one overriding purpose. If that is not evident from the list the writer makes, then he or she should give some more thought to the letter itself.

Following closely on the purpose for writing the letter is the action expected of the recipient. Again, the letter writer should ask a question: "What do I want the reader to do after reading the letter?" Sometimes the answer is a simple one and comes directly from the purpose of the letter. At other times, the intended action of the reader may not be apparent. Again, the writer should have this clearly in mind before starting to write the letter. In any case, the action of the reader should be as specific as possible.

The table on the next page shows some examples of purposes and intended actions for a letter.

Once the purpose of the letter and the intended action on the part of the reader is established, the writing can begin. One of the first and most important considerations a writer should give to a letter is its tone. The proper tone is essential to the effectiveness of a letter. In most cases of business correspondence, a letter must be both personal and professional; they must show the right mix of these qualities. A letter that is too personal—especially if the writer and recipient are not personal friends—may offend the recipient as an invasion of privacy. A letter that is too formal may make the recipient feel that he or she is not very important to the writer.

What do we mean by being "too personal" in a letter? Here are some things to do to avoid that:

Don't be obsequious. The dictionary defines obsequious as "exhibiting a servile attentiveness or compliance." In letter writing, this means not thanking someone too much (twice is the maximum for a letter; once is better); don't keep apologizing; not saying "please" more than once in a letter; not using or repeating phrases such as "I hope you'll understand." All of these things irritate the reader; most people want to be spoken to, or written to, in a straightforward manner.

Don't be too complimentary. Depending on the purpose of the letter, compliments can ring hollow very quickly. In a letter telling a job applicant that he or she didn't get the job, this might be appropriate:

```
The experience listed on your resume shows
that you are very well qualified for a number
of positions.
```

But this would be too much:

```
The experience listed on your resume shows
that you are very well qualified for a number
of positions. You made an excellent impres-
sion on all of us when you interviewed for
the position, and we were glad that you know
so much about our company. People like you
would be a credit to our company, and we're
just sorry that we had only one position to
fill.
```

A letter like that is likely to leave the reader asking, "If they thought so much of me, why didn't I get the job?" In that case, the letter would not have accomplished its purpose. Long compliments are usually reserved for friends. They have only limited effectiveness in a business letter.

Generally, don't try to be funny. Humor is not expected in business correspondence and is likely to get in the way of your purpose for writing the letter. In addition, few people can write humor well enough to be understood, so the best rule is: Don't try.

Avoid referring to the personal characteristics, habits, or feelings of the reader. If you are dealing with someone on a professional basis, you probably do not know much about their personal habits or feelings. And even if you think you do, you shouldn't make too many assumptions about them. In the letter above telling a person that he or she did not get a job, what if the writer had said:

```
I know this news will disappoint you.
```

It is possible that the recipient would actually be glad not to have gotten the job offer. The recipient may have gotten a better offer from another company. In that case, the writer looks pretty silly.

To avoid sounding too formal in your letters, here are some things you should consider:

Use personal pronouns. Used appropriately—that is, not too much—personal pronouns can humanize a letter without letting it become too personal. A reader wants to be recognized as a human being with attitudes and feelings. The use of personal pronouns, especially *you* to address the reader, is a good device for business correspondence.

Avoid impersonal constructions. Impersonal constructions are those such as "It is . . ." and "There is . . ." These constructions also include those that place the blame on "it," as in "It has been decided . . ." "It" does not decide anything; some person or group does. Writers use these constructions in the hope that readers will not attribute an action to a particular person (especially themselves). Readers are usually sharper than that, however, and can see right through this ploy.

Avoid the passive voice. The passive voice—in business letters as in

Figure 8-2 Letters —————————————————————————————
The table below shows the variety of purposes and intended actions that letters might have. Letter writers should have a good sense of both of these concepts.

Letters: Purposes and Intended Actions

The purpose of the letter is	The intended action on the part of the reader is
to answer a complaint from a customer	to understand why the situation occurred
to explain a policy to a member of the organization	to know what the policy is
to announce a new procedure for applying for promotion	to follow the new procedure when applying for promotion
to persuade someone to subscribe to our magazine	to fill out the subscription card
to ask someone to join our organization	to fill out the membership card
to get someone to pay a bill	to send the payment
to tell someone that he or she didn't get a job	to know that he or she didn't get the job but still to feel that he or she received fair treatment

all other forms of writing—deadens writing. It robs any piece of writing of its vitality. Active verbs make a letter much more likely to be read and understood.

Be careful about referring to policies, rules, and regulations. If a policy or rule is the reason that something occurred and that needs to be explained in the letter, the policy or rule should be stated in the simplest terms possible. In many large, bureaucratic organizations, such rules are written in an obscure form of bureaucratese. The writer needs to translate this for the reader into the plainest terms possible. In most cases, the writer should not make technical references, such as "Regulation 33.b states. . . ." unless that is something the reader will readily understand.

Avoid using technical language that may mean nothing to the reader. A person who has a complaint will not be pacified by a letter that he or she does not understand. In fact, it is likely to confirm the feeling that the complaint is valid. Such a letter is also likely to offend the reader by its condescending tone.

Avoid wordiness. Lots of words, long sentences, and long paragraphs will obscure the message of the letter. They may sound impressive to the person who writes them, but they will not impress the reader. One of the best ways to strike that mix of the formal and personal necessary to a good letter is to write in simple, down-to-earth language.

Company publications

News releases and letters are very important and common forms of public relations writing, but they are by no means the only ones. Organizational publications abound, and the public relations people in an organization are usually responsible for them.

In dealing with these publications, the public relations practitioners may be responsible for more than writing. They should know about editing, typography, layout, photo selection and cropping, and other parts of the publication process. Those topics are not covered specifically by this book. Rather, the focus here is on the basic writing skills that are a part of any of these jobs.

Three major kinds of publications that organizations produce are newsletters, pamphlets and brochures, and company reports.

Newsletters. The newsletter is a basic term for a wide variety of publications a company may produce. The newsletter may range from a single mimeographed sheet to a slick, full-color magazine. The form that a newsletter takes will depend on the company, the amount of money that is spent on it, and, most importantly, the audience.

Newsletters are directed at a particular audience, and a writer for a newsletter must keep this in mind to be successful. Most company newsletters are internal; that is, they are targeted for audiences within the company. One of the most popular types of newsletters is the employee newsletter. This one is directed toward the employees of an organization, giving them information about the company and focusing on their interests and concerns. Newsletters may be specialized to the point of aiming at a certain set of employees in a company. The point is that newsletters should always be directed at a particular audience, and they must be written and edited with that audience in mind.

The style of writing a newsletter uses will depend on the audience and its purpose. Many newsletters are purely informational. They try to get as many facts to the audience as quickly as possible. Other newsletters are for information and entertainment. Either way, the writing in a newsletter must be concise and precise. No newsletter should waste the reader's time. Few companies will *require* that their employees read a newsletter. Rather, they are encouraged to do so, and one of the means of encouragement is an efficient writing style.

Because of the advent of desktop publishing (DTP) technology, organizations are more likely to produce newsletters for their publics. Desktop publishing technology is computerized editing equipment that allows the users to write, edit, and design a publication on the same computer screen. With DTP, newsletters are an even more efficient means of getting current information to an audience quickly. DTP allows newsletters to be produced efficiently and at a lower cost than was possible just a few years ago. The leading computer for this activity is the Apple Macintosh, but many other computer hardware and software companies are designing products for the DTP market. An understanding of this technology is necessary for the person wishing to become a PR practitioner. That person needs to know how to write but in addition needs to know how to design and lay out a publication.

Newsletters are most effective when they are consistent in their writing, design, and publication schedule. Those who read them should know what to expect in them and when to expect it. The PR practitioner who publishes a newsletter must understand the value of this consistency to the effectiveness of the newsletter.

Pamphlets and brochures. Unlike newsletters, pamphlets and brochures are usually directed at external audiences—people outside an organization. They are not published periodically as a newsletter is. Rather, they are published once and for a specific purpose. These kinds of publications are important because they are often the first and sometimes the only contact a person may have with an organization. These publications must catch the eye of a potential reader and then deliver content that is substantial and well written. Like an advertisement, the appearance of a pamphlet or brochure will promise something; that promise should be kept with the content. Public relations people are often put in charge of producing as well as writing these publications.

There are two kinds of pamphlets and brochures: informational and persuasive. The informational brochure tells about an organization or procedure. The writing in this kind of brochure must be down to earth, practical, and efficient. A brochure on how to hang wallpaper, for instance, should take the reader through a step-by-step process, giving the reader enough information to do the job but not wasting the reader's time. The persuasive brochure is one that tries to make a point, to sell an idea, or to persuade readers to adopt a certain point of view. Many examples of this kind of brochure exist: An American Cancer Society brochure on the evils of smoking is one. Writing style may vary in this kind of brochure, but one thing the writer should remember is that opinions should be based on information. A writer may express opinions very strongly, but these expressions are not nearly as persuasive as facts. For instance, a writer may say, "You ought to give up smoking because it is bad for your health." The writer would be more effective by saying, "Doctors say more than half the cases of lung cancer that they treat are caused by smoking." The second statement is much stronger because it gives the reader facts, not just opinions.

(For the rest of this section, the term brochure will to refer to both pamphlets and brochures. A pamphlet is usually smaller than a brochure, has a narrower purpose, and often has a shorter life. Beyond that—for the purposes here, at least—the differences between a pamphlet and brochure are not significant.)

The brochure is a common means of introducing an organization to the public. Its strength is that it can be designed for and delivered directly to an audience of the organization's choosing. That means that it is efficient in holding the attention of a particular audience. It can be designed for maximum effect on the audience.

The design is a very important part of a brochure and has a great deal to do with the writing in it. There is a wide variety of formats and an infinite number of designs that can be applied to a brochure. In thinking about put-

Figure 8-3 Company publications
The examples below show a variety of kinds of publications that a company may produce. Every company has to deal with a "public" in public relations terms, and most have more than one of these constituent groups. Targeting them with a variety of publications is a common way for an organization to communicate quickly and efficiently.

Figure 8-4 Producing a brochure
The producers of a brochure or pamphlet have to decide on the publication's purpose and message first. Writing and design decisions are then made – often simultaneously.

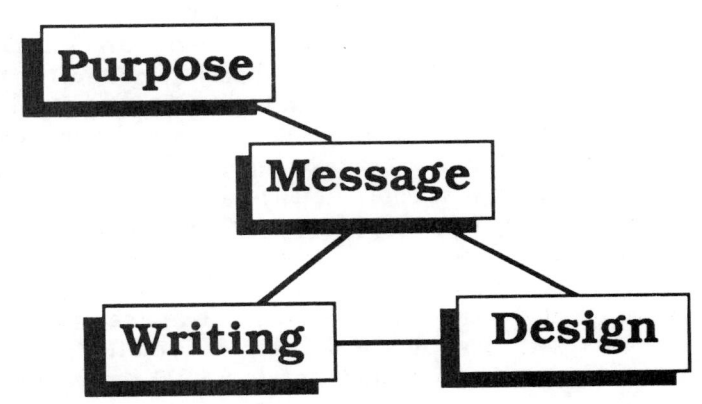

ting together a brochure, it is useful to follow the diagram on this page. Those in charge of the production of the brochure need to decide first on the purpose it is to serve. They should ask, "Why is this brochure necessary? What problem will it solve? What audience is it directed to?"

Following closely on these questions is the message that the brochure is to convey. Is the brochure supposed to describe the organization in general, or does it have a more specific message? Is it to persuade its audience to do something, or is it simply to inform? (The thinking that goes into a brochure is much like the thinking that goes into an advertisement. In fact, a brochure can be considered a kind of advertisement for an organization. For a more in-depth review of this process, see Chapter 7.)

Once the purpose and message of a brochure are decided, the design and writing decisions are made. These decisions may be simultaneous; that is, the writing and design may take place at more or less the same time. A PR practitioner who is proficient at both writing and design will often do this. Or one decision could follow the other. For instance, a designer may come up with a design for a brochure and then give it to a copywriter; or a writer may write the copy first and hand it over to the designer. In any case, the design and writing are closely linked.

Many people make the mistake of thinking that simply presenting information is a good persuasive method. While information is necessary for a persuasive argument, it usually needs to be crafted in a way that will emphasize its persuasive factors. Sometimes that can be done by the order in which the information is presented. Very often it is done by the graphic techniques in the brochure. If a PR practitioner is not good with design and layout, he or she needs to find someone who is and work closely with that person.

Annual reports and other types of reports. Companies that sell stock to the public are required by law to produce an annual report. Many other organizations that do not come under this requirement also produce annual reports. These reports give people inside and outside the company an idea of what the company is all about and how the company is doing financially. Many companies, particularly larger companies, consider the annual report one of the most important forms of communication they have. One legal requirement for annual reports is that they must be truthful. While a company may try to put on its "best face" in an annual report, the information the report contains must be factual.

The writer of an annual report—usually someone in the company's public relations department—is often required to translate a lot of complicated financial data and industry jargon into a simple, clear account of the company's activities and position. The writer must use understandable English and write for an audience that does not know the ins and outs of the company.

Other kinds of reports a company may require are quarterly or semiannual reports or reports about an organization's activities that are directed to a special audience. Nonprofit organizations may compile these kinds of reports when they embark on fund-raising campaigns. Writing these kinds of reports takes a lot of intelligence and skill in using the language.

Annual reports must contain financial information about the organization and some descriptive information about the company's structure and activities for the year. Beyond that, companies have wide latitude in what they may include in an annual report. Large organizations sometimes put thou-

Figure 8-5
Two approaches for brochures
Here are two brochures about the same organization, but they use different approaches. The top one is informational; the bottom one is persuasive. The persuasive brochure is aimed at a narrower audience — potential students of the department. The informational brochure could be given to anyone interested in the department.

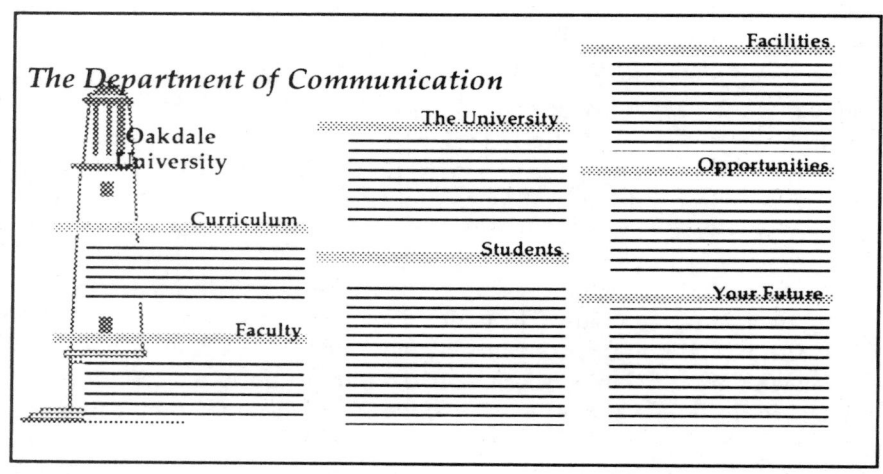

sands of dollars into the production of an annual report, and they target these reports for specific audiences and purposes, such as attracting investors, holding onto stockholders, and creating a stable image within a field of competition; for non-profit organizations, the purpose of an annual report might be to attract members, increase visibility in the community, and report on otherwise hidden activities.

Oral presentations

Speeches, statements, and other oral presentations are among the most common forms of public relations writing. The major difference between this kind of writing and the writing that we have discussed previously is that, like writing for broadcasting, oral presentations are written for the ear, not the eye. They are written to be spoken, not read silently.

Consequently, many of the principles of broadcast writing apply to this kind of writing. Oral presentations should be written in simple, clear, concise language. Sentences should be short. Modifiers and modifying phrases should be kept to a minimum. The content of the speech should be simple; the points made should be easy to follow.

In writing any oral presentation, the PR practitioner must take three major factors into consideration: the audience, the speaker, and the subject of the presentation.

The writer should know, as precisely as possible, who will be listening to the speech. For instance, a company president may be asked to speak at a high school graduation. The writer should understand that while the speech may be directed to the graduates, the audience will also contain their parents and other relatives. This may make a difference in how the speech is structured. The writer will also need to have some idea of what the audience is "expecting" to hear and how important it is to meet those expectations. For instance, if the local college football coach is asked to make a speech before the Lion's Club in early August, the audience will expect him to comment on the upcoming season. They are likely to be disappointed if most of his speech is devoted to the previous season.

The speaker is an important part of how the writer approaches a speech. His or her personality will have much to do with the content of the speech. For instance, the writer may need to know if the speaker is comfortable telling funny stories or if the speaker likes to quote certain people. The speaker may have some ideas he wishes to use in the speech, or he or she may even want to write a draft of the speech for the writer to polish.

The subject of the oral presentation, of course, is an all-important factor for the writer. The subject matter is usually connected with the position of the speaker, although that is not always the case. In the case of the high school graduation speech just mentioned, the company president is not expected to talk much (if at all) about his company. Too many comments about the organization might be inappropriate in this setting. In other cases, however, the audience will expect to hear about the organization that the speaker represents.

Three of the most common types of oral presentations that PR practitioners are asked to write are slide presentations, statements, and speeches.

The **slide presentation** (or presentation using transparencies) is very popular with many organizations, and its use is very likely to increase. Slide presentations are an effective means of presenting information, particularly to small groups of people. They are especially helpful in sales presentations. Slides can supplement the words of the speaker and can help focus the attention of the audience on the points that the speaker wants to make.

One of the reasons that slide presentations are growing in popularity is technology. With DTP equipment, it is much easier and less expensive than it was only a few years ago to produce quality graphics that can be made into slides. Producing such graphics, as well as writing the presentation, may become the duties of the PR person—yet another reason for the PR student to become knowledgeable about DTP technology.

The writer of a script for a slide presentation needs to understand the relationship between the script—that is, what the presenter will say —and the slides themselves. In almost all presentations, the slides are used to supplement and enhance what the speaker is saying, but the main information comes from the speaker. The slides themselves should be simple and uncluttered and should have a consistent format. The script contains the major part of the information in the presentation.

Another concept the writer of a slide script needs to understand is that of pacing. Pacing simply means how fast the slides appear to the audience. Some presentations need to be fast-paced; that is, the slides are shown rapidly throughout the presentation, possibly as many as ten per minute. A fast-paced script means that the slides contain no detailed information that the audience must absorb. If the slides do contain such information—such as graphs that indicate something about an organization's progress—the presentation should be at a slower pace. Some presentations call for slides to be shown at a rate of only one or two per minute. For most presentations, a minute per slide is probably too slow; the audience will expect a faster pace than that.

A **statement** is a short oral presentation; its length depends on the forum in which it is presented. A statement that precedes a question-and-answer session at a press conference should be relatively short—one to two pages at most. A statement that is read to a legislative committee might be longer, depending on the subject and the time allotted to the speaker. A statement has few of the formalities of a full-blown speech. It is an attempt to summarize facts and make points as efficiently as possible. It often sets the stage for what is to come later, particularly if it precedes a news conference. A statement should be cleanly and efficiently written. It should present its facts and make its points and then stop.

Speeches come in a wide variety of forms. They may be informative, persuasive, entertaining, or a combination of all three. They may last only a few minutes or all day (although modern Western audiences are likely to think a speech is too long if it exceeds thirty minutes). Many of our most memorable sayings were delivered in speeches. For instance:

> And so, my fellow Americans, ask not what your country can do for you; ask what you can do for your country.
> John F. Kennedy
> Inaugural address, 1961

> The only thing we have to fear is fear itself.
> Franklin D. Roosevelt
> Inaugural address, 1933

I never met a man I didn't like.

> Will Rogers
> Speech in Boston, 1930

Four score and seven years ago, our fathers brought forth on this continent, a new nation, conceived in Liberty, and dedicated to the proposition that all men are created equal.

> Abraham Lincoln
> Gettysburg Address, 1863

I have a dream.

> The Reverend Martin Luther King, Jr.
> Civil rights march in Washington, 1963

Writing a speech is not an easy task, but it is a common one for many PR practitioners. Writers may begin their work by thinking of a speech as consisting of three parts: an opening, a middle, and an ending.

The opening should do a number of things. It should allow the speaker to introduce himself or herself to the audience with some sort of personal reference. In most cases, an audience will already know something about a speaker; the speaker may have been formally introduced by someone else. The opening allows the speaker to say something about himself or herself and establish a relationship with the audience.

Many speakers also use the opening to "warm up" the audience with a humorous story. Such a device works best when the point of the story can be directly related to the points that the speaker is trying to make in the speech. A funny story for its own sake may help the speaker get going, but it is not as effective as the one that is part of the speaker's message.

Most important, the opening of a speech should establish the speaker's subject and should give the audience clues to the direction in which the speaker is headed. An audience should detect in a speech a logical progression of thought, and that progression should be evident from the very beginning of the speech.

The middle of the speech should take whatever points are made—or alluded to in the opening—and expand on them. A speaker may use a variety of techniques to do this. One of the most effective is telling a story. People of all ages like to hear stories; they enjoy following narratives. The stories, of course, should support the points that the speaker is trying to make in the speech, and they should do so in a fairly obvious way. A speaker who tells a story and then tries to explain what that has to do with the points in a speech has failed in using this device.

Another useful technique for a speech writer is the striking quotation. A speaker who can use quotations from other sources can add interest, strength, and credibility to his or her own remarks. Consider these remarks from a Vietnam combat veteran who was asked to speak to a local civic club about his war experiences:

```
    Occasionally, I am asked to describe what
it was like to be in Vietnam. From the per-
spective of those who lived in America during
```

that time, Vietnam was somehow a different
kind of war. It has often been pointed out
that it was the first war we saw on television. To the combat soldier, however, that
made little difference. We knew that all wars
are essentially the same. William Tecumseh
Sherman, speaking more than a hundred years
ago, summed up our feelings about war when he
said, "I am tired and sick of war. Its glory
is all moonshine. It is only those who neither fired a shot nor heard the shrieks and
groans of the wounded who cry aloud for
blood, more vengeance, more desolation. War
is hell."

Adapting an ancient quote to a modern purpose is another useful way to
add interest to speeches. A person speaking on the environment used a bibli-
cal quote in this way.

The Book of Ecclesiastes says there is "a
time to cast away stones, and a time to gather stones together." Generations before us in
this century have been casting away the
stones of our environmental systems. I firmly
believe that it is the charge of our generation to gather those stones together. Now is
the time.

Making a striking statement is another technique that speakers can
use to make a point and gain the attention of their audience. Sometimes that
statement can come in the form of challenging conventional wisdom, like the
following:

Most people believe that the Golden Rule—
"do unto others as you would have them do
unto you"—is the simplest and best formula
for good human relations. I'm here to tell
you that it isn't. In fact, that formula, despite the best intentions of some people, is
a disaster.

Sometimes an obscure but striking fact can gain the attention of the audience in the same way. The following is from a speech about how people can
rebound from failures early in life and go on to success later:

Back in 1919, the New York Yankees were
looking for an outfielder who was also a good
hitter. They thought they had a promising
young man, but he managed only two hits in
twenty-two at bats. The Yankees then went out
and purchased Babe Ruth from the Boston Red
Sox. Everybody knows what Babe Ruth accomplished, of course. But what about that young

man who only got the two hits? Whatever happened to him? He decided that baseball wasn't
his game after all, so he gave football a
try. That game was obviously better suited to
his abilities, and he became a star. In fact,
many consider him to be the father of professional football. His name was George Halas,
the long-time owner of the Chicago Bears.

These are just a few of the techniques that a writer can use to expand
the body of a speech. Whatever techniques are used, the speech should follow
a logical line—one that the audience can follow, too. If the speech goes off on
tangents and never returns, the points will be lost and the audience will be
dissatisfied.

The closing of a speech can be used to make the final, major point of the
speech or it can offer the audience a summary of what the speaker has already said. The same rhetorical devices that you can use in any other parts of
the speech—telling stories, using quotes, making striking statements—can be
used to close a speech. Speech writers should remember, however, that a good
speech does not need a dramatic flourish at the end. It can simply end with a
story that summarizes the subject of the speech, a listing of the points already made by the speaker, or a conclusion that can be logically drawn from
what the speaker has said.

Figure 8-6
Speakers and speeches
Speaking before an
audience demands a
different set of skills than
writing for the pulbic. The
writer of a speech must take
into account the person who
will be delivering the speech
as well as the content of the
speech and the makeup of
the audience.

Conclusion

Public relations work is mostly writing. Employers will look for people who can write to fill their public relations jobs. Public relations writing requires a versatility on the part of the writer that is demanded in few other jobs. While it is exciting and rewarding, the field of public relations is one that demands intelligence, skill, and hard work.

Points for consideration and discussion

1. At the beginning of this chapter, the author describes the field of public relations and some of the things that public relations practitioners do. From this description and what you know about the field, what is the most attractive thing about public relations work to you? What is the part of the work that you would like the least?

2. Many people who work in journalism and elsewhere have a very negative opinion of the field of public relations. Why do you think they have such an opinion?

3. A public relations practitioner has to have a wide range of knowledge and understanding to do his or her job well. What other courses in the curriculum of your college or university would you think a person should take if he or she is interested in becoming a public relations practitioner?

4. What are the advantages and disadvantages of writing a letter as opposed to making a telephone call when you want to make personal contact with someone?

5. The author says that the design and the content of a brochure or pamphlet are closely related. Try to find some examples of brochures or pamphlets and see if you think the people who put these together did a good job of relating the design and content.

6. The author lists several techniques for writing speeches, such as adapting ancient quotes and telling personal anecdotes. Can you think of others?

Further reading

Allen H. Center and Scott M. Cutlip, *Effective Public Relations,* 5th ed., Englewood Cliffs, NJ: Prentice-Hall, 1978.

George A. Douglas, *Writing for Public Relations,* Columbus, OH: Charles E. Merrill, 1980.

Richard Weiner, *Professional's Guide to Public Relations Services,* New York: Richard Weiner, Inc.

James J. Welsh, *The Speech Writing Guide,* New York: Wiley, 1968.

EXERCISES

The following section contains a variety of public relations writing exercises. You should follow your instructor's directions in completing them.

News releases

Write news releases based on the following information. Follow the directions given to you by your instructor.

YMCA

You work for the YMCA in your city, and as part of your job you have to write news releases about the organization's many recreational and educational programs. One such program is an on-going series of swimming lessons for children, young people, and adults. You have to write a release including the following information about the fall series:

Children's classes begin August 25 and are held on Mondays, Wednesdays, and Fridays. One class is held for each of five different age groups: tiny tots (ages one to three); kindergarten (ages four to six); elementary (six to nine); youth (ages ten to thirteen); and teens (ages fourteen to seventeen). All of these classes meet twice each week until November 30 on the following schedule:

Tiny tots meet on Mondays and Wednesdays from 1 p.m. until 2 p.m.

The kindergarten class meets on Mondays and Wednesdays from 2 p.m. until 3 p.m.

Elementary students meet from 3:30 p.m. until 4:30 p.m. on Mondays and Wednesdays.

The youth class runs from 4:30 p.m. until 5:30 p.m. on Mondays and Fridays

The teen class meets from 5:30 p.m. until 6:30 p.m. on Mondays and Wednesdays.

Two classes are held for adults (ages eighteen and older). One meets on Monday and Tuesday nights from 7 p.m. until 8 p.m. The other meets on Saturday from 1 p.m. until 3 p.m.

Registration will be held at the YMCA office from August 15 until August 22. Classes are limited to fifteen students each, and the registration cost is twenty dollars per child or twenty-five dollars per adult for YMCA members, thirty dollars per child or thirty-five dollars per adult for non-members.

Information: Mrs. Bertha Bucher, 774-4567.

Registration: See Mr. Bob Driver at the YMCA office.

No cash refunds for registration fees will be given. Those who register for classes but find it necessary to cancel should be sure to notify Mrs. Bucher immediately so that a credit memo may be issued for the amount of the registration fee. This memo can be applied to registration for other YMCA classes at some future date.

Department head leaves

You are public relations director for a local private hospital, Mountain East Medical Center. During the past few months, there has been considerable friction between the hospital's board of directors and the head of the purchasing department, Bob Wilkinson. Wilkinson's tight-fisted purchasing practices have been criticized by some of the medical staff in spite of the fact that the board of directors had ordered him to cut costs by 15 percent.

Write a press release using whatever of the following information you feel is important.

Wilkinson's resignation is effective immediately. He will be replaced by the assistant head of the department, Johnny Toler, who has been with the hospital for thirteen years.

Wilkinson was a 1972 graduate of the state university's school of hospital administration. He came to Mountain East Medical Center in 1975 after working for a small rural community hospital as purchasing chief. He will take a job as a purchasing agent with the City Memorial Hospital.

Toler's background is in pharmacy. He began as an assistant druggist in the hospital pharmacy 13 years ago and was moved to the purchasing department in 1978 as an assistant after the hospital pharmacy closed. Toler's wife, Carolyn, is head of the gynecology department at MEMC. They have two children.

Hospital administrator Harry Illscott had this comment: "Bob's abilities will be greatly missed at this hospital, but I know that Johnny Toler is a person we can all depend on to do whatever is necessary to keep his department going. I have great faith in him and in this hospital."

Toler gave the following statement: "This hospital means a great deal to me and my family, and I will give my best efforts to making our purchasing department the best. I learned from a fine man—Bob Wilkinson—and I hope I can continue to build on the foundation he established."

Honorary degrees

Each year, your university awards honorary degrees to people who have made outstanding contributions to the state or to society in some way. This year two honorary degrees will be awarded at the commencement exercises, which will be held at 11 a.m. on May 14 in Memorial Coliseum.

You work part-time at the university's public relations depatment, and your boss asks you to write a press release announcing that the following people will be receiving honorary doctorates at the Saturday morning ceremony:

George T. Hale, sixty-three, a 1945 graduate of the university who established the state's first cable television system back in the early 1960s, will be cited for his "ability to envision the future and make it a reality for the state's telecommunications industry." When he retired from the presidency of Hale Communication, Inc., last year, the company had more than 40 percent of the cable market. Hale, a multimillionaire, has donated thousands of dollars to the development of educational television at both major universities in the state. In addition, he built a camp for physically handicapped adults on his mountain estate and sends more than 300 individuals there each spring and summer for an extensive recreation training program. Hale lives in Birmingham with his wife of thirty years, Elizabeth. They are the adoptive parents to two Korean children: Lee, twenty-one, and Ben, eighteen.

Rachel Cabanis, forty-four, an Alabama native and 1956 graduate of Goucher College, completed law school at Harvard after a twenty-year career as a legal secretary with her husband's law firm in Montgomery. Her famous book about her decision to go to law school and her experiences there, *Breaking Through*, has been lauded as "the greatest statement of one woman's choices written in this decade." It won her a Pulitzer Prize (and at least a year's worth of speaking engagements). Mrs. Cabanis, now separated from her husband, Roy Cabanis, will return to Montgomery as a full partner in another law firm. She is being honored by the university for her "honesty and integrity in making difficult choices in a complex world and succeeding despite numerous obstacles."

New plant

You work for the Holesome Donut Company of Wilmington, Delaware. Your company wants to open as many plants as possible in the Sunbelt, and company officials have decided to establish a new doughnut factory in Repton, Alabama.

Write a press release announcing plans for the complex. Include as much of the following as you feel is significant.

Repton city officials had been bargaining for the new plant for two years. At least twelve small towns in Tennessee, Georgia, and Mississippi also wanted to be the site of the new plant. Repton was chosen because of its desirable location, the low interest rates local banks offered for development, and the willingness of city officials to help build roads and sidewalks, waste disposal facilities, and recreation areas near the plant.

Repton currently has a 14 percent unemployment rate, slightly below the state average. However, its main industry, a shoe factory, is reducing its payroll by half at the beginning of next year.

Construction on the $3 million doughnut factory is slated to begin on March 31. A tentative completion date of November 15 is set, and the factory should be in full operation by the beginning of next year.

The plant will provide 700 jobs for local people, and more than 100 families are expected to be brought in to work for the company.

The plant will make and package doughnuts for shipping to all parts of Alabama.

Company president Lonny Joe Underwood, an Alabama native who once owned a grocery store in Repton, made the following comment: "We believe that the future of America, like its past, lies in small towns like this. We want to be an integral part of this community and make it just as prosperous as it should be."

Tuition decrease

You are working in the public relations department of your university. The board of trustees is about to meet to consider tuition costs for next year. One of the proposals before the board is that tuition be lowerd by 10 percent for all students, in-state, out-of-state, graduate students, and undergraduates. The president of the university has already polled most of the board on this issue and has general agreement from the board on this action. Your first assignment is to prepare a news release on this action with an embargo time of 11:45 a.m. Friday, which is when the board meeting will be finished.

You can use the following information to prepare your news release:

The president's statement: "I am extremely pleased that the board has seen fit to follow our recommendations on lowering tuition costs. During the past several years we have had to raise tuition a number of times for all of our students. Out-of-state students have been particularly hard hit. For some time we have been afraid that we have been pricing ourselves out of the market, even with in-state students. With more and more people attending junior colleges and other universities in the state, we have recognized that those who want to come to this university must have some relief.

"Unfortunately, of course, the board's actions will have some negative effects on some parts of the university. Cutting tuition means a reduction in our income, and that reduction will have to be made up in other areas. No faculty or staff member will lose his or her job because of these cuts, but we will not be able to offer as many of the programs as we have in the past. The faculty and staff members whose programs will be eliminated will be absorbed into other areas of the university. I am very pleased about that. The students attending these programs, of course, must find alternatives."

Programs to be cut: Women's Studies, Ornithology Department, Arts and Sciences Honors Program, Women's Golf Team, Men's Golf Team, Human Resources Management Institute, University Hosts and Hostesses Program, and the Department of Eastern Languages; the Geology Department will be merged with the Geography Department.

Tuition costs during the last five years:
Tuition per semester

Undergrad (in-state)	$500	$550	$650	$800	$1050
Undergrad (out-of-state)	$800	$800	$1000	$1200	$1400
Graduates (in-state)	$600	$650	$750	$900	$1200
Graduates (out-of-state)	$850	$1000	$1100	$1200	$1700

Each of the final figures in the table above will be reduced 10 percent for the next term.

Overall enrollment increased at the university in the last five years from 14,500 students five years ago to 16,275 this year; however, last year the total enrollment was 16,700. Applications for next semester are down, and if they continue at the current rate, a 10 percent drop in enrollment from this year's figure is anticipated.

After the news release, you are to prepare two advertisements to run in the state's major newspapers telling about the new tuition rates at the university.

Press Association

You are the public relations officer for your state's Press Association. This association counts as its members all of the state's daily and weekly newspapers, and it performs a number of services, such as a statewide advertising bureau (if an advertiser wants to advertise in all of the state's newspapers, he or she can come to the Press Association and place the ad rather than going to the individual newspapers), information about the state's newspapers, a professional training program with a local university for people who work with the state's newspapers, and a lobbying service in the state legislature on bills that affect the press.

Recently, the Press Association board of directors decided that your office should do some special promotion for National Newspaper Week. Also, the press association has recently hired some university professors to conduct a survey about newspaper leadership in your state. That survey has been completed, and the board has decided to release the results and have them serve as the basis for this promotion.

Consequently, the Press Association has called a press conference for next Monday, the first day of National Newspaper Week. The press conference is scheduled for 10 a.m. The executive director of the Press Association, Ken Billiard, and this year's president of the Press Association, Slade Luketon, editor of the Rogersville Register, will be there to announce the results of the survey and to talk about newspapers.

Here are some facts about the survey: The survey was conducted during a two-week period in the fall by a polling organization at the state university. The number of people surveyed was 500, randomly selected from all across the state. The margin of error for the results is plus or minus 4 percent. The survey showed the following things: Newspaper readers are a "quality audience" (they tend to be married, more highly educated than the average person, have more annual income, own their own home, and vote regularly); newspaper readership is positively linked with income (only 43 percent of those with incomes of less than $30,000 read a newspaper regularly while 96 percent of those with incomes of more than $30,000 read a newspaper regularly); and 80 percent of everyone in the state reads a newspaper regularly; on the average, two newspapers are read in each home; more than half the people in the state read a newspaper every day; newspapers were named by 70 percent of the people as the most "thorough" medium (that is, giving the most complete reports), by 65 percent as the "most trustworthy" media (as opposed to television, 25 percent, and radio, 10 percent); and about 85 percent of the people in the survey said

they regularly made decisions based on newspaper advertising.

Luketon's statement, to be released at the time of the press conference: "The results of this survey show that newspapers are a trusted and useful medium. We believe that a newspaper is the best buy that an advertiser or a consumer can make in today's market. Newspapers have been hiding their lights under a bushel for a long time. We haven't bothered to tell people how good we are and what we can do for them. We hope that our attention to National Newspaper Week will help us tell this story."

Billiard's statement: "These results clearly show that newspapers are here to stay. While a few have gone out of business elsewhere, the newspapers in this state have a strong following among many people. Those newspapers plan to continue to provide the excellent service to advertisers and readers that we have provided in the past."

You are to prepare a 250-word press release incorporating these statements and summarizing the results of the survey. The press release will be handed out to other media in the state.

You are also assigned to prepare two advertisements based on the survey results. At least one should be for print and will run in the state's newspapers. The other may be for print, radio, or television.

Speeches and statements

The following situations require that you draft speeches or statements. Follow the instructions below or those given to you by your instructor.

Commencement speech

You are writing in the public relations department of a local company which manufactures computers, computer parts, and computer-related equipment. The president of your company has been asked to be the commencement speaker for this year's high school graduation ceremony. The president asks you to draft a speech for him which should be about five to ten minutes long. He says he wants to bring a hopeful message—one that says that despite a period of locally high unemployment, the future looks bright for today's high school graduates.

Kiwanis speech

Look at the press release on page 229. The president of American Southern has been invited to make a short speech to the Midville Kiwanis Club after this announcement has been made. He wants to tell them a little more about why his company chose Midville for the location of the plant. Here are some of the reasons:

• the educational system; Midville has one of the best in the state; a high percentage of students graduate from high school and go on to college (85 percent and 62 percent, respectively; the company feels that this is the kind of community that it can ask its managers and their families to live in.

• the waterways; the manufacturing process used in the new plant will require abundant sources of water; it will also require rivers that can be navigated to major shipping areas; the Blount River in Midville is such a river.

• a generally favorable business climate; the state has some of the lowest business taxes in the region and that's what prompted American Southern to look at the state for a location here in the first place.

You may also use information found in the press release.

The Kiwanis Club is a service organization. The members get involved in a lot of community projects. They will want to know about American Southern's planned involvement in the community. The president wants to tell them that community involvement is important to the company; they offer to contribute money and people to causes such as the United Way; they generally sponsor YMCA soccer, basketball, and baseball teams in the youth leagues. He wants to tell them that once American Southern is located there, they will see what the needs of the community are and try to help out.

The speech should be 750 to 1,000 words long.

College day

The Chamber of Commerce in your hometown is sponsoring "College Day," and the president has asked you to come back and tell them about your experiences in college. You'll be one of three people who have been asked to speak at the meeting that day on this subject. The president tells you that he wants you to talk purely from your own experiences. Try to give the listeners a flavor of what it was like to go to the college you attend; how you felt about going to your first class; when and how you made friends; how much money it costs; what some of the things are that they could tell their high school-age children about college.

The speech should be 500 to 750 words long.

Letters

Write letters based on the following information. Follow the directions given by your instructor.

Letter of apology

Just after Christmas, a large department store receives a letter from a woman complaining about the rudeness of the sales people in the women's ready-to-wear department. The woman is not specific about her complaints but says that she was in the store twice before Christmas and she was ignored completely once and spoken to rudely by a young sales girl the other. The department head, on seeing the letter, says that Christmas was a very busy season, the store always seemed to be crowded, and the department had to hire some temporary and untrained people to work during that time. She says she doubts that the woman would feel slighted by the regular employees. Draft a letter of at least 150 words for the store manager's signature responding to the woman's complaint.

Employee dinner

You are working in the public relations department of the home office of an insurance company. The company is planning an employee appreciation dinner for home office employees. This is the fifth year the company has had such a dinner. One of them will be named Outstanding Home Office Employee for the year. Another will receive the Community Service Award, which is given to the home office employee who has contributed the most to the community. A string quartet from the local university will provide the entertainment for the dinner, and Paul Harvey, the radio commentator and newspaper columnist, will give a speech. You should draft a letter to all the employees to encourage them to attend. The dinner will begin at 6:00 p.m. at the Hilton Hotel on April 5. Employees who plan to attend should inform their supervisors by April 1.

Fund-raising letter: Consolidated Giving fund drive

The president of your university wants to send out a letter to all employees encouraging them to support the annual community Consolidated Giving fund drive. As a member of the PR department, you have been assigned to draft the letter. The letter should make the following points (but not necessarily in this order):
• contributing to the Consolidated Giving fund is easy and convenient; employees can sign up for a monthly payroll deduction; the card to do this with will accompany the letter;
• the university has always been a major contributor to the community's Consolidated Giving fund; last year, more than $200,000 was raised from university employees also; this year's goal is $250,000;
• Consolidated Giving supports more than fifty community projects; more than 95 percent of the contributions will stay within the community;
• each department within the university has been given a goal; it is important for every individual employee to respond.
The letter should be between 150 and 200 words.

Fund-raising letter: Public radio

The manager of the local public radio station (for which you are a volunteer) has asked you to draft a letter announcing an on-air fund-raising campaign for the station. The campaign is to begin in two weeks and will run for five days. The goal is $50,000 from the listeners. The letter that you are drafting will go to people who contributed last year. These people already have supported public radio, and they know the kind of programming that public radio has: the news shows "Morning Edition" and "All Things Considered" from National Public Radio; the classical music during the weekdays and the jazz and bluegrass on the weekends; the special broadcasts of musical events in the community.

This year's fund-raising campaign is particularly important, and it's important that the station get off to a good start with early contributions from previous supporters. It's important for the following reasons:
• the station needs a new emergency generator; bad weather had knocked the station off the air a number of times;
• the station needs to purchase a new compact disk player so it can play many of the new releases, some of which are available only on compact disks;
• the cost of many of the programs that the station has to buy has gone up during the past year—some by as much as 25 to 30 percent; some of these programs may have to be dropped if the station doesn't get more money.
The letter should be between 150 and 200 words.

Pamphlets and brochures

Swimming

Below is the design for a pamphlet that the local YMCA wants to publish and distribute about the benefits of a regular swimming program. The purpose of the pamphlet is to get people to join the Y and begin swimming or doing some form of exercise. The pamphlet will be distributed to local businesses, especially those close to the Y.

The pool at the YMCA is open during the following hours: 7–9 a.m., 11 a.m.–1:30 p.m., and 4:30–7:30 p.m. on Mondays through Fridays; 3–6 p.m. on Saturdays. People who want to join the Y should come by or call, 876-0987. A year's membership costs thirty-five dollars.

Here are some of the benefits of swimming:

• it's aerobic exercise, meaning that it conditions the heart and lungs; this exercise can help prevent heart disease, the nation's number-one killer;

• it can help control body weight;

• it can help to build up stamina in a person;

• it can relieve tension; many doctors believe that exercise is a good antidote for depression and other emotional stress;

• swimming is a particularly good exercise because it is not hard on your joints; this is important especially for elderly people who are more likely to suffer from arthritis; swimming often offers a lot of relief for arthritis;

• swimming exercises almost all the major muscles of the body;

• regular exercise is good for the self-image; you just feel better about yourself.

YMCA officials also caution that people may need to consult their doctors or physicians before beginning an exercise program.

You need to write about 300 words of copy for this brochure.

Travel brochure

The Chamber of Commerce for the county next to the one you live in wants your public relations agency to design and write a short travel pamphlet about the sights in the county. This pamphlet will be distributed by the State Department of Tourism and will be found in hotels, travel bureaus, and agencies and interstate rest stops.

Write about 300 words that would persuade a traveler to visit that county. You may also want to suggest a general design for the pamphlet. Here are some facts that you can use:

Probably the major scenic attraction of the county is the four covered bridges; all have been well preserved and date back to the 1800s; they are (1) the Morton Mill Bridge, the highest covered bridge above water (about seventy-five feet), located five miles east of Smithville on Highway 6; it's 220 feet long; built in 1877 and restored in 1976; located next to the bridge was Morton Mill, where farmers brought their corn and wheat to be ground from about the time the bridge was built until the 1930s; (2) the Ensley Bridge, the oldest one in the county, built in 1821; legend has it that there was a skirmish between companies of Confederate and Union soldiers during the Civil War; several were killed, and locals say you can hear the ghosts rustling through the grass and trees at dusk; it's located on Highway 42 west of Springtown; (3) the Swann Bridge, built in 1921, is the newest of the four bridges; it is on the Old Barterville Highway, just south of Masontown; there was also a mill located next to it, and part of that mill building has been restored and is open to tourists; (4) the Nactor Bridge was built in 1900 and is to be found in the western part of the county on Highway 69 west of Smithville; the reason it was built is unclear, although some say a mill was located next to it for a while; if that's the case, it wasn't there very long because there are no records of it. Just why covered bridges were built is not exactly clear, although the ones that were located next to mills were probably built so that farmers would have some protection from the weather while waiting to get their wheat and corn ground. Since this is a small and still mostly rural county, the covered bridges are a big part of the heritage of the people.

The county offers some other attractions. It has several lakes and recreation areas, plus Rickwill Caverns, a 280-acre state park that is open all year around. The park features a restaurant that is actually located inside the cavern; you can also explore the caverns for a small admissions fee.

Finally, every October, there is the "Old Times Festival," a week-long fair that features everything from a tennis tournament to a quilt show; special tours of the covered bridges are conducted then.

APPENDIX A

Copy-editing symbols

The following is a standard listing of editing symbols that you should learn as quickly as possible.

Indent paragraph	The president said
Take out letter	occassionally
Take out word	the red hat
Close up words	week end
Insert word	take it run (*and*)
Insert letter	encyclopdia (*e*)
Capitalize	president washington
Lowercase letter	the President's cabinet
Insert hyphen	up to date
Insert period	end of the sentence
Insert comma	He said "I'll stop
Insert quotation marks	the "orphan quote
Abbreviate	the United States
Spell out	Gov. Sam Smith
Use figure	one hundred fifty-seven
Spell out figure	the 3 horses
Transpose letters	pejoartive
Transpose words	many problems difficult
Circle any typesetting commands	bfc clc
Connect lines	the car wreck xxxxx injured two people

Appendix B
The media and the law

This section is divided into two parts. The first gives some guidelines about the relationship of the news media to the law. The second introduces the the concepts of regulation of broadcasting and advertising.

News media and the law:

Some introductory guidelines

By Dwight Teeter, University of Tennessee

Journalists are people too, although non-journalists may sometimes have their doubts. Journalists show up at awkward times and ask unwelcome questions, and they seem to be around at times when lawyers enter people's lives.

Also, think about news coverage of your own family and friends. When persons you know well are in the news, are their names spelled right? Are the facts correct, and are all the words in the story spelled (or pronounced) correctly? When Aunt Tillie died in an automobile accident which killed three other people, were the facts straight? If reporters called, were they polite and sympathetic, or did they seem brusque and uncaring?

If, in your own experience, you or your friends and family have encountered press performance that is less than admirable, it follows that many other people—non-journalists—have had similar experiences. And it is from these non-journalists that juries in libel cases are formed. If press credibility is suffering, it is in part because of problems with inaccuracies.

There are no "small errors" in the news business. Misspelling one name can damage the credibility of a newspaper or magazine, at least in the eyes of people who know the person whose name was misspelled. Omission (or addition) of just one word can make an enormous difference. For example, compare the terms "guilty" and "not guilty." Many effective journalists have a kind of self-protective paranoia. Check the facts, and then check them again. Recheck all spellings. Remember,

there's only a one-space difference between "therapist" and "the rapist."

If you are accurate and do your best to be fair, those characteristics will go a long way toward keeping you out of the legal difficulties that many journalists find so threatening: Defamation (Libel), Invasion of Privacy, and Copyright Infringement.

Some cautionary notes

This introduction to media law is not intended to be a comprehensive listing of everything a journalist needs to know about media law. This will not and should not make journalists comfortable about their knowledge of legal matters. They should learn as much as they can about the law on their own, and they should endeavor to keep up with this rapidly changing field.

Journalists place themselves and their employers in legal peril when they "play lawyer." Journalists should not assume they know all they need to know about media law. When in doubt, seek advice from an attorney who is knowledgeable about communications law.

Perhaps the most important thing to remember about media law is this: What is legal may not be ethical. To say it another way, just because you can get away with something does not necessarily make it right. There is a general rule, for example, that citizens—including journalists—may publish material found in public records. That seems to mean, at least as of this writing in June of

1989, that journalists can lawfully publish the name of a rape victim if that victim's name was found in a public record. In ethical terms, however, it is difficult if not impossible to justify publishing the identity of a living rape victim.

Newspapers depend on access to information and are guaranteed the right to print and distribute the news. In general, the press of this nation is immune to pre-publication censorship—except in extremely limited situations involving vital information during wartime, publication of obscenity (whatever that is), and incitement to violence or overthrow of the government. After news has been published, however, punishment may be applied by courts under various criminal laws (e.g. the Espionage Act in time of declared war, or federal or state obscenity statutes).

Some legal terms

Keep in mind the difference between criminal law and civil law. *Black's Law Dictionary* (every newsroom should have one) defines a crime as an offense against the state. A crime can be committed by omission (e.g. not paying income taxes, not registering for the draft), or by commission (e.g. intentionally injuring or killing someone).

Civil law includes lawsuits (personal damage actions) in which a person asks for "recovery or redress," seeking "damages" (or payment). If, for example, a publication injures a person's reputation by publishing a false and harmful statement, that person may go to court with a libel lawsuit. Libel is a civil tort. (*Tort* is a French word meaning "wrong.") Civil libel is a tort. Invasion of privacy is a tort.

Constitutional law represents the basic governmental framework. The federal Constitution is the highest law of the land and divides government into three branches: legislative, executive, and judicial. (Similarly, state constitutions provide basic charters with similar divisions of powers.) In addition to apportioning powers of government among the three branches, the document also lists, in the Bill of Rights (the first ten amendments — powers that the U.S. government may not bring to bear upon residents of this country.

Keep in mind that there are fifty-one constitutions and legal systems in the United States of America: the federal Constitution plus the fifty state constitutions. Remember also that the federal Constitution is the highest law in this nation. Any state constitutional provision in conflict with the U.S. Constitution is not enforceable. Similarly, if a law or a decision by a state court, a U.S. District Court, or a U.S. Court of Appeals is held to be "unconstitutional" by a decision of the Supreme Court of the United States, that law or lower court decision is nullified.

Statutory law is now the most important source of law in this nation. Statutes are laws passed by legislatures, from Congress to state legislatures on down to city councils and county boards.

Common law refers to the decisions and precedents set by courts. (In England centuries ago, judges—lacking all the law books and precedents available today—"found" or "discovered" the law.) And once a decision was made on a point of law—and that decision was written down—then under common law that decision became a precedent which could be followed in deciding similar cases in years to come.

Equity is an area which began in England hundreds of years ago. The Chancellor (the Monarch's right-hand man) set up courts called "Chancery" or "Equity" to settle disputes which somehow fell outside the concerns of the "regular" courts of law. Some fragments of "equity" remain and may be found in the law of today's United States. For example, when a court grants an injunction forbidding an action, or a cease and desist order, those are examples of equity. So is a court order known as mandamus (Latin for "we demand"), directing that some specific action be taken.

Administrative law has grown rapidly in the United States over the past century. When business and industrial development became too complex for Congress to legislate effective controls, Congress began in 1890 to create administrative agencies. These agencies, which have legislative, executive, and judicial powers, include units which have a direct impact on the media: the Federal Trade Commission (FTC, established 1914), once a major regulator of advertising, and the Federal Communications Commission (FCC, established in 1934).

The federal Executive branch can set forth edicts with the force of law; these are known as executive orders. An obvious example of this is the classification of secret/confidential documents in 1951 by President Harry S. Truman: Top Secret, Secret, and Confidential.

Defamation: civil libel

Civil libel is one of the two torts included under the more general term of defamation; the other tort is slander. Libel, in general, covers communication in written, fixed, or permanent form. Slander refers to oral communication. (In most states, because of the great diffusion of broadcast messages, plus, presumably, recognition of recording techniques, broadcast defamation is treated as libel rather than as slander. This matters because slander suits tend to be more difficult to win and generally result in smaller damage awards when they are won.)

Libel law changed drastically during the 1970s, and the change is continuing in the 1990s. Because change will occur, this discussion deals only with the basics libel disputes. Intricacies such as constitutional defenses to libel actions will be left for attorneys once a publication or station has been hit with a lawsuit.

What is defamation? The late William L. Prosser, dean of the University of California Law School, provided this definition:

> Defamation is an invasion of the interest in reputation and good name, by communication to others, which tends to dimish the esteem in which a person is held, or to excite adverse feelings or opinions against him.

If something is published or broadcast, it could be the source of a libel suit. Take these examples:

a) Pictures can lie. Pictures—photos and cartoons—can cause libel suits. Cameras do play tricks, and the innocent-looking photograph when viewed from one angle may have an off-color effect when viewed from another. An embarrassing optical illusion, for example, can make a fully clothed person appear to be indecently exposed. Also, be sure to check picture captions and cutlines. Do they go with the photo for which they are intended? Is that hometown florist misidentified as mobster?

b) Headlines can be libelous. Even standing by itself, a headline over an otherwise praiseworthy story can cause a libel suit. For example, an Iowa newspaper ran a headline which said, "Murderer Freed by Trial Jury." Actually, the man charged with the murder—the defendant—had been acquitted of a murder charge by a jury.

c) Editorials can cause libel suits.

d) Letters to the editor must be handled with great care. Cautious editors will try to speak in person to the author of every letter to ensure that the individual whose name is signed really did write it. If face-to-face conversation is not possible, the procedure used by *Newsweek* magazine might help.

Newsweek editors telephone persons whose names are signed to letters, asking them whether they have written to the magazine recently. And what was in the letter?

e) Quotations from others: Keep in mind that accuracy and truth are not synonymous. Just because you have quoted someone accurately when that person makes a defamatory statement does not protect your publication or broadcast station. You and your employer can be sued along with the source of the defamatory quotation. The law of defamation assumes that the person who spreads a harmful falsehood—like the person who invented the falsehood—be held liable for it.

f) Classified advertisements can be trouble. Watch out for double meanings. Avoid personal advertisements where the word meaning is suspicious in the slightest degree. If personal ads are run by a newspaper, persons should not be identified. (Avoid full names, or first names or nicknames which are so unusual as to identify a specific person.)

If a (possible) libel occurs. . .

When a publication discovers that it has libeled someone, it usually prints a prompt correction or retraction, often accompanied by an apology. The correction should be prominently displayed in order to be a factor in reducing damages. However, since a retraction is, in effect, a confession of error, its wording should be approved by an attorney with real expertise in communication law. The person offended also may be asked to sign a release, in effect promising not to sue.

If threatened with a libel suit, or if someone demands a retraction, a reporter, news producer, editor, etc., should make no apologies or admissions. Talk courteously to the complaining person, gather needed information, and then discuss the problem with a supervising editor, producer, or news director. Do not write any correction or retraction until instructed to do so by a supervisor; chances are, an attorney may be asked to lend a hand with the wording. Whatever you do, don't make insulting responses to a complaining caller, and do not assume that such complaints come from "cranks."

The first response to a person threatening a libel suit may be the most important response, according to *Libel Law: Myth and Reality*, the famed Iowa Libel Project by Randall Bezanson, Gilbert Cranberg, and John Soloski. In such situations, it may be, as the Bible says, that a soft answer turneth away wrath. Threats of a suit are serious business and should be treated as such.

Let your bosses know immediately that there could be a problem. Don't hide the problem, because what bosses hate most of all is getting hit from the blind side.

The elements of libel

Perhaps a simplistic formula may help here:

L = D + U

Libel = a publication which is Damaging to reputation and which is Untrue.

For a libel suit to be brought successfully, the person bringing it (the plaintiff) must plead and prove five things:

(1) Publication
(2) Identification
(3) Defamation
(4) Fault
(5) Injury

(1) Publication means distribution of a statement, whether in oral, written or printed, pictorial, or broadcast form. Although publication is generally thought of in the mass media sense, technically it takes only three people to accomplish publication in a defamation suit: the publisher or speaker, the target of the statement, and a third party.

(2) Identification means that if a person wishes to sue for defamation, he or she must show that the false statement complained of singled out that one individual.

Most of the time, it is evident whether or not a person has been identified: the person's name was published, the person's picture was broadcast. Also, a person can be said to be identified if he or she is a member of a small group. Legally, one can get away with publishing statements such as "all medical doctors in Chicago" are incompetent quacks, or "all lawyers in Milwaukee" are ambulance-chasing shysters. (Again, the ethics of such sloppy statements must be questioned.) There are thousands of physicians in Chicago, and more than a thousand attorneys in Milwaukee. With such a large group, there can be no individual identification.

But if a small group (or a sub-group of a larger group) is named, identification can occur. How big does a group have to be before there's no identification? That seems to vary from place to place. In a federal court, for example, it was held that publishing a rumor about one unnamed member of a twenty-one-person police force did not create identification. [*Arcand v. Evening Call Pub. Co.*], 567 F. 2d 1163 (lst Cir., 1977). In New York, however, members of a group of fifty-three unnamed policemen were held to have been identified. *Brady v. Ottaway Newspapers*, 84 A.D.2d 226, 445 N.Y.S.2d 786 (1981).

NOTE: The *Brady v. Ottaway Newspapers* case obviously contradicts the oft-repeated rule of thumb that identification can't occur in a group larger than twenty-five.

(3) Defamation. Is the publication defamatory? That is, did it really damage reputation, or, in some instances, cause emotional distress? A court will rule whether words are defamatory. If words are plainly, obviously defamatory, they are said to be libelous *per se* [by itself]. But if the words are ambiguous, having both innocent and defamatory meanings, then the jury will decide how the words are to be understood.

In addition, sometimes innocent-appearing words can be made defamatory by the context in which they are used. That is called libel *per quod*. For example, a note in a newspaper's record column that a daughter was born to Josephus Q. Doe and his wife looks acceptable. But suppose that Josephus Q. Doe is a Catholic priest who has not broken his vow of celibacy. The "extrinsic fact" that Doe is a priest would make the publication defamatory.

In general, any publication that says that someone has been doing something illegal, immoral, or unethical could expose a newspaper broadcast station to a libel suit.

Here are some "red flag" words and phrases that could result in a libel suit: [Suggested by Bruce Sanford's *Synopsis of the Law of Libel and the Right of Privacy,* 1981 ed., pp. 25-26.]

adulterer	gambling house	paramour
AIDS victim	gangster	paranoid
alcoholic	gay	peeping Tom
ambulance chaser	grafter	perjurer
atheist		pervert
attempted suicide	herpes	pimp
	hit-man	plagiarist
bad morals	homosexual	price cutter
bankrupt	hypocrite	profiteer
bigamist		pockets public funds
blackmail	illegitimate	prostitute
bordello	illicit relations	
briber	incest	rapist
brothel	incompetent	recidivist
	infidelity	rogue
cheat	influence peddler	
collusion	informer	sadist
communist	insane	scam-artist
con man	intemperate	scandal monger
convict	intimate	scoundrel
corrupt		seducer
coward	Jekyll-Hyde personality	short in accounts
	junkie	shyster
drunk		skunk
death-merchant	kept woman	sneak
divorced (when not)	Ku Klux Klan	stuffed ballot boxes
drug addict or druggie		
	lewd	underworld connections
embezzler	lascivious	unethical
ex-convict	liar	unmarried mother
		unprofessional
fascist	mental disease	unsound mind
fink	mental incompetent	
fixed game	molester	vice den
fool	moral degenerate	villain
fornicator	murderer	viper
fraud		
	nazi	

(4) Fault: To win, the plaintiff in a civil libel suit is required to show some kind of "fault" on the part of the publisher or broadcaster. In effect, key libel decisions by the Supreme Court of the United States since 1964 have told media defendants, "We've got some good news and some bad news." First, the good news. That includes the important idea, expressed in *New York Times v. Sullivan*, 376 U.S.254, 84 S.Ct. 710 (1964), that public officials will not be allowed to use the law of civil libel to inhibit discussion of the public's business.

That is, Alabama courts could not uphold a $1,000,000 libel verdict against the *New York Times* for publishing an advertisement by civil rights advocates denouncing racist law enforcement actions during the Freedom Marches in the South. Instead, the Supreme Court found constitutional protection against libel suits for the news media.

The constitutional guarantees require, we think, a federal rule that prohibits a public official from recovering damages for a defamatory falsehood relating to his official conduct, unless he proves that the statement was made with "actual malice" (that is, with knowledge that it was false or with reckless disregard of whether it was false or not) [376 U.S. at 279-280, 84 S.Ct. at 710 (1964).

That's the "Sullivan rule," which many have criticized as too protective of the media or as declaring "open season" on the reputations of public officials. Under that rationale, public officials can't collect damages simply because published falsehoods injure their reputations. They have to prove that the defamation was published with knowing falsity or with "reckless disregard for the truth," (e.g. failure to investigate, use of untrustworthy or obviously biased sources).

After 1964, the Supreme Court expanded its Sullivan Rule protections, saying, for example, that former public officials would have to meet that higher ("actual malice") standard of proof to win in a libel case. In 1967, the Court said that "public figures" must meet a higher standard of proof than ordinary private persons. And in 1971, the Court said that even ordinary "private figures" who were caught up in newsworthy events would have to meet that tougher test. [See, e.g., *Rosenblatt v. Baer*, 383 U.S. 75, 86 S.Ct. 669 (1965); *Curtis Pub. Co. v. Butts*, 388 U.S. 130, 87 S.Ct. 975 (1967); *Rosenbloom v. Metromedia*, 403 U.S. 29, 91 S.Ct. 1811 (1971).]

Such decisions indeed were good news for the media, saying, in effect, that if a persons were prominent or through misadventure got themselves thrust into the news, they would have to meet the "actual malice" standard of proving publication with knowledge of falsity or reckless disregard for the truth.

Then, with 1974's *Gertz v. Robert Welch* decision, the U.S. Supreme Court gave the media some bad news by narrowing the range of persons who would have to meet the "actual malice" test in order to collect. In the future, private person libel plaintiffs would have to prove mere "negligence" to prevail in a libel suit. Also, the Gertz decision said that there would be two kinds of "public figures": 1) the person with pervasive fame, an "all purpose public figure (cf. Carol Burnett), and 2) the limited or special-purpose public figure, who is a public figure only as there is involvement in trying to affect the outcome of a public issue or controversy.

Defining negligence is like trying to nail custard pie to a wall. Negligence, a concept taken from tort law, means—in the view of a jury—that one person has harmed another by not taking reasonable care. In libel, if a negligence "standard" is to be used, that means that a jury made up of non-journalists will decide whether a journalist was acting as a "reasonable person" when he or she published a defamatory falsehood. Suffice it to say that it is easier for a plaintiff to convince a jury of negligence (lack of reasonable care) than it is to get a jury finding of "actual malice" (publication of a defamatory falsehood with knowledge of falsity or reckless disregard for the truth).

Categories of libel damages

There are three general categories of damages awarded to winners of libel suits:

1) Compensatory or General Damages. Such damages are reflected in a jury's monetary award, based on the jury's estimate of the amount of reputational harm, humiliation, pain and suffering, etc. A sub-category here is called nominal (in name only) damag-

es, where a jury in effect decides that the publisher was at fault but that little real reputational harm has been done. Compensatory damages may run into hundreds of thousands of dollars; nominal damages could be one dollar or three cents.

2) Actual or Special Damages. Here, plaintiffs must prove actual monetary loss resulting from a publication.

3) Punitive Damages. This is the "big money" category, with sympathetic juries sometimes making multimillion-dollar awards. This category of damages is awarded as a matter of public policy to punish outrageous behavior on the part of the publisher, and to make an example of the publisher. (This category of damages is sometimes called "Exemplary Damages.")

By mid-1989, the largest media libel award to survive appeal was $3.05 million, in the case of *Brown & Williamson Tobacco Corp. v. Walter Jacobson and CBS*, 827 F.2d 1119 (7th cir. 1987), cert. den. by Supreme Court of the United States, 1098 S.Ct. 1302 (1988).

(5) Actual Injury. The final element that a libel plaintiff needs to prove (at least to a jury's satisfaction) is "actual injury." Every plaintiff must demonstrate some kind of reputational harm or loss. This harm could include a showing of monetary loss, or loss of contact with friends and acquaintances after the publication, humiliation, or mental anguish.

Defenses to libel

Just because it appears that you've published or broadcast a libel, all is not lost. There are defenses which may be of help. "Complete" defenses to libel include the following:

Statute of limitations. This is an entirely passive defense. Every state has statutes which set time limits for the filing of lawsuits to prevent the filing of stale legal claims.

The statute of limitations in about half the states—plus the District of Columbia—is one year. States with two-year statutes of limitations include Alabama, Alaska, Connecticut, Delaware, Hawaii, Idaho, Indiana, Iowa, Maine, Minnesota, Missouri, Montana, Nevada, North Dakota, South Carolina, South Da-

kota, Washington, and Wisconsin. Arkansas, Massachusetts, New Hampshire, and Vermont's limits are three years, and the Florida statute of limitations is four years. In Tennessee, strangely enough, the statute of limitations is six months for slander and one year for libel.

Truth. This is the "glorious defense," but it is more than that. It should be the goal of every journalist. Truth is a complete defense, in most states, regardless of the motives behind publishing it. (In some states, the truth must be published "for good motives and justifiable ends.")

Knowing that something is true is not enough for a journalist. To use truth as a defense, it must be provable in court, and that means that you will need credible witnesses (who stay healthy!) willing to testify in your behalf. Or, you will need airtight documentation in terms of records which courts will allow to be admitted as evidence.

Truth, as important as it is philosophically and practically, is not the most-used defense to libel, at least not in court. In another sense, truth may be the best defense because if a person who has been bruised by the press knows that his reputation has been damaged by statements which are provably true, that person won't sue.

Privilege of the participant ("Absolute Privilege"). Participants in a public official proceeding can not be used successfully for defamation. No words relevant to the proceeding will support an action for damages. This is done as a matter of public policy because in some circumstances it is crucial that people be allowed to speak without having to fear a defamation suit. Examples: witnesses under oath, testifying in court; legislators speaking while a legislature is in official session, or during an official session of a committee of that legislature.

Privilege of reporting ("Qualified Privilege"). As a practical matter, this may be the most useful defense against libel suits. Public policy in an open society demands that the people be able to discuss what their public officials are doing. The privilege of reporting ("qualified privilege") holds that anyone who reports public official proceedings has an immunity from successful suit for defamation. This is true even if the report quotes a member of the Milwaukee City Council as he defames a citizen of Brewtown.

Note that this is a qualified privilege. The qualifications are that it must be a public official proceeding, in session, and that the report must be fair and accurate. If the city council member makes his defamatory remark during a recess, then it is not privileged. Or, if a witness makes a defamatory remark during courtroom testimony and the judge strikes it from the record, it is not privileged.

Even with those qualifications, this "privilege of reporting" makes it possible to cover and to report on government bodies and officials.

Fair comment. This is an old defense which allows criticism of things which are offered to the public. Historically, it has been useful in protecting both criticism of government activities and officials and also critical comments, as by reviewers of plays, books, etc. This defense protects opinion, and it is still used as a defense (despite reports of its demise). The major problem with this defense is that the opinion must be based on facts truly stated. If the underlying facts are misstated, then this defense will fail.

Compare this defense to the *New York Times* Rule, discussed briefly below and on page 260. That rule holds that when public officials or figures are involved in a story relating to public interest, it is not enough for a "public plaintiff" to prove falsity. The public plaintiff needs to prove that the defamatory falsehood was published with "actual malice," that is, with knowledge that it was false or with reckless disregard of whether it was false or not.

The New York Times rule (the Constitutional defense). This defense is discussed in summary form on page 260. This rule was crafted by Justice William J. Brennan, Jr., in 1964, in an effort to prevent public officials from using civil libel to harass the news media. Without that famed case of *New York Times v. Sullivan* (1964), public officials who could get a jury to agree with them that a publication was false could get enormous libel judgments. Fear of such judgments, Justice Brennan reasoned, could lead the news media into debilitating self-censorship.

Consent. If one consents to publication of a libel (and the journalist can prove that consent), there can be no successful lawsuit for defamation. An example (actually from a privacy lawsuit): a Pittsburgh Steeler fan, full of beer, kept yelling convivially at a *Sports Illustrated* photographer, asking that his picture be taken. The photographer did so, capturing Joe Sixpack the fan with his fly open. It was held that the fan had consented to have his picture taken, and that he had brought upon himself whatever humiliation the publication of the picture caused.

Self-defense. This is the "right to fight back," and it runs through much of Anglo-American law. If you punch me, I can defend myself. However, if you bump into me on Wisconsin Avenue and I respond by blasting you with my Clint Eastwood model .357 Magnum, that obviously would be an excessive response.

But if, say, city council member Tom Trashe makes some defamatory remarks about realtor Mabel Acres, he would be covered by absolute privilege. As a citizen and reporter, you have a qualified privilege to report what Trashe said. Ms. Acres—under the concept of self-defense—could respond to the remarks made by Trashe.

Ethically, a reporter—who is able to report the charges without fear of being sued—should try to talk with the person attacked to see if that person wants to speak up in self-defense.

Broadcasting and Advertising Regulation

By Perri Colley
University of Alabama

While the First Amendment says, "Congress shall make no law . . . abridging the freedom of speech, or of the press . . . .", the First Amendment has not stopped the government from becoming involved with many matters concerning the mass media. Since the beginning of broadcasting, the government has been concerned with regulating the industry and the airwaves, and that regulation has sometimes concerned what has been written for the airwaves.

Regulation of advertising is also considered to be a legitmate government function for two reasons: promoting the concept of fair trade and protecting the consumer

What follows gives you a brief introduction to the two government agencies that have the most to do with regulating the mass media, the Federal Communications Commission and the Federal Trade Commission.

Federal Communications Commission

Each element of broadcast regulation is based on the understanding that you and I own the airwaves. We control the lifeline of all broadcast communication through the Federal Communication Commission. The FCC acts as our protector, making sure that radio, television, wire, satellite, and cable use our property to promote our well-being.

If it sounds like broadcasters are in a precarious position, they are. As operators of the only government-licensed medium, broadcasters operate under legal duty to the public. If a station doesn't fulfill that duty, the FCC replaces it with one that will.

Monitoring transmissions amounts to a mammoth responsibility. The investigative and enforcement work requires six regional offices and thirty-six field offices, as well as a nationwide fleet of mobile radio direction-finding vehicles for technical enforcement purposes. The field staff provides continuous surveillance of the radio spectrum to detect unlicensed operation and activities or nonconforming transmissions.

As an airwave owner, you have more influence than you might imagine. The field offices enforce specific FCC regulations, but the public participates in the enforcement of the FCC's most basic requirement: Broadcasters must serve the public interest, convenience, and necessity. The catch is that the "public" is not the entire U.S. population. It pertains to the specific demographic group that the station considers its audience.

To assure the fulfillment of this public duty, the FCC operates a strict regulatory structure to control the industry. The power to license stations, particularly its power to revoke or to refuse to renew, is the Commission's most intimidating tool for guaranteeing that stations serve the public interest. The FCC has two different license renewal processes, one for renewing an existing license and the other for requesting a new license. The first and simplest step in determining if a new license will be granted is to determine if a frequency is available. If an assignment can be granted and the applicant is a U.S. citizen, the battle for a new license ensues. This extremely complicated request requires the applicant to convince the Commission of his or her character, financial standing, technical capability, programming plans, nondiscrimination in employment, and non-ownership of conflicting media.

The few applicants who can meet these stringent qualifications are limited in their potential range of influence. No single broadcast outlet is allowed to reach more than 25 percent of the total U.S. population as a market. In addition, no single owner can control more than thrity-six stations: twelve AM stations, twelve FM, and twelve mixed television stations. The Commission may bump that number up to fifteen of each if the owners employ a sufficient number of minorities in their corporate structure.

The public wields considerable influence when it comes to renewing a station's licence, a task that must be accomplished every seven years for a radio station and every three years for a television station. As a matter of fact, the only time the FCC seriously considers a prospective broadcaster's challenge of an existing station is when the public voices dissatisfaction and documents evidence to challenge the station's licence. Common complaints include inappropriate jokes, absence of public service notices, biased public affairs programming, and malfeasance in billing. The public also guards the only specific content regulation enforced by the FCC that prevents broadcasters from airing anything indecent.

The two dirty words in broadcast, payola and plugola, are usually subtle violations, thus they are more difficult for the public to detect and document. Payola is an illegal situation in which external benefit is added as incentive for special treatment. An example is a record company or concert house that rewards disc jockeys for giving special play to certain songs or artists. Plugola involves an external benefit for plugs or announcements. As long as the audience clearly understands that the plug is an advertisement, plugs are perfectly legal. Foul play occurs when the audience is mislead.

Public ownership of the airwaves complicates the issue of politics in broadcast. Print media can accept or refuse political advertisements with no government intervention. Politicians have no share in the ownership of paper, ink, and printing presses as they do in the ownership of the nation's airwaves. Therefore, a station must accept ads from all candidates if it accepts an ad from one. The Equal Time provision forbids broadcasters from editing ads and also protects them from liability. If an employee who is running for office appears on the air, all other candidates must be given equal and comparable time slots. Bona fide news uses are exempt from Equal Time.

The FCC protects the rights of both politicians and non-politicians with the Person Attack provision. Anytime someone is attacked on the air, the station is obligated to notify that person and provide him or her with a script, tape, or summary of the attack. Secondly, the station must provide them with an equal opportunity to respond publicly. This notification must be sent to the person attacked through registered mail within one week of the attack.

As a record for both the station and the public, the FCC requires stations to keep a detailed public inspection file. This requirement upholds the theory that the marketplace is the most efficient regulator for broadcasters. The public inspection file must contain a copy of the official license, minutes from the most recent board of directors meeting, a list of shareholders, the titles and home addresses of the station's programming decision makers, a list of problems facing the community that is updated every six months, the station's response to those problems, a summary of all complaints, and the insertion orders of all political ads run with a notarized statement that the person who sponsored the ad was duly authorized to place it.

Federal Trade Commission

The attitude of "let the buyer beware" died long ago. With the recognition of advertisements as the initiation of a contract, advertising is now protected under contract law by the Federal Trade Commission. Any advertisement which is false, deceptive, or misleading constitutes a fraudulent contract and may be prosecuted under law. The relationship between contract law and advertisements is the key to understanding FTC regulations.

Prior to the 1970s, the Supreme Court flatly refused to give First Amendment protection to "mere commercial speech," as Justice William O. Douglas called advertising. But in 1975, a case called *Bigelow v. Virginia* completely changed the way courts view advertising. Instead of protecting it as a speaker's right to speak, the protecting now lies in the consumer's right to receive information in the ad. This process of speaker-message-receiver creates a contract situation controlled by law.

The responsible party is, of course, the FTC. Consumer protection is one of the two main missions of the Commission. It prevents the use of unfair or deceptive advertising and marketing practices. Again, contract law is the fundamental principle. A contract is invalid if it is based on fraudulent information.

The Commission's second major mission is to encourage competitive forces in the national economy. It attempts to prevent mergers of companies if the result may be to lessen competition. The FTC also guards companies from unfair practices that may keep one company from competing with others.

As with the FCC, the FTC depends heavily upon the watchful consumer. Private remedies are an advertiser's nightmare. Juries generally sympathize with the individual, not the agency or the manufacturer. Costly law suits drain the agency's financial as well as creative energy. Advertisers are most vulnerable to ads that pose a health hazard. The ad may show a product being used incorrectly, it may fail to disclose important facts, and the product itself may pose a health hazard. Other advertising pitfalls are hazardous packaging, claims that are impossible to prove, and ads aimed at children or other vulnerable subsets such as the elderly, the sick, or the poor. Nutritional claims, direct product-to-product comparisons and the use of trademarks also pose legal problems for advertisers.

Not only must advertising executives be students of word connotations, they must also have the sophistication to foresee any poten-tial harm in a message. Because the public assumes that a trained advertiser is a communication expert, an ad agency or individual may be held partially responsible for harm caused by the client's product. The advertiser has a duty to the public as well as to the client.

The FTC requires manufactures to substantiate claims and to make explicit all warning disclosures. The Commission denies the existence of a "reasonable" consumer who has a certain degree of common sense when using products. Manufacturers cannot assume that consumers will not use the hair dryer in the shower; they have to print a warning.

Cases before the Commission may originate through complaint by a consumer or a competitor, or they may be initiated by the government itself. No formality is involved in submitting a complaint. The FTC requires only a letter giving the facts in detail, accompanied by all supporting evidence. The Commission begins a prompt investigation, and the results may be disastrous. The dissemination of a false advertisement of a food, drug, device, or cosmetic, for example, constitutes a misdemeanor if the product could be a health hazard or the intent was to defraud or mislead.

Appendix C
Problem words

This section contains a variety of words and phrases that often give writers difficulty. Much of this section is about words that have similar sounds but that have different meanings.

accede, concede
To *accede* is to agree, and is often used with the preposition *to*. To *concede* is to yield without necessarily agreeing.

access, excess
Access is a noun meaning "a way in"; *excess* is a noun meaning "too much."

adjured, abjured
To *abjure* is to renounce; to *adjure* is to entreat or to appeal.

opponent, adversary
While an *opponent* is simply on the opposite side, an *adversary* is openly hostile.

effect, affect
Effect is a change or result; *affect* is always a verb that means to pretend to feel or be, to like and display, or to produce an effect.

afterward, afterwards
Use *afterward*. The dictionary allows use of *afterwards* only as a second form.

aisle, isle
Aisle is a noun refering to a passageway; *isle*, also a noun, is a shortened form of *island*.

all right
That's the way to spell it. The dictionary may list *alright* as a legitimate word, but it is not acceptable in standard usage.

altar, alter
An *altar* is a tablelike platform used in a church service; to *alter* is to change something.

annual
Don't use *first* with it. If it's the first time, it's not *annual* yet.

anyone, any one
Anyone means any person as in "Did anyone come?"; *any one* refers to any member of a group as in, "Any one of you is welcome to come."

apprised, appraised
Apprise means to inform; *appraise* means to give or place a value on something.

arbitrator, mediator
An *arbitrator* is one who hears evidence from all persons concerned, then hands down a decision. A *mediator* is one who listens to arguments of both parties and tries by the exercise of reason to bring them to an agreement.

as, like
As is used to introduce clauses; *like* is a preposition and requires an object.

atheist, agnostic
An *atheist* is a person who believes there is no God. *Agnostic* is a person who believes it is impossible to know whether there is a God.

auger, augur
Auger, a noun, is a tool used for boring into wood or the ground. *Augur*, a verb, is used to imply foretelling.

adverse, averse
Adverse means unfavorable or hostile. One who is *averse* is reluctant.

biennial, biannual
Biennial means every two years. *Biannual* means twice a year and is a synonym for semiannual.

bloc, block
A *bloc* is a coalition of persons or a group with the same purpose or goal. Don't call it a *block*, which has some forty dictionary definitions.

bored, board
Bored is an adjective that means lacking interest; *board* is a noun that may refer to lumber or food or a group of people.

bullion, bouillion
Bullion is gold or silver in the form of bars, while *bouillion* is a clear broth for cooking or drinking.

cannon, canon
A *cannon* is a weapon; a *canon* is a law or rule. The books that are in the Bible are referred to as the canon.

Capitol, capital
Capital refers to a seat of government, generally a city. A *Capitol* is the building in which a legislature sits. It should be capitalized.

carats, karats
Carats are used to measure the weight of precious stones. *Karats* measure the ratio of gold to the mixed alloy.

censor, censer
Censor, the verb, means to prohibit or restrict; as a noun it means prohibitor. A *censer* is an incense burner or container.

chairwoman, chairperson
Under *AP* Style, *chairwoman* is used for a female; *chairman* is used for a man. *Chairperson* is used only when it is the organization's formal title.

cite, site
Cite is a verb that means to acknowledge; *site* is either a noun meaning location or a verb meaning to place.

complement, compliment
Complement is a noun and verb denoting completeness or the process of supplementing something. *Compliment* is a noun or verb that denotes praise or the expression of courtesy.

comprises, composes
Comprise means to contain, to include all or to embrace. It is best used in active voice, followed by an object. *Compose* means to create or put together.

conscience, conscious
Conscience is a noun which means a sense of right and wrong; *conscious* is an adjective meaning "aware."

consul, counsel
A *consul* is a diplomatic emmisary residing in a foreign country, overseeing his country's interests there. A *counsel* is an attorney.

continuous, continual
Continuous means unbroken. *Continual* means repeated or intermittant.

couple of
You need the "of." It's never "a couple tomatoes."

demolish, destroy
They both mean "to do away with completely." You can't partially *demolish* or *destroy* something; nor is there any need to say "totally destroyed."

denotes, connotes
Denotes implies a specific meaning; *connotes* means to suggest or imply.

dietitian, dietician
Dietitian is the correct spelling for someone trained in the field of nutrition planning, not *dietician*.

different from
Things and people are *different from* each other. Don't write that they are different than each other.

difference, differential
Difference is a noun that refers to the amount by which two things are dissimilar. *Differential* is an adjective that means distinctive or making use of a difference. The two words are not interchangeable.

discomfiture, discomfort
Discomfiture is uneasiness or embarrassment, while *discomfort* is inconvenience or a physical lack of comfort.

disinterested, uninterested
Disinterested means impartial; *uninterested* refers to someone who lacks interest or doesn't care.

dissent, descent
Dissent is disagreement; it can be a verb or noun. *Descent* is the past tense of "to descend," or "to go down."

drown
Don't say someone *was drowned* unless an assailant held the victim's head under water. Just say the victim *drowned*.

due to, owing to, because of
Prefer the last. Wrong: The game was canceled *due to* rain. Stilted: *Owing to* rain, the game was canceled. Right: The game was canceled *because of* rain.

dyeing, dying
Dyeing refers to changing colors. *Dying* refers to death.

ecology, environment
They are not synonymous. *Ecology* is the study of the relationship between organisms and their environment. Right: The laboratory is studying the ecology of man and the desert. Right: There is much interest in animal ecology these days. Wrong: Even so simple an undertaking as maintaining a lawn affects ecology. Right: Even so simple an undertaking as maintaining a lawn affects our *environment*.

effective, efficient
Effective means producing an effect with emphasis on the process of doing so; *efficient* means producing results with minimum effort or time.

either
It means one or the other, not both. Wrong: There were lions on *either* side of the door. Right: There were lions on each side of the door.

elude, allude
Elude means to escape from. *Allude* means to refer to or mention.

eminent, imminent
Eminent is an adjective meaning prominent, important; *imminent* is an adjective that refers to something about to happen.

enervate, energize
To *enervate* is to drain or weaken, while to *energize* is to invigorate.

equal, equitable
Equal is an adjective that has no comparatives; that is, you cannot say that something is "more equal" or "less equal." The adjective *equitable* does have comparatives.

exaltation, exultation
Exaltation is high praise or to have raised in honor. *Exultation* is celebration or the act of rejoicing.

feign, fain
To *feign* is to pretend; *fain*, an adjective or adverb, means glad or willing.

flare, flair
Flare is a verb meaning to blaze with sudden, bright light or to burst out in anger; it is also a noun meaning a bright burst of light. *Flair* is conspicuous talent.

flout, flaunt
Flout means to mock, to scoff, or to show disdain for. *Flaunt* means to display ostentatiously.

fliers, flyers
Flier is the preferred term for both an aviator and a handbill.

Funeral service
A redundant expression. A *funeral* is a *service*.

gibe, jibe
To *gibe* means to taunt or sneer. *Jibe* means to shift in direction or, colloquially, to agree.

goodbye, goodby
It's *goodbye*, not *goodby*.

gourmet, gourmand
A *gourmet* is a person who is a judge of fine food; a *gourmand* is a person who eats to excess, a glutton.

grizzly, grisly
Grisly means horrifying; *grizzly* means bearish.

head up
People don't *head up* committees. They head them.

half-mast, half-staff
On ships and at naval stations ashore, flags are flown at *half-mast*. Elsewhere ashore, flags are flown at *half-staff*.

hopefully
One of the most commonly misused words, in spite of what the dictionary may say. *Hopefully* should be used to describe the way the subject feels—for instance, "Hopefully, I shall present the plan to the president." This means that I will be hopeful when I do it, not that I hope I will do it. And it is something else again when you attribute hope to a nonperson. You may write, "Hopefully, the war will end soon." What you mean is that you hope the war will end soon, but this is not what you are writing. What you should write is, "I hope the war will end soon."

human, humane
Human means referring to people; *humane* is an adjective meaning kindly.

hanged, hung
Hanged is used for people; *hung* refers to objects. One exception is the term "hung jury."

illicit, elicit
An *illicit* activity is illegal or unseemly. To *elicit* is to invoke.

imply, infer
Imply means to suggest or indicate; *infer* means to draw a conclusion from.

in advance of, prior to
Use "before"; it sounds more natural than either of the above.

indiscreet, indiscrete
Indiscreet means lacking prudence. *Indiscrete* means not separated into distinct parts.

it's, its
It's is the contraction of *it is*. *Its* is the possessive form of the word *it*.

leave, let
Leave alone means to depart from or cause to be in solitude. *Let* alone means to allow to be undisturbed. Wrong: The man had pulled a gun on her, but Mr. Jones intervened and talked him into leaving her alone. Right: The man had pulled a gun on her but Mr. Jones intervened and talked him into letting her alone. Right: When I entered the room, I saw that Jim and Mary were sleeping, so I decided to leave them alone.

lectern, podium, pulpit
A speaker stands *behind* a *lectern*, *on* a *podium* or rostrum, or *in* the *pulpit*.

fewer, less
Use *fewer* with countable items; use *less* with amounts or things not countable.

lie, lay
Lie is a state of being (John chose to *lie* in the sun), while *lay* is the action or work (He started to *lay* down the books). *Lay* needs an object to be used correctly.

like, as
Don't use *like* for *as* or *as if*. In general, use *like* to compare nouns and pronouns; use as when comparing phrases and clauses that contain a verb. Wrong: Jim blocks the linebacker like he should. Right: Jim blocks the linebacker as he should. Right: Jim blocks like a pro.

lineage, linage
Lineage means descent or ancestry. *Linage* means number of lines; newspapers often refer to the amount of advertising they have as "ad linage."

mantel, mantle
A *mantel* is a shelf, and a mantle is a cloak. *Mantle* also refers to a symbol of preeminence or authority.

marshall, marshal
Generally, the first form is correct only when the word is a proper noun: John Marshall. The second form is the verb form: Marilyn will marshal for forces. And the second form is the one to use for a title: fire marshal Stan Anderson, field marshal Erwin Rommel.

Mean, average, median
Use *mean* as synonymous with *average*. Both words refer to the sum of all components divided by the number of components. *Median* is the number that has as many components above it as below it.

noisome, noisy
Noisome means offensive or noxious. *Noisy* means loud or clamorous.

off, off of
When using *off*, the word *of* is not necessary. *Off* is an adequate preposition to carry the phrase.

official, officious
Something that is *official* is formally authorized; one who is *officious* is impertinent or meddlesome.

over, more than
Over and *under* are best used for spatial relationships. When using figures, *more than* and *less than* are better choices.

palate, palette
Palate is the roof of the mouth. A *palette* is an artist's paint board.

parallel construction
Thoughts in series in the same sentence require *parallel construction*. Wrong: The union delivered demands for an increase of 10 percent in wages and to cut the work week to thirty hours. Right: The union delivered demands for an increase of thirty percent in wages and for a reduction in the work week to 30 hours.

parole, probation
Parole is the release of a prisoner before the sentence has expired, on condition of good behavior. *Probation* is the suspension of a sentence for a convicted person.

passed, enacted
Bills are *passed*; laws are *enacted*.

peacock, peahen, peafowl
Peacocks are male, *peahens* are female, and *peafowl* are both.

peddle, pedal
When selling something, you *peddle* it. When riding a bicycle or similar means of locomotion, you *pedal* it.

pour, pore
Pour means to flow in a continous stream; *pore* means to gaze intently.

prescribe, proscribe
To *prescribe* is to order or recommend the use of. To *proscribe* is to forbid, denounce, or prohibit.

pretext, pretense
They're different, but it's a tough distinction. A *pretext* is that which is put forward to conceal a truth. Right: He was discharged for tardiness, but this was only a pretext for general incompetence. A *pretense* is a "false show," a more overt act intended to conceal personal feelings. Right: My profuse compliments were all pretense.

principal, principle
Principal means someone or something first in rank, authority, or importance. *Principle* means a fundmental truth, law, or doctrine.

prone, supine
Prone means lying face-down; *supine* means lying face-up. Prone can also mean inclined toward while supine can mean passive.

prophesy, prophecy
Prophesy is the verb; *prophecy* is the noun form.

survey, questionnaire
A *survey* is another word for a public opinion poll. A *questionnaire* is the set of questions that the respondents in the poll answer. Survey is not a synonym for questionnaire.

ravaged, ravished
To *ravage* is to wreak great destruction; to *ravish* is to abduct, rape, or carry away with emotion. Buildings and towns cannot be ravished.

raze, raise
To *raze* is to destroy or to demolish. To *raise* is to lift up or to increase.

reeked, wreaked
To *reek* is to permeate with an offensive or strong odor. To *wreak* means to punish or to avenge; it connotes destructive activity.

refute
The word connotes success in argument and almost always implies an editorial judgment. Wrong: Father Bury *refuted* the arguments of the proabortion faction.

rein, reign
The leather strap for a horse is a *rein*. *Reign* is the period a ruler is on the throne.

reluctant, reticent
If she doesn't want to act, she is *reluctant*. If she doesn't want to speak, she is *reticent*.

shut off, shut-off
Shut off is the verb form. The noun form, *shut-off*, is hyphenated.

stanch, staunch
Stanch is a verb that means to stop. *Staunch* is a adjective meaning strong.

stationary, stationery
Stationary means to stand still; *stationery* is writing paper.

suite, suit
Suite refers to a set of rooms and furniture; a *suit* refers to clothes, cards, or a law suit.

temperatures
They may get higher or lower, but they don't get warmer or cooler. Wrong: *Temperatures* are expected to warm up on Friday. Right: *Temperatures* are expected to rise on Friday.

their, there
Their is a possessive pronoun; *there* is an adverb indicating place or direction.

that, which
That tends to restrict the reader's thought and direct it in the way you want it to go; *which* is nonrestrictive, introducing a bit of subsidiary information. For instance: The lawnmower that is in the garage needs sharpening. (Meaning: We have more than one lawnmower. The one in the garage needs sharpening.) The statue that graces our entry hall is on loan from the museum. (Meaning: Of all the statues around here, the one in the entry hall is on loan.) The statue, which was in the hallway, survived the fire. (Meaning: The one statue survived the fire. It happened to be in the hallway.) Note that *which* clauses take commas, signaling that they are not essential to the meaning of the sentence.

troop, troupe
A *troop* is a group of people or animals. A *troupe* is an ensemble of actors, singers, dancers, etc.

under way,
Not underway. But don't say something got *under way*. Say it started, or began.

unique
Something that is *unique* is the only one of its kind. It can't be very unique or quite unique or somewhat unique or rather unique. Don't use it unless you really mean unique.

up
Don't use it as a verb. Wrong: The manager said he would *up* the price next week. Right: The manager said he would raise the price next week.

venerable, vulnerable
Venerable means respected because of age or attainments; *vulnerable* means open to attack or damage.

oral, verbal
Oral is used when the mouth is central to the idea, as in "He made an *oral* presentation." That means he spoke. *Verbal* may refer to spoken or written words.

versus, verses
Versus means to go against or abberate; *verses* are lines of poetry.

whom, who
A tough one, but generally you're safe to use *whom* to refer to someone who has been the object of an action: A 19-year-old woman, to whom the room was rented, left the window

open. *Who* is the word when the somebody has been the actor: A 19-year-old woman, who rented the room, left the window open.

whose, who's
Whose is the possessive form of who. *Who's* is the contraction of who is.

would
Be careful about using *would* when constructing a conditional past tense. Wrong: If Smith would not have had an injured foot, Thompson wouldn't have been in the lineup. Right: If Soderhelm had not had an injured foot, Thompson wouldn't have been in the lineup.

your, you're
Your is a pronoun that means "belonging to you"; *you're* is a contraction of "you are."

APPENDIX D — Exams

The exams in this section are meant to help students discover various writing, editing, and grammar problems. The key to these exams may be found in the Instructor's Manual to the book. That manual may be obtained from Prentice Hall or from the author of this text.

Grammar Exam

A Note to Instructors: This exam has been designed to test a student's ability to recognize correct grammatical formations. Students should be given about fifty minutes to complete the exam.

1. There_____many possible candidates. (a) is (b) are (c) was (d) none of the above

2. None_____ so blind as he who will not see. (a) is (b) are (c) either of the above (d) none of the above

3. Both of your excuses_____ plausible. (a) sound (b) sounds (c) either of the above (d) none of the above

4. Several of the members_____ absent. (a) was (b) were (c) either of the above (d) none of the above

5. Few of my family really_____ me. (a) understand (b) understands (c) either of the above (d) none of the above

6. Many_____ surprised at the final score. (a) was (b) were (c) either of the above (d) none of the above

7. Some of the money_____ missing. (a) is (b) are (c) either of the above (d) none of the above

8. All of the cherries_____ ripe. (a) look (b) looks (c) either of the above (d) none of the above

9. _____ any of this evidence been presented? (a) Has (b) Have (c) either of the above (d) none of the above

10. Mary Sloan, one of the brightest girls, _____to represent the school in the contest. (a) were chosen (b) was chosen (c) have been chosen (d) none of the above

11. Baker took the handoff,_____ his way within one foot of the goal line. (a) bulldozes (b) bulldozing (c) bulldozed (d) none of the above

12. I will_____ you to swim. (a) learn (b) teach (c) either of the above (d) none of the above

13. Fans cheered as the touchdown _____(a) had been made (b) was made (c) either of the above (d) none of the above

14. The team plans_____ tomorrow. (a) to celebrate (b) to have celebrated (c) either of the above (d) none of the above

15. _____ the tickets, Mr. Selby took the children to the circus. (a) buying (b) having bought (c) either of the above (d) none of the above

16. It is customary for ranchers_____ their cattle. (a) to have branded (b) to brand (c) either of the above (d) none of the above

17. The pond has begun freezing because the temperature_____ (a) has dropped (b) dropped (c) either of the above (d) none of the above

18. They_____ Mary from the invitation. (a) accepted (b) excepted (c) either of the above (d) none of the above

19. The citizens_____ many reforms. (a) affected (b) effected (c) either of the above (d) none of the above

20. A large_____ of disgruntled men barred the entrance. (a) amount (b) number (c) either of the above (d) none of the above

21. What honor is there_____ the forty thieves? (a) among (b) between (c) either of the above (d) none of the above

22. You have_____ friends than she. (a) fewer (b) less (c) either of the above (d) none of the above

23. Is an author to blame for what the public_____ from his work? (a) infers (b) implies (c) either of the above (d) none of the above

24. My house is_____ his. (a) different from (b) different than (c) either of the above (d) none of the above

25. It is handy for everyone to know how to cook for _____. (a) hisself (b) himself (c) theirselves (d) themselves

26. The old man fascinated_____ children with stories of his adventures. (a) them (b) us (c) we (d) none of the above

27. Between you and_____, the food could have been much better than it was. (a) I (b) me (c) she (d) none of the above

28. Why don't you get_____ some lunch? (a) your selves (b) yourselves (c) yourselfs (d) none of the above

29. Judy has just as much time to wash the dishes as_____.(a) I (b) me (c) them (d) none of the above

30. _____ and_____ dad have the same hobbies. (a) She, her (b) Him, his (c) Them, their (d) none of the above

31. The reforms_____ many citizens. (a) affected (b) effected (c) either of the above (d) none of the above

32. The construction of fallout shelters_____ being considered. (a) was (b) were (c) are (d) were not

33. Your contribution, in addition to other funds,_____ the success of our campaign. (a) have been assuring (b) assures (c) assure (d) were assuring

34. A combination of these methods_____ sure to succeed. (a) were (b) are (c) is (d) none of the above

35. Each of their children_____ a different instrument. (a) have (b) play (c) plays (d) either a or b

36. Val_____ me the very record I would have _____. (a) give, choosed (b) gave, choosed (c) give, chosen (d) gave, chosen

37. By the time the sun_____, we had_____ nearly a hundred miles. (a) rised, drove (b) raised, driven (c) rose, driven (d) had raised, driven

38. As I_____ there, my hat was_____ into the river. (a) sit, blowed (b) sit, blown (c) sat, blown

39. Mr. Greenfield's lost eyeglasses_____ the object of everyone's search at the church picnic. (a) were (b) was (c) is (d) be

40. He is one_____ broke it. (a) who (b) that (c) either of the above (d) none of the above

41. _____ of class standing, everyone will take the test. (a) Regardless (b) Irregardless (c) either of the above (d) none of the above

42. I must_____ find a job. (a) try and (b) try to (c) either of the above (d) none of the above

43. The theater was_____ full by seven o'clock. (a) already (b) all ready (c) either of the above (d) none of the above

44. The cast was_____ for the curtain call. (a) already (b) all ready (c) either of the above (d) none of the above

45. Everything will be_____.(a) alright (b) all right (c) either of the above (d) none of the above

46. Don't pay the bill_____ you received the goods. (a) unless (b) without (c) but (d) whether

47. Both the doctor and his nurse_____to work on foot. (a) come (b) comes (c) has come (d) has came

48. If you_____, you would have passed easily. (a) would have took my advice (b) had taken my advice (c) had taken my advise (d) would have took my advise

49. If you will_____ me your radio, I'll fix it for you. (a) bring (b) take (c) either of the above (d) none of the above

50. Why don't you_____ someone else have a turn? (a) let (b) leave (c) either of the above (d) none of the above

51. Phil_____ and waited for his turn. (a) sit (b) set (c) sat (d) none of the above

52. Will they let_____ fellows use the pool? (a) us (b) we (c) either of the above (d) none of the above

53. Andy shot two more baskets than_____ .(a) he (b) him (c) her (d) either b or c

54. I_____ back in my chair and relaxed. (a) lie (b) laid (c) layed (d) lay

55. Dick_____ his books on a vacant seat. (a) layed (b) laid (c) lay (d) lie

56. I_____ down and waited for the dentist to call me in. (a) set (b) sat (c) sit (d) sitted

57. I lay awake, wondering where I had_____ the receipt. (a) lay (b) laid (c) lain (d) layed

58. The meat was still frozen, though I had_____ it on the stove to thaw. (a) set (b) sat (c) sit (d) layed

59. Glen_____ me the pictures he had taken at the game. (a) brung (b) bringed (c) bring (d) brought

60. I_____ past a house on which a tree had fallen. (a) drived (b) drive (c) driven (d) drove

61. The new teacher,_____ I met today, came from the South. (a) who (b) whom (c) whose (d) who's

62. The new teacher,_____ has taken Mr. Breen's position, came from the South. (a) who (b) whom (c) in formal usage, either would be correct (d) none of the above

63. Leroy feels quite_____ about getting a scholarship. (a) hopeful (b) hopefully c) either of the above (d) none of the above

64. The detective's solution to the crime was_____ right. (a) altogether (b) all together (c) all to gather (d) all too gather

65. Henry is the_____ of the two. (a) more strong (b) strongest (c) stronger (d) most strong

66. You cannot vote_____ you are eighteen. (a) unless (b) without (c) unless being (d) without being

67. Ann_____ three lessons. (a) taking (b) taken (c) has taken (d) has took

68. Cross the streets_____.(a) careful (b) carefully (c) most careful (d) carefuller

69. There is no use feeling sorry_____ the vase is shattered on the floor. (a) for (b) as (c) besides (d) because

70. The weather looks_____ it is about to change for the better. (a) like (b) as (c) like as (d) as if

71. The girl waved goodbye,_____ her mother did not see her. (a) because (b) whether (c) but (d) since

72. It was_____ paid the bill. (a) her who (b) she who (c) her whom (d) her who

73. The two students assigned to this project are you and me. (a) Correct as is (b) you and I (c) I and you (d) me and you

74. Will you please tell me_____ I can solve this problem? (a) in as much as (b) whenever (c) with that which (d) so that

75. He walked right_____ the trap we set for him. (a) up on (b) in (c) into (d) in upon

76. She gets a larger allowance_____ she is older. (a) being that (b) because (c) being because of (d) none of the above

77. Too much food and rest_____ circus animals lazy. (a) make (b) makes (c) either of the above (d) none of the above

78. The footprints under the window_____ burglary. (a) suggests (b) suggest (c) either of the above (d) none of the above

79. Tracy Avenue is the only one of our streets that_____ from one end of the city to the other.   (a) run (b) runs (c) either of the above (d) none of the above

80. The man acts as though he_____ the owner. (a) is (b) was (c) were (d) none of the above.

81. If he_____ registered later, he would have had the right classes. (a) would have (b) had (c) either of the above (d) none of the above

82. Each one of the ladies_____ splashed by the passing car. (a) was (b) were (c) are (d) a and c above are correct

83. The natives believe that noise, smoke, and dancing_____ away the evil spirits. (a) drives (b) drive (c) drived (d) none of the above

84. Please tell me_____ you_____ during the winter. (a) at where, live (b) where, live at (c) where, live (d) where at, live

85. _____ he_____yet? (a) Have, ate (b) Has, ate (c) Have, eaten (d) Has, eaten

86. The *New York Times* still_____ a wide circulation. (a) has (b) have (c) either of the above (d) none of the above

87. Athletics_____ required of every student. (a) are (b) is (c) either of the above (d) none of the above

88. On the wall_____several posters. (a) was (b) were (c) is (d) either a or b

89. He failed _____ not studying. (a) due to (b) because of (c) owing to (d) because

90. She _____ her new clothes as if they made her superior to the rest of us.
(a) flouted (b) flaunted (c) had flouted (d) flautened

91. He misspelled _____ words on this exam. (a) less (b) fewer (c) lesser (d) more fewer

92. Sue had_____ the cake on a kitchen chair. (a) sat (b) set (c) sitted (d) sit

93. The police will not_____ you park there. (a) leave (b) let (c) either of the above
(d) none of the above

94. The gift from_____ and Bert came on Christmas Eve. (a) she (b) her (c) either of the
above (d) none of the above

95. Norm and_____ share the same locker. (a) he (b) him (c) either of the above (d) none
of the above

96. Ron doesn't live as far from the school as_____.(a) us (b) we (c) they (d) either b or c

97. The children amused_____ by asking riddles. (a) theirselves (b) themselves
(c) either of the above (d) none of the above

98. I was sitting all by_____ in that last row. (a) my self (b) myself (c) either of the
above (d) none of the above

99. Four of the committee members_____ married. (a) were (b) is (c) are (d) either a or c

100._____ and_____are good friends. (a) Her, me (b) He, she (c) She, I
(d) either b or c

Diagnostic Exam

Note to Instructors: This test has been designed to help you determine levels of understanding about knowledge and use of the language. The final ten questions on copy-editing symbols may or may not be relevant to your instruction.

1. Robert_____ from his bike.
(a) had fell (b) had fallen (c) fallen (d) falling

2. The plane with its crew_____ trying to take off now.
(a) is (b) be (c) are (d) been

3. Is the atmosphere on the moon_____ the atmosphere here on earth?
(a) different from (b) liken to (c) different than (d) as different as

4. Why is the referee so_____ the players?
(a) angry at (b) angry with (c) angry in (d) angry over

5. Why_____ allowed to join?
(a) was Ann and he (b) was Ann and him (c) were Ann and he (d) were Ann and him

6. Someone_____ turned on the automatic sprinkler.
(a) must of (b) might of (c) must to (d) must have

7. I noticed the dog as he_____ on the porch.
(a) laid (b) lay (c) lain (d) lied

8. Share the work_____ all the workers.
(a) between (b) amongst (c) betweens (d) among

9. The trunk was_____ heavy_____carry.
(a) to, to (b) too, too (c) too, to (d) to, too

10. Will you_____ come?
(a) try and (b) try to (c) be trying and (d) trying to

11. It was Ann who_____ the book on the table.
(a) layed (b) laid (c) lain (d) lay

12. The committee_____ holding an open meeting on Thursday.
(a) are (b) is (c) been (d) be

13. The new suit is_____.
(a) alright (b) al right (c) allright (d) all right

14. I am happy to_____ your offer to go to the games.
(a) accept (b) except (c) have excepted (d) having accepted

15. He spoke very_____.
(a) strange (b) stranger (c) strangest (d) strangely

16. He speaks_____.
(a) good (b) goodly (c) well (d) more better

17. She_____ finished the job in half the time.
(a) could of (b) can't of (c) could have (d) could had

18. Please_____ here.
(a) set (b) sit (c) to be set (d) to be sitted

19. He_____ a pint of milk.
(a) has drank (b) have drank (c) has drunk (d) have drunk

20. Either you or your friends_____ to blame for the accident.
(a) is (b) are (c) been (d) was

21. Neither Barbara nor Sara_____ homework on Saturdays.
(a) do (b) does (c) are doing (d) were doing

22. None of the programs_____ free from station breaks.
(a) is (b) are (c) be (d) being

23. Why are you still angry_____ me?
(a) at (b) with (c) by (d) against

24. If everyone does_____ share, we shall certainly finish on time.
(a) their (b) his or her (c) there (d) they're

25. _____, the majority of the board members promises to support him.
(a) Regardless of who is chosen (b) Regardless of whom is chosen
(c) Irregardless of who is chosen (d) Irregardless of whom is chosen

Choose the correct style in exercise 26 through 35:
26.   (a) in a baptist church
         (b) in a Baptist Church
         (c) in a baptist Church
         (d) in a Baptist church

27.   (a) a Mother's Day gift
         (b) a Mother's day gift
         (c) a mother's day gift
         (d) a Mother's Day Gift

28.   (a) the new Fall colors
         (b) the new fall colors
         (c) the New Fall Colors
         (d) the New fall colors

29.   (a) the Brother of mayor Bates
         (b) the brother of Mayor Bates
         (c) the Brother of Mayor Bates
         (d) the brother of mayor Bates

30.   (a) a brazilian pianist
         (b) a Brazilian Pianist
         (c) a Brazilian pianist
         (d) a brazilian Pianist

31.   (a) at Eaton High School
    (b) at Eaton high school
    (c) at Eaton high School
    (d) at eaton high school

32.   (a) on the North Side of Pine Lake
    (b) on the north Side of Pine Lake
    (c) on the North side of Pine lake
    (d) on the north side of Pine Lake

33.   (a) Dodd tool company
    (b) Dodd Tool company
    (c) Dodd tool Company
    (d) Dodd Tool Company

34.   (a) any Sunday in July
    (b) any sunday in july
    (c) any Sunday in july
    (d) any sunday in July

35.   (a) a College Football star
    (b) a college football star
    (c) a college Football star
    (d) a College Football Star

36. Mabel asked, "To which colleges has Joan_____
    (a) applied."
    (b) applied"?
    (c) applied".
    (d) applied?"

37. _____ should be free of loose dirt and paint.
    (a) Before you paint the surface, of course,
    (b) Before you paint the surface of course,
    (c) Before you paint, the surface, of course,
    (d) Before you paint, the surface, of course

38. All the _____
    (a) students, whose reports were not handed in, failed.
    (b) students, who's reports were not handed in, failed.
    (c) students who's reports were not handed in failed.
    (d) students whose reports were not handed in failed.

39. "Before starting to write your _____ Miss Wright advised.
    (a) composition plan what you are going to say,"
    (b) composition plan what you are going to say"
    (c) composition, plan what you are going to say,"
    (d) composition, plan what you are going to say",

40. Choose the correct possessive case:
    (a) everyones friend
    (b) childrens' toys
    (c) the school's reputation
    (d) Is this your's?

41. Built in 1832,_____ is now a museum of early American life.
    (a) Dunham Tavern at 6709 Euclid Avenue in Cleveland, Ohio,
    (b) Dunham Tavern, at 6709 Euclid Avenue in Cleveland, Ohio,
    (c) Dunham Tavern, at 6709 Euclid Avenue in Cleveland Ohio
    (d) Dunahm Tavern, at 6709 Euclid Avenue in Cleveland, Ohio

42. "When you come to the stop_____"make a full stop."
    (a) sign", Dad repeated,
    (b) sign: Dad repeated,
    (c) sign," Dad repeated
    (d) sign," Dad repeated,

43. Every_____ lose his license.
    (a) motorist, who is caught speeding, should
    (b) motorist who is caught speeding should
    (c) motorist who is caught speeding; should
    (d) motorist, who is caught speeding should

44. _____ stimulates the heart and raises blood pressure.
    (a) Caffeine which is present, in both tea and coffee,
    (b) Caffeine, which is present in both tea and coffee,
    (c) Caffeine, which is present in both tea, and coffee
    (d) Caffeine, which is present in both tea and coffee

45. Choose the correct possessive case:
    (a) Barton's and McLean's store
    (b) Jack and Tom's responsibility
    (c) moons rays
    (d) editor-in-chiefs' opinion

Choose the correct spelling in exercises 46 through 65.

46. (a) fullfil (b) fulfil (c) fullfill (d) fulfill

47. (a) seperate (b) sepurate (c) separate (d) saperate

48. (a) defenitley (b) defientely (c) definitely (d) definitly

49. (a) calander (b) calandar (c) calendar (d) calender

50. (a) acomodat (b) accomadate (c) accommodate (d) accomodate

51. (a) amatur (b) ameteur (c) amateur (d) amater

52. (a) defisite (b) deficit (c) deficite (d) defecite

53. (a) auxelary (b) auxilary (c) auxiliary (d) auxilairy

54. (a) conceintous (b) consientius (c) conscientious (d) consentious

55. (a) presedent (b) presedant (c) precedent (d) precedant

56. (a) superentendent (b) superintindent (c) superintendint (d) superintendent

57. (a) recieve (b) riceive (c) ricieve (d) receive

58. (a) adaptability (b) adaptabilaty (c) adaptibility (d) adaptibilaty

59. (a) alegance (b) allegance (c) alegiance (d) allegiance

60. (a) privilege (b) priviledge (c) previledge (d) preveledge

61. (a) concede (b) conceed (c) consede (d) conceede

62. (a) elegible (b) eligible (c) elegeble (d) eligeble

63. (a) camoflauge (b) camouglauge (c) camouflage (d) camalage

64. (a) athleet (b) athlete (c) athelete (d) athilete

65. (a) genarosity (b) generosity (c) genatousity (d) generousity

66. Copy-editing symbol for "new paragraph": (a) ⎡The (b) ⎣The (c) Par The (d) → The

67. Copy-editing symbol for "deletion":
    (a) painᵍted (b) painᵡted (c) painᵔted (d) painᵔted

68. Copy-editing symbol for "spell out a number": (a) 6̲ (b) ⑥ (c) ⑥ (d) 6ˢᵖ

69. Copy-editing symbol for "use numerals": (a) (forty) (b) ⎡forty⎤ (c) num forty (d) ~~forty~~

70. Copy-editing symbol for "eliminate space":

    (a) ques/tion (b) ques͡tion (c) ques//tion (d) ques͡tion

71. Copy-editing symbol for "insert comma":

    (a) howeverᵒ (b) howeverₐ (c) howeverᵛ (d) however,

72. Copy-editing symbol for "retain copy":
    (a) stet ~~never~~ (b) never ~~never~~ (c) Keep ~~never~~ (d) (never)

73. Copy-editing symbol for "center copy":

    (a) ⎡John Doe⎤ (b) |John Doe| (c) ⎤John Doe⎡ (d) →John Doe←

74. Proper mark to indicate that the story does not end on this page:

    (a) More,   (b) add,   (c) continued,   (d) —

75. Proper mark to indicate the end of the story:

    (a) end,   (b) —   (c) –30–   (d) ––

APPENDIX E

Advertising Copy Sheets

Copy platform sheets
Copy sheets
Radio script sheets
Television script sheets
Television storyboard sheets

COPY PLATFORM

Ad subject:

Ad problem:

Product characteristics:

Advertising objective:

Target Market:

Competition:

Statement of benefit and appeal:

Creative theme:

Supportive selling points:

COPY PLATFORM

Ad subject:

Ad problem:

Product characteristics:

Advertising objective:

Target Market:

Competition:

Statement of benefit and appeal:

Creative theme:

Supportive selling points:

COPY SHEET

Product:
Medium:
Client:
Writer:

Headline:

Subhead:

Body copy:

Subhead or slogan:

Signature:

COPY SHEET

Product:
Medium:
Client:
Writer:

Headline:

Subhead:

Body copy:

Subhead or slogan:

Signature:

RADIO SCRIPT SHEET

Product:
Client:
Title:
Writer:
Length:

Source   **Audio**

TELEVISION SCRIPT SHEET

Product:
Client:
Title:
Writer:
Length:

Video   **Audio**

TELEVISION STORYBOARD

Product:
Client:
Title:
Writer:
Length:

Video   **Audio**

Frame time

Frame time

Frame time

Frame time

Frame time

Frame time

Frame time

Index